GENDER: A CROSS-CULTURAL PERSPECTIVE

GENDER

A CROSS-CULTURAL PERSPECTIVE

KANWAR SONALI JOLLY-WADHWA

FOREWORD BY:

V. MOHINI GIRI

GYAN

GYAN PUBLISHING HOUSE

NEW DELHI-110002

GENDER : A CROSS-CULTURAL PERSPECTIVE

(*Women Studies, Gender Studies, History, Sociology*)

ISBN: 81-212-0695-2

Published in 2000 in India by
Gyan Publishing House,
5, Ansari Road, Darya Ganj
New Delhi-110002

Laser Typesetting at: A.S. Printers, Delhi.

Printed at: Mehra Offset Press, Delhi.

His Holiness Baba Virsa Singh Ji
from whom all knowledge and learning
flows like a natural spring

To women, across cultures,
all individuals in their own right, yet, bound by ties of
common experiences, shared emotions, similar constraints
and a common desire to spread our wings
and soar up in the sky.

CONTENTS

SECTION 3
WOMEN AND FAMILY

SECTION 4
WOMEN AND RELIGION

SECTION 5
GENDER AND THE STATE

SECTION 6
GENDER AND WORK

FOREWORD

Long ago Schopenhauer forced us to believe that man was the stronger and the superior sex and the woman was mentally inferior to him. In fact, the great philosopher had intentionally or unintentionally, given a boost to the ongoing gender battle which has continued for ages. He reminded the world of the low stature of women. However, recent events and developments definitely disprove the German thinker's theory.

Advocates of woman's liberation and the believers in the rights of women thought, spoke, wrote and acted otherwise to prove their point in creating a niche for the womenfolk in the new world.

In today's world—the women still do not avail and enjoy all rights at par with men. However, the bright aspect is the recent women's movement to keep the flame of revolution on.

One more effort, in the same direction—in the form of this book scribed by Kanwar Sonali Jolly-Wadhwa, a budding scholar and authoress.

Sonali has dealt with the subject in a mature manner and brought her point home in a very empirical manner.

She has brought to the forefront the struggle of various fighters and advocates for the eradication of poverty, slavery, bondage, and turmoil of women, who have been victims of the silent revolution which is taking place all over the world—be it America, China, Japan, India or elsewhere.

The book is exhaustive in its details. The book is the story of the advancement of women from the grassroots to the modern world.

Sonali has made it possible to trace the course of this development of women in a clear and crisp fashion.

Since the dawn of civilisation, women have been the theme for poets, writers, artists and sculptors. Sonali has based her study on original sources like diaries, personal accounts, public records and contemporary novels and poetry. Interestingly, this work describes women of almost all great nations and races, living through the ages. Here I should take liberty to say that not many people know about the exact course of development which eventually changed the lot of the women to the present status. The author of "GENDER: A CROSS–CULTURAL PERSPECTIVE" has made a sincere and powerful attempt to enlighten people on the subject.

I find the book to be an objective study of the conditions of the women, living in some great countries through the past centuries and in particular of the Women's Movement of Liberation in United States of America—where the authoress is based—and of its grand success to bring women to their current position in that country. In a significant move, the authoress has also studied, analyzed and projected the state of Indian-Amercian women community—a part of which she herself is—in such a logical manner which makes it one of the best chapters in the book.

Sonali, while writing the book must have certainly worked in a large spectrum, which proves that she has an understanding of all the issues involved. She has, I feel, researched meticulously and penned thoughtfully.

I am not supposed to pass any judgement on the merit or rank of the young authoress, still, I cannot refrain myself from recording it that this book of hers is a typical example of hard earned knowledge, painstakingly done research and a promising style of writing.

No doubt, Sonali is a prolific writer in the making. I would like to congratulate her for this work of worth on a good subject—departing from the milieu—which is bound to stir the calm waters and at least create an awareness among the people—scholars and laymen alike—regarding the real problems of women, the world over.

"Let's not measure a sapling, as it may hamper its growth"—goes an old adage. Hence, I do not want to say much at this initial stage. I simply wish the upcoming scholar-writer, all success, and bless the sapling to flourish into a revolution.

V. Mohini Giri

PREFACE

In recent years, studies on gender have reached a prominent focal point within the discipline of social history and have also attracted the attention of various scholars around the world. This book represents, yet, another humble attempt in this direction. I have chosen this subject, because I consider gender to be an integral part of all human experiences. Since gender is so omnipresent in human life, shaping the decisions, choices and lifestyles of individuals, it is a good idea to study the role of gender in varied perspectives, across boundaries of time and place. Consequently, I have tried to look at the different ways in which gender plays a crucial role in the lives of human beings, especially women, as they are usually in a disadvantageous position *vis-á-vis* the males.

The essays in this collection transcend geographical and spatial divisions to provide diverse perspectives on the role of gender as an agent in the historical process of the development of society and social institutions. The present work incorporates various aspects of gender, from its subversion to its role in shaping the experiences of migrant communities; from marriage and motherhood to status of women in religious orders, state politics and work, through the lanes and by-lanes of history. This study covers a vast spectrum, filled with vivid colours which converge to form the bright rainbow of womanhood. It unearths various moods and achievements of women from the Far East to Northern Europe and covers Central and North America as well. The experiences of women in one region find parallels in other areas of the world, across cultural boundaries.

In this academic research, an attempt has been made to cover the quntessential woman of Rabindra Nath Tagore also.

> "I am no goddess to be worshipped nor the object of common pity to be brushed aside like a moth of indifference. If you desire to keep me by your side in the path of danger and daring, you allow me to share the great duties of your life then you will know my true self".

I owe a great debt of gratitude to the librarians at the J. Paul Leonard Library of the San Francisco State University, the Bancroft Library at the University of California, Berkeley, and the San Francisco Public Library, (USA). I would also like to extend my thanks to the authorities at the Asian Art and the de Young Museum as well as the Legion of Honour in San Francisco, California, (USA). I also express my heartfelt gratitude to the staff of the library of the National Museum and the National Archives, the Central Library of the Delhi University and the library of the Institute of Women's Studies and the National Gallery of Modern Art in New Delhi.

I shall fail in my duty, if I do not utilize this opportunity to thank certain individuals whose support has been a crucial determinant behind the success of this venture. First and foremost, I would like to thank my teachers at Mater Dei and Lady Shri Ram College (New Delhi) who laid within me the foundations of knowledge and learning and created the base for higher academic studies. I especially thank my professors at the San Francisco State University, (USA). Prof. Hsu, Prof. Loomis and Prof. Peard for initiating me into this field of knowledge and for guiding me.

Special thanks to Revered Gyaniji for his constant blessings and love.

Further, I thank my parents, whose eyes see dreams and whose hearts strive towards realizing them. I thank them for inculcating the values of prayer, work ethic and sincerity which are essential ingredients for the initiation and completion of any assignment in life. I thank Papa for believing in me. His timely reminders that this work is a blessing of God rejuvenated me during the most trying times. I would especially like to thank my Mama for having an incredible amount of faith in my abilities and for encouraging me to reach for higher goals. in life. Her visits with me to the museum, her midnight meals, and company through long and cold winter nights, while I worked on the book must not go unmentioned.

I thank my husband, Amit without whose support, my views and thoughts could not have been channelized into academic writings. His confidence in my intellectual capacity, an almost parental attitude towards my academic development and a constant support have been crucial in completion of this book. I also thank him for his critical reviews of my essays and their placement on a scale of excellence which compelled me to put even more effort into my work. Not to forget his hauling books to and from the library, his midnight dashes to the printer and copier, and his visits to my favourite restaurant to bring me sustenance during highly exhaustive sessions before the computer, have kept me going through the mentally and physically demanding task of writing this book.

My heartiest thanks go to my grandparents, *Barepapa* and *Barimama*, who although separated from me by vast oceans and continents, have yet, been a constant presence in my life through their countless prayers and letters filled with blessings and good wishes.

I also thank my parents-in-law for their cooperation and for showing an avid interest in my work.

I send a warm note of thanks to my sister Supreet, whose hard work and dedication are a source of inspiration to me and whose prayers and pride in me filled me with a desire to work even harder. A very special thanks to my brother Prabhnoor, who rendered invaluable assistance not only by helping with the typing, but who also, with his wonderful sense of humour, created many light moments and brought laughter to my heart and eased the long process of compilation and computing.

Last but not the least, I owe a special thanks to my publishers, M/s Gyan Publishing House, without whose persistent motivation and cooperation, this work could not have been published within the limited span of time.

Kanwar Sonali

INTRODUCTION

I propose to bring forth the multi-faceted role played by gender in the lives of individuals, across ethno-cultural lines. I believe that gender is the central aspect of every human experience even though it may act in different ways at different places and at different times. In keeping with this central belief, I have approached the study of gender as an historical agent from diverse perspectives and in varied situations. I have studied the role and impact of gender in the lives of women within the traditional venues of home and family, at the convent, and in the more contemporary scenario, I have tried to analyze the role of gender in the lives of women in politics and at work. The underlying theme in all these seemingly diverse subjects lies in the determination of women's role by society on the basis of her gender. Society's expectations from women have been shaped by historical processes in which the agency of gender acts as a crucial catalyst. Society works in myriad ways and unlike legal and scientific developments which proceed within the bounds of fixed rules and laws, and can be documented in decrees and treatises, social developments on the other hand are rarely codified in chronicles. Hence, the task of going back in time and teaching the process of the birth, growth and ageing of social customs and conventions which have shaped today's society requires the use of special tools and sources by which the history of social processes such as the interaction of gender with other socio-economic and political forces can be reconstructed.

This reconstruction entails the use of both archaeological sources such as old monuments, pottery and coins as well as literary sources of the time such as written accounts of a period. Sources such as paintings and engravings reflect significantly on the lives of people. Pictorial expressions of human feelings and emotions undoubtedly play a crucial role in the process of writing the history of periods for which no literary sources are available or for those civilizations whose script has not been deciphered yet, as, for instance, the Indus Valley Civilization. However, the importance of such sources did not end with the invention of the script. As various historical studies based on such pictographic evidences have shown, even today, the use of sources such as paintings has continued to hold the interest of historians of the contemporary world. One of the essays in the collection uses paintings and Engravings to shed light on the position of women within marriage and society in eighteenth Century England. This use is based on the premise, that from the period of the earliest cave paintings right until today, art encompasses within itself, the deepest essence of human emotions, reactions, responses and expectations. In this context, art then in fact is society represented on canvas. It is in this light that I have used the paintings of Arthur Denis and engravings of William Hogarth as crucial sources reflecting the poignancy of women's state in Eighteenth Century England.

The second category of sources is madeup of literary documents. In their research for reconstructing the history of periods after the invention of the script, historians have begun to rely heavily on literary evidence. Apart from providing additional information, written sources also help in corroborating evidence from archaeological sources. For instance, a study of Lord Hardwick's Marriage Act of 1753, helps in understanding the situation of the prospective bride and groom in the face of a law which reinforced patriarchal authority in the arena of marriage. Literary sources can be divided into public and private documents. The former include state records such as laws, decrees, ordinances, chronicles and other government documents belonging to the period under study. However, the inherent nature of such sources which makes them excellent reference material for legal and political history, often renders them inadequate as source material for other aspects of history, most noticeably social history. As a result, social historians employ other sources, which can be categorized as private documents such as religious texts, church laws and edicts, novels, epics, lyrics, poetry, letters and diaries, to shed light on the societies of the past. Such literary sources supply scholars with a rich documentation of the customs, traditions, attitudes and behavioural norms of the people in previous centuries. One of the most interesting characteristics of such sources is that often while writing such accounts, the authors are usually unaware of the fact that they are soldering links in the chain of historical reconstruction, because later on, historians use such writings as tools to paint an approximately accurate picture of society in the past centuries.

Writings of the women of earlier periods, which previously had been excluded from the mainstream of historical sources, have since the last century become a focus of analysis and interpretation by many historians. In particular, social historians and biographers have tended to study documents such as letters and diaries in their attempt to shed light on various aspects of popular culture and everyday life, prevalent in the years gone by. Keeping such views in mind I have used selections from the letters of Eliza Southgate Bowne which were published in 1887, to show an example of how unconventional sources such as letters can be used to reconstruct aspects of social history. Written by an ordinary girl, leading an ordinary life, these letters, if scrutinized closely, reveal a great deal of information about various aspects of the society, social norms and conventions extant in the late nineteenth century. One such aspect reflected to certain depth in these letters is—the strategic role played by the parents in the daughter's marriage.

In a country which stressed the importance of individual liberty and pioneered the movements of the 'Hippies' and the 'flower children', propagating notions of free sex, it is indeed surprisingly revealing to read older literature, in this case letters which preached the exact contrary as the acceptable way of life. Eliza Southgate represented the entire community of young girls in the newly-formed American nation when she wrote a letter to her mother introducing the subject of her marriage. The letter, dated September, 1802, echoed very clearly the hesitant and shy attitude of the daughter as she approached the matter for the very first time.

> 'I know not, my dearest mother, how to introduce this subject, yet as I fear you may hear it from others and feel anxious for my welfare, I consider it a duty to tell you all'.

Such an attitude regarding the parents' right to know every detail of the daughter's life and the belief of the daughter in it being her infalliable duty to share everything with them shows the pattern along which children, especially daughters, were raised. They were taught to confide everything in their parents, more so in their mothers.

Following almost as a natural corollary was the idea that the parents knew best and so their approval was very important, in fact, absolutely essential. Thus, right from childhood the daughters were indoctrinated with a firm belief in the wisdom of their parents. Thoroughly in keeping with such a faith, Eliza Southgate recounted her different experiences with Mr. Bowne, the gentleman she believed "is serious" in his attentions towards her. Right from her first encounter with him, which cam about by virtue of his staying in the same house as hers, all the way through different outings where he accompanied her, Eliza felt that she was obligated to narrate each and every meeting to her parents.

> 'At Albany, on our way to Ballston, we put up at the same house with a Mr. Bowne from New York; he went on to the Springs the same day we did, and from that time was particularly attentive to me; he was always of our parties to ride, went to lake George in company with us, and came on to Lebanon when we did...'

Further, on the letter gave the impression that it was as though after this narration, Eliza realized that her acquaintance with Mr. Bowne seemed too short to meet with her parents' approval and so she decided to defend her position by adding that,

> '...for four weeks I saw him every day and probably had a better opportunity of knowing him than if I had seen him as a common acquaintance in town for years'.

Shy and reticent as most girls even today feel while bringing up the subject of their marriage in societies where dating is not the acceptable mode in the social milieu, Eliza probably could foretell her parent's response to her situation and therefore she went on to address their fears as her very own,

> 'I left myself in a situation truly embarrassing. At such a distance from all my friends, —my Father and Mother a perfect stranger to the person, —and, prepossessed in his favour as much as so short an acquaintance would sanction, his conduct was such as I shall ever reflect on with the greatest pleasure, —open, candid, delicate and generous'.

Then she tried to dispel them by describing Mr. Bowne's disposition:

> 'He is a man in whom I could place the most unbounded confidence, nothing rash or impetuous in his disposition, but weighs maturely every circumstance...'

Having made clear that a short acquaintance was, in fact, much more revealing, and having fulfilled the arduous task of describing Mr. Bowne's various virtues, Eliza supplemented her information with excellent references from "so many *New Yorkers*" and Mr. and Mrs. Derby. "Mr. and Mrs. Derbey were very much pleased with him... they both approve my conduct," believing as would any other girl in her age and situation that such excellent addresses would undoubtedly strengthen her case. Evidently in that period, the parents of a girl were more interested in knowing the views of some remote "*New Yorker*" whom they had never met before in their life and probably never will again. In fact, the approval of their friends was more significant than the views of their own daughter—the person most intimately associated not only with them but also with the immediate issue being discussed. Hence the approbation of the society and the seal of acceptance given by its members and not feelings and emotions of the parties concerned seemed to have played a decisive role in matters as crucial as marriage.

Notions of social conformity and convention being inextricably woven into the pattern of her thought processes, the young girl Eliza felt it essential to include her prospective beau's views regarding such matters,

> '...he knew I was not at liberty to encourage his addresses without the approbation of my

> parents, and appeared as solicitous that I should act with strict propriety...He advised me like a friend and would not have suffered me do anything improper.'

The conventionality, cautiousness and the desire to strictly follow the pattern of proprieties laid down by the society, thus reflected in the boy's attitude would go a great way in deciding the matter in his favour before the jury of the girl's parents, jury indeed! they constituted, because their decision was final and overbearing. The girl's role ended at hinting and pleading her case,

> 'That I feel deeply interested in Mr. Bowne, I candidly acknowledge and from the knowledge I have of his heart and character I think him better calculated to promote my happiness than any other person I have yet seen; he is a firm, steady, serious man, nothing light or trifling in his character, and I have every reason to think that he had well weighed his sentiments towards me, —nothing rash or premature.'

Her views and desires could be overruled by her parents.

Considering the standards set by the nineteenth century society, perhaps Eliza believed herself to be really audacious to recommend her choice to such great extent, and therefore she reiterated at regular intervals the fact that no matter how she felt, the ultimate decision lay with her parents and that her best interest lay in their decision:

> 'He only required, I would not discourage his addresses till he had an opportunity to make known to my parents his character and wishes—this I promised and went so far as to tell him, but the decision must rest with my parents, their wishes were my law...And now my dearest mother, I submit myself wholly to the wishes of my Father and you, convinced that my happiness is your warmest wish, and to promote it has ever been your study...I have referred him wholly to you, and you, my dearest parents, must decide...(I) will depend on your advice...I wish my Father

> would write to Mr. Derby and know what he says of Mr. B's character. I don't know but 'tis a subject too delicate to give his opinion, but I can conceive that my Father might request it without any impropriety...'

The last sentence of the quote states in almost explicit terms that it would be highly proper for the "Father" to request an account of the man's character from a third party because it must be a common practice those days, for the parents to have detailed background searches regarding the life, family, profession of their prospective son-in-law, a practice, Americans today would consider as personally insulting and denigrating.

These lines where Eliza keeps referring to her parents also suggests feelings similar to filial piety. The words "Father", "Mother" and "Parents" all begin with capital letters, a form now used only while referring to "God". This either meant that the people in the late nineteenth century practised the use of this form of honour more liberally, extending it to their parents as well, or perhaps they held their parents in such high veneration and revered them as one would revere God 'the giver of life' that they chose to express this filial worship by using the same technique of capitalizing the first letter of the words used to address their "Parents" as they would do with the word, "God".

From a sociological point of view such strong faith reflects the tremendous premium, the young nineteenth century American nation placed on age and the rigidly set hierarchy of familial relationships. Parents were accorded the highest honour possible just short of crediting them with divinity. Unlike contemporary America, where parents usually are only 'informed' for their daughter's decision to marry a particular person, the nineteenth century or at least the former half of it presented a contrasting picture of marriages, which cannot be called anything but "arranged", a concept most Americans today view with derision and scorn. Thus, a custom most often called medieval and archaic was indeed prevalent in that country till just the other century whereby American girls married according to their parents' wishes, love could or could not be involved as a secondary factor as is much visible in this set of contemporary private documents, belonging to during that period. But then it appears that it did not matter because as this letter reveals, it was the girls' faith in their parents which provided the momentum for the marriage rather than the concept of falling in love. The existence of this faith depended on the fact that families then were closely knit cohesive units of the society and therefore, parents were better acquainted with their children's disposition and this put them in a much better position for finding suitable partners for their daughters. Indirectly, therefore, this letter reflects that the "American family" which today many consider as falling apart was indeed a very cohesive and strong unit in the nineteenth century American society, where all members of the family were bound together "...with sentiments of duty and affection" although "sentiments of affection" represent a rather new set of values, compared to bonds of submission or obedience.

Hence it is clear as to how important every piece of historical evidence is. No matter how narrowly confined the subject of discussion is, as in this case where the whole letter centered around the matter of a daughter bringing up the subject of her marriage. Even though it is a letter written in strict confidence to her mother by an ordinary girl and not by a great political figure or a statesman and the matter being discussed is trivial indeed when compared to matters of national and international political and economic significance and seems remote from the possibility of being of any historical importance, a closer, more careful look will reveal that this seemingly trivial and ordinary letter is, in fact, an account of the past, documenting the social norms and conventions prevalent in the late nineteenth and early twentieth century America. Ranging from the form of marriage, right through the status of parents in the individual's life, up to describing the role of the parents in the marriage of their daughter, the letter reveals it all. And, therefore, the likes of such commonplace everyday household accounts of social practices are crucial to the work of a social historian and in fact the historical interpretation of such information could be further stretched out to reflect on the nature of the corresponding political and economic structures that would coexist with and sustain such a social structure. Today more than ever when history is no longer the story of heroic battles and biographies of kings but has expanded its horizons to incorporate the people's history, such documents are rendered indispensable and will continue to be crucial pieces of the puzzle of the reconstruction of the past as long as the Elizas of the world continue writing history without their ever knowing so.

In keeping with the tradition of popular history of the common people, this collection of essays relies very heavily on such private and personal documents as: diaries in which women confided their innermost thoughts and feelings, in stories and novels, which form testimonials to women's observation of society, and their reaction to it, and finally poetry which flows from their heart and is the manifestation of their souls, portraying or bringing out the suppressed emotions which otherwise would find it difficult to come out in a repressive society. These personal writings were created by women, and whether knowingly or unknowingly, particularly for women to read. In a society which was like a dark, closed room, these writings formed windows through which expression and creativity entered as whiffs of fresh air and rays of light to rejuvenate women and to give them the strength to accept their lot and to strengthen their resolve to make the best of their lives despite all odds.

Such private documents also form the basis of my secondary sources, which I have used in my study of the theoretical aspect of gender. In the first section of the book, I have discussed five major historical controversies on the subject of gender. First and foremost, I discuss the relevance of the concept of 'separate spheres', which delineates two distinct arenas of activity and autonomy for men and women, as a useful tool of analysis in the study of women's history. The two regions under study are the USA and China. The discussion of scholarly debate in the United States of America is important because this is where the debate initially originated. Scholars have studied the diaries and letters of eighteenth and nineteenth century American women and have discerned two distinctly 'separate spheres' of activity for men and women. They refer to the division of economic activity and daily chores of men and women and present a very convincing argument that 'separate spheres' are in fact basic to the study of women's history. However, historians such as Nancy Hewitt counter argue that women in fact, did not form a monolithic bloc, and as such, the experiences of one class of women cannot be generalized or extended to include all women. She delineated two most important exceptions to 'separate spheres'—working class women and slave women who worked alongside men and were not confined to any one particular sphere. The discussion closes with Rosalind Rosenberg's argument that, indeed women's history today needs to go beyond the concept of 'separate spheres'.

The other region chosen for examining the relevance of separate spheres to the study of women is China. I chose the traditional Chinese society as my field of study, because the general view regarding Chinese women is based on two misconceptions, so aptly outlined by Dorothy Ko. The first being that Chinese women were cloistered and completely isolated from the outside world, and the second, being that their bound feet rendered them helpless and confined them to the inner quarters. The chapter briefly discusses the metaphysical grounding of *nei* (inner) and *wai* (outer) in the traditional concepts of *yin* and *yang* and moves on to the discussion mainly by Dorothy Ko and Susan Mann, that the two spheres are in fact interrelated and had constant interaction with each other. Thus, it is incorrect to assume that Chinese women were doomed to spend their lives cloistered, rather, in their bid to improve their situation and fulfil their thirst for intellectual learning, they pursued education, studied traditional texts and entered in lively discussions with their husbands.

The third chapter in this section studies the question of the relevance of gender in social history. I have chosen immigration to the USA in the nineteenth and twentieth centuries as my field of study to prove that gender is indeed crucial to any study involving human experiences because society is made up of two distinct, gendered identities—male and female. Hence, any study of society should not be genderless, rather it should include both male and female experiences. The research for this paper covered myriad sources belonging to various racial and ethnic settings, because I aimed at providing a comprehensive picture, spanning across chronological, geographical and ethnic boundaries using sources such as fiction, poetry and films.

The next chapter once again engages with the study of gender. Only in this case, I study the process of gender subversion through history as reflected in the eighteenth century Chinese novel—The *Dream of the Red Chamber*. This essay testifies to the relationship between literature and society, as Yi-tse Mei Feuerwerker has very correctly noted, "The novel stands at the point where social history and the human soul intersect". Writing this chapter has been a highly enjoyable experience, since I spent countless hours reading all the five volumes of the novel, finding myself drawn to all the characters, placed in moving plots. By the time I actually got down to writing the essay, I thought that I had lived among them and knew each of the characters personally.

The last chapter of this section brings out the true nature of the Puritan and Victorian views on sexuality. I chose to include this chapter in this anthology on gender not only because sexuality is an integral part of the gender, but also because any study of society's attitude on sexuality also reflects on attitudes towards gender as well. Contrary to popular use of the words, Puritan and Victorian as interchangeable synonyms for prudery, this study reveals how different the two periods in fact were from each other and from the notion of prudery itself.

The next section of the book is characterized by the common theme of women's position within marriage. I have chosen three areas of study in chronological order across the globe. The first chapter studies the position of women in Roman society, the law and literature during the first and second centuries A.D. I study the status of women in the Roman legal codes governing marriage and adultery and reflect on the plight of women under patriarchal authority, as portrayed in contemporary literature by Ovid, Apuleius and Seneca.

In my next essay, I have once again used unconventional sources such as medieval Japanese literature and writings by women. The essay adopts an interesting approach towards women within marriage. I have studied the response of Japanese women to male domination, with the help of diaries of elite women. These diaries known as *Onna-de* reveal moving accounts of women's lives and represent their private response while there were public responses also in the form of spirit possession. Another important channel open to women who were disillusioned by a dominant male society was the Buddhist convent, which housed women as nuns who had renounced the world in favour of spiritual pursuits. In this essay, I take the relationship between the shift of residence from the father's house to the husband's house during the Heian to the Kamakura periods and the consequent change in the nature of women's response which began with diaries and the desire for revenge through possession, but in the end tapered off in terms of its insurgent quality, when women chose the quiet and secluded life of the monastery.

The last chapter of this section studies women within the institution of marriage in eighteenth century England. I have used both archaeological and literary evidence in my study. The paintings and engravings by William Hogarth supplement and reinforce the information received by studying the literature of the time, which includes official documents as well as the popular fiction of the time, the personal correspondence between women, and writings by pioneers of women's rights in England. All the sources reveal the inferior position to which women were relegated *vis-á-vis* men and how well-read, learned women like Mary Wollstonecraft and Mary Montagu were raising a cry to protest male dictatorship within the house at a time when countries were executing monarchs and creating democracies.

Motherhood has been an experience as central to women's lives as marriage, consequently, the next section of the book focuses on the concept of motherhood. The first chapter in this section brings out the role of the Chinese mother as the moral guide and the first teacher of the child. The essay emphasizes the importance, which traditional Chinese texts and tradition place on the significance of the role of mothers. Traditional Chinese medical treatises stress on the importance of correct moral conduct for expecting mothers. Many Chinese texts were written around the theme of women's education, because it was believed that a family's purity and its future were tied to the education of its women especially in the classical texts. My study of the writings of women in the early twentieth century reveals that such as idealistic view regarding women's role as mothers was not just a guideline present in traditional texts, but rather was transferred to social reality even as late as the present century.

The second chapter of this section is perhaps one of the most moving papers of the entire collection. The research which I undertook before writing this essay proved to be a memorable experience. Being an Indian studying in the USA I am a part of the Asian-Indian American community and so I could identify with these women. In the process of reading the writings of these women, I perused through a vast amount of literature, even though I knew I could not include everything in my essay. However, I could not stop reading. The poetry especially, that by Chitra Bannerjee Divakaruni often moved me to tears. Nevertheless all the proverbial sweat, toil and tears proved very fruitful and enriching in the end, when I finally finished writing the essay.

Women have often been called the preservers of values and tradition, which also includes the tradition of religion and moral learning. While most women are obligated to fulfil their familial duties and thus, are lay followers of religion, there also are women who renounce the world and take up the spiritual path. The next section of the book focuses on one such group of Chinese Buddhist nuns during the Six Dynasties period—I trace the reasons for their joining the convent and the intellectual, spiritual and religious activities of the nuns, as revealed in their biographies.

While convents formed a major outlet to public life for women in the earlier periods, since the last century women have had access to a number of other channels, because of their connection with the state and law making bodies. The next three chapters study women's involvement with the state and the state's role towards women. The first chapter studies the development of the feminist movement in the USA from its birth in the nineteenth century to the present day. While the pioneer feminists had to struggle for rights as basic as the right to vote, the later feminists already had the ground prepared for them. As rightful citizens equipped with constitutional equality, they now lobbied for legal and economic rights and were successful in getting the Equal Rights Amendment (ERA) and Equal Employment Opportunities Law (EEOL) passed. Finally, women also sought reproductive rights, as being rights over their own body, and also questioned the traditional assumption that women were supposed to do the housework and that men only "helped out".

The most significant factor behind the rise of the feminist movement was rooted in women's demand for the right to vote. The next chapter in this section examines the Suffrage movement in the American State of California.

The final chapter of this section studies the position of women under the Communist regime in the People's Republic of China. Initially, the Chinese Communist Party gained the support of women by promising them a genderless regime. After the Revolution, the Chinese Communist Party even tried to improve women's lot by passing laws such as the Marriage Act of 1950. However, feudal and patriarchal notions of male superiority have continued and women's presence in the fields of education and politics is negligible. Moreover, as my study will show, today women are the worst-hit section of the Chinese society in the context of the One-Child Policy enacted since the early 1980s.

Not all women participate in political movements or in politics. However, the concept of work touches the lives of most women in the world. The last section of this book examines the much discussed and highly controversial subject of women and work. In the world of post-Second World War corporate capitalism, women have constituted a large part of the work force. In this section I have studied two groups of women. The first group consists of Japanese mothers. I have placed this essay in this particular section, instead of the section on motherhood, because I see the rise of motherhood as the ideal form of womanhood in post-war Japan as, being the product of the capitalist ambitions of the Japanese corporations, rather than being a mere cultural model. Japanese women stay on the so-called M-curve, whereby, they finish their education and join the work force, leave to marry and have children and then return as part time workers. Thus they fulfil the requirements of the companies and perform their duty towards their families.

The last essay of the collection examines the life of the Mexican women who work in the Maquiladora (off shore production units). I view their life as a battleground made up of daily struggles against the triple forces of *Marianismo* (Latin American version of 'separate spheres'), patriarchy and capitalism.

As my readers will see, each day in the lives of these women, no matter where their battle ground lay, whether in the house, in politics or at work, was filled with new challenges, struggles, disappointments and successes. However, the journey is not yet over. This work is just a milestone on the long and winding road of the discovery of the past and present, as well as the prediction of the future role of gender in building and rebuilding human experiences. As I take leave from my readers before they embark on this road where each chapter represents a milestone in the fascinating world of gender and human relationships I sincerely hope that my readers will enjoy reading this book as much as I have enjoyed writing it.

SECTION 1

THEORETICAL ASPECTS OF GENDER

1

MYTH OR REALITY

The Relevance of 'Separate Spheres' in the History of Women in the United States

On his visit to the USA Alexis de Tocqueville had discerned "two closely distinct lines of action" sexes. Unknowingly so, he outlined the basis of the theory of 'separate spheres.'This theory attempts to explain the construction of arenas of autonomy and influence and the ways in which women and men differ in their attitudes and behaviour. The concept of spheres, the public open men and the private being women's domain has been a major orienting principle for women's history. Increasingly historians found that notions of women's sphere had permeated the language and its usage was widespread in the nineteenth century. This directed the twentieth century historians to use the metaphor in their description of women's role in the American culture. The theory received a psychological foundation when in 1964, Erik H. Erikson formulated the theory of "Inner and Outer Space" based on a study of the play patterns of children.[1]

Laurel Thatcher Ulrich argues that in the pre-industrial and pre-Victorian period,there existed division of labour along gendered lines but this division had not yet crystallized into a cultural notion of separate spheres.[2] Her study of Martha Ballard's diary reveals that houses still belonged to men, whereas when separate spheres were more solidly in place, a visiting woman might have said that she was visiting so and so woman's house. However, with the onset of industrialization, work patterns shifted and greater distinctions between the work places of men and women created greater divisions in their area of activity.[3]

In early 1800s, this division between the arenas of male and female activity began to get a cultural tint. One such person who is regarded as being most instrumental in and responsible for defining the basic tenets of the traditional women's spheres is Catherine Beecher. The life of Catherine Beecher, who was born in 1800 has been analyzed by Kathryn Kish Sklar in her book *Catherine Beecher: A Study in American Domesticity.*[4] Sklar's study reveals that Beecher oulined these tenets as being--domesticity, nurture and education. Beecher believed that the dichotomies of masculine and feminine identity could be channelised to conform to both -- "a standardized cultural score and a specialized personal Calling." Moreover, she believed that womanhood was a unifying force which could overcome regional, lineage or class distinctions. A similar public world could be chalked out for men. The private sphere of women did not encompass politics. Beecher also addressed elements of the physical location of the women's sphere as being in "classroom" and in "the home" and laid out explicit and original plans for "The American Woman's Home."[5]

In the mid 1960s, historians began substantially reinforcing the centrality of the metaphor of Separate spheres. In 1966 Barbara Welter published the *Cult of True Womanhood*, in which she studied nineteenth century women's fiction and popular prescriptive literature and identified a general nineteenth century stereotype which she called the *Cult of True Womanhood*[6]. She associated certain values with the cult of true womanhood--domesticity, piety, purity and submissiveness, the home was referred to as the women's proper sphere. However, in spite of finding Separate spheres to be a useful tool for studying women's experiences, Welter judged the sphere to be a negative development and said that the separation denigrated women and hence the "cult" had a deprecatory connotation, which symbolized the subordination of women to men.[7]

In 1975, Carroll Smith-Rosenherg presented a reinterpretation of 'separate spheres', and said that gender-role differentiation led to the emotional segregation of women and men.[8] She wrote that there existed a distinctive women's culture where women helped and assisted each other in times of pregnancy, childbirth, menopause and illness. This framework of social construction was built around a network of sigle sex or homo-social relationships which lent women with a physical and emotional intimacy. She used the testimony of printed and manuscript sources to support the hypothesis that eighteenth and nineteenth century Americans assumed the existence of distinctly male and female spheres.[9] She alludes to the fact that women did not form an isolated or suppressed sub-category within a male society, rather the letters and diaries of women revealed that the women's sphere had a integrity and dignity emanating from their shard experiences and mutual affection.[10]

Both Rosenberg and Sklar emphasize that the women's spheres formed the basis for the development of a sub-culture among women, which proved to be a source of strength and identity for them and contributed to the creation of sisterly relations. Thus according to Sklar, the ideology owed its tenacity as much to women's motives as to the imposition of men's or society's wishes.[11]

Nancy F. Cott has examined the letters of New England, middle class women's letters and diaries and found that they had a distinctive "orientation towards gender," that derived from shared patterns of work.[12] Cott believes that the domestic sphere become more conspicuous and more clearly articulated as women's prerogative towards the end of the eighteenth and the beginning of the nineteenth centuries. She points out that the shift of production and exchange away from the household and the gradual tightening of functional "spheres" led to greater specialization in the economy and society at large and made it seem "separate." She has consulted numerous sermons of ministers delivered during tht period and concludes that they attached a halo to the significance of the home and family and reconnected women's "separate" sphere with the general well-being of society.[13]

Reflecting on the positive influence of 'separate spheres,' Cott argues that the doctrine of 'separate spheres' opened to women or rather reserved for them, the avenues of domestic influence, religious morality and child nurturing, thus articulating a social power based on special female qualities. This represented an advance over the earlier belief of overall male dominance at home and outside. More importantly, Cott believes that the ideology of woman's 'sphere' formed a necessary stage in the process of shattering the hierarchy of sex and more directly, in softening the hierarchical relationship of marriage. Hence, she ended by proposing that the feminist political movement of the nineteenth century had grown out of the separation of 'spheres' and had taken its distinctive shape and interests from that separation.[14]

Cott asserts that domesticity and feminism were linked by a "woman's perception of womanhood"[15]. This consciousness, argues Cott was a necessary precondition for feminism. By stressing their difference from men, women got around the question of inferiority and superiority. Proponents of women's 'sphere' largely agreed with feminists' demands of enhancing self-esteem and freedom from obeisance to men's whims.

In the 1980s, Suzanne Lebsock published her work on antebellum Petersburg (Virginia) and rejected the notion of contributing history advocated by Gerda Lerner, which says that women should be tested on how they measure up on a masculine scale of achievement.[16] Lebsock believes that women all along created cultures of their own and that with enough imaginative research it should be possible to reconstruct women's cultures or their own 'spheres' and this, she believes would help in understanding how women experienced change and how their gender influenced their choices as active agents in history.[17] Relating separate spheres to industrialization, Lebsock believes that in pre-industrial society, the home was the center of economic production and men and women worked there in tandem, as has also been pointed out by Thatcher-Ulrich.[18] After industrialization, men went out to work while middle class women's stayed within the house and so the *cult cf true womanhood* was invented to make a virtue out of women's confinement to the home. While some historians saw this confinement as a decline on account of the economic aspects of women's status, Lebsock sees it as a sign of progress.[19] She agrees with Scott Smith and Carl Degler, who say that sexuality, affection and family relationships suggest a progress in women's position. Lebsock sa,s that the doctrine of 'separate spheres' may look sexist but it was an improvement over the sex-role ideology of the colonial period when women were held to be inferior in every way. Lebsock refers to Smith and Degler's view that the glorification of domesticity, greater social prestige to women's traditional roles of marriage and motherhood were now treated as sources of power. So relationships between wives and husbands became more companionate and less hierarchical. Degler describes the drive for autonomy within the family as a form of domestic feminism. Lebsock argues that women did gain power within the family without the assistance of a politically oriented discourse of organized feminism.[20]

L. Thatcher Ulrich studied the diary of Martha Ballard, a midwife in the late eighteenth and early nineteenth century and comments that men and women in early America had to work in tandem in order to complete any single life sustaining chore. However, in the next sentence she contradicts herself saying that a closer examination of that economy revels that its most striking feature is the independence of men and women's labours in production, management and utilization of resources. Laurel-Ulrich's study reveals that the financial accounts of Martha Ballard and her husband are "harmoniously separate," the former dealing with lumber and the latter with cabbage, textiles and midwifery. Similarly, the diaries maintained by men and women of the same period and place reflect upon the distance existing between the worlds of the two. While men recorded events of major political significance, such as the president's visit, Martha's diary recorded an account of the arduous, daily task of crossing the Kennebec river. The diary also highlights the gender-linked patterns of work with women -- daughters and nieces being borrowed and lent to do chores like weaving.[21] Even patterns of visiting showed gender segregation,husbands and wives seldom visited together. All these day to day needs, argues Thatcher-Ulrich, gave women a collective consciousness and defined their separateness from the men's world. Moreover as Linda Kerber suggests, the long absences such as those of Martha's husband, which were dictated by work patterns, perhaps reinforced the need to aintain the boundaries of a 'separate women's sphere.'

However, at this juncture, it is important to point out that many women also succeeded in expanding their sphere through means of education and learning and later on by joining professions, initially dominated by men. Thus, they transcended traditional gender-lines and could not be classified in any one sphere. Moreover, through their role as teachers and instruetresses, providing both secular and moral education, women created links between the 'public and the private spheres.' Hence, the two 'spheres' emerge as overlapping entities, rather than watertight compartments.

Nancy Hewitt, one of the leading critics of the theory of 'separate spheres' studies two exceptions to the concept of 'separate spheres'-- slave women, who did not define themselves in opposition to their male counterparts, rather they forged bonds of sisterhood and used these bonds as a weapon in the fight for black community survival.[22] From the perspective of slave experience, there existed strong communal ties among women. These ties were not rooted in any culture-bound concept of 'separation of spheres' but rather found their basis in material realities of a sexual division of labour. Slave women formed a collective power which was welded in defence of same-class men and in defiance of other class women. The second exception to the concept of 'separate spheres' is represeented by working class women, whose bonds were also forged due to a material or economic necessity.[23] Once again, like slave women, working women too formed bonds in the interest of men as well as women.

Moreover, even within middle class, women did not form a unified body in mid-nineteenth century, there were critical divisions along lines of economic and social interests. Moreover, as Cott argues, even in case of middle class women, if 'separate spheres' reserved certain avenues, it also barricaded against other options of advancement.[24] Lebsock also relents that greater power and autonomy within the house, resulting from 'separate spheres' would automatically mean, the creation of new forms of subordination in the public sphere.[25] Thus, the adherence of women of the privileged class, to a narrow and class-bound definition of women's proper 'sphere' though helped develop their own sense of community, was a barrier against the inclusion of women form other economic and social circumstances. Thus, middle class women advocated single-sex associations thereby alienating working class women, who did not want to create divisions within the heterosexual labour unions which operated within the working class community.

Thus, Hewitt concludes that there were cross-class aliances

which negated the existence of any single, women's culture or sphere.[26] There was only a culturally dominant definition of sexual spheres promulgated by an economically, politically, socially dominant group and was firmly grounded in, the sexual division of labour appropriate to that class alone. A final analysis by Hewitt insists that no such universal sisterhood existed, rather the development of a sense of community among various classes of women posed as a barrier to an all-embracing bond of womanhood. Louise Tilly agrees with Hewitt and believes that gender relations and interests which grow out of them, as well as the call location of women influence their political activism.[27]

The Marxist interpretation represented by Kraditor, Lerner and Fox-Genovese also argues that the concept of 'separate spheres' is a myth, rather than a historical reality.[28] They see it as tool of the dominant class and trace its origin to the Industrial Revolution which increased the difference between different classes and thus they conclude that 'separate spheres' served only the interests of the dominant classes. The central argument of the critics of 'separate spheres', therefore is that it is not a result of cultural accident or biological determinism, rather it was a conscious social construction serving the interests of a dominant class.

Linking the development of 'separate spheres' to the growth of industrialization, Kraditor and Lerner argue that industrialization affected work patterns and thus created greater distinction between women's and men's work. Men's work now became time disciplined and women's still remained task oriented. Cott also subscribes to this view saying that, industrial development affected pattern of work differently for men and women, and hence, led to the formation of separate spheres, which as Cott interprets as being the result of economic changes more than a construction of social forces.[29]

In the past decade, the historiography regarding women's history has emphasized the move beyond the concept of 'separate spheres'. Writings such as those by Rosalind Rosenberg mark the beginnings of modern studies of sex differences in the Progressive era. These studies which challenge the role of 'separate spheres', are based on the most significant critique of the notion, which as-sociologists, anthropologists, and psychologists are concluding is a result of socialization and not a biological creation. In this light, Rosenberg imagines a culture, which has not been divided into separate spheres. She believes that aproaches which look for the "women's problem" in a domain apart, fail to explain how men and women together participate in the creation of institutional forms.[30] She asserts that the language of 'separate spheres' denies reciprocity between gender and society and imposes a static model on dynamic relationships.

Linda Kerber echoes such views as she discusses the 'unpacking' of the metaphor of 'separate spheres' and embedding women's experience in the main course of human development. Men influenced 'separate spheres', yet at the same time, women's activities defined and influenced 'separate spheres' and set limitations on men's activities. Thus, 'separate spheres' were socially constructed both for and by women.[31]

Moreover, as Hewitt points out, such a theory is not universally applicable because many communities are often fashioned along social and economic divisions, rather than along lines of gender. Hence material considerations are more important than ideology.[32] Hence 'separate spheres' are useful only if used in consideration of the social and economic circumstances of the community of women under study. The theory of separate spheres can prove to be useful for a certain section or a particular community as is evident from Studies such as those by Cott and Lebsock about middle and upper class communities in New England and Petersburg. In these communities, women's experience was often limited only to the domestic sphere, hence a history of women's daily life in these communities would be best written if it is based on their role within their own sphere, rather than within the larger sphere of a society dominated by men. Thus, the role of the concept of 'separate spheres' in forging women's history cannot be negated, as emphasized by Cott, it acted as a major instrument in the creation of women's consciousness, as the guiding light of American women's suffrage movement, Elizabeth Cady Stanton very rightly proclaimed that not until they saw themselves thus classed by sex would women join to protest their common sexual fate.

REFERENCES

1. Erik Erikson, *Childhood and Society* (New York: Norton, 1964).
2. Laurel Thatcher Ulrich, *A Midwife's Tale: The Life of Martha Ballard Based on her Diary, 1785-1812* (New York: Vintage Books, 1990).

3. *Ibid.*
4. Kathryn Kish Sklar, Catherine Beecher: A Study in American Domesticity, (New Haven: Yale University Press, 1973).
5. *Ibid.*
6. Linda Kerber, *Toward an Intellectual History of Women: Essays* (Chapel Hill: University of North Carolina Press, 1997).
7. *Ibid.*
8. Carroll Smith-Rosenberg, *Disorderly Conduct: Visions of Gender in Victorian America* (New York: A.A. Knopf, 1985).
9. *Ibid.*
10. *Ibid.*
11. Sklar, *Catherine Beecher.*
12. Nancy F. Cott, *The Bonds of Womanhood: "Woman's Sphere"* in *New England*, 1780-1835 (New Haven: Yale University Press).
13. *Ibid.*
14. *Ibid.*
15. *Ibid.*
16. Suzanne Lebsock, *The Freewomen of Petersburg: Status and Culture in a Southern Town, 1784-1860* (New York: Norton, 1985).
17. *Ibid.*
18. Thatcher Ulrich, *A Midwife's Tale.*
19. Lebsock, *Freewomen of Petersburg.*
20. *Ibid.*
21. Thatcher Ulrich, *A Midwife's Tale.*
22. Nancy Hewitt, "Beyond the Search for Sisterhood: American Women's History in 1980s," *Social History* 10, No. 1. (1985): pp. 299-321.
23. *Ibid.*
24. Cott, *Bonds of Womanhood.*
25. Lebsock, *Freewomen of Petersburg.*
26. Hewitt, "Beyond the Search for Sisterhood."
27. *Ibid.*
28. Kerber, *Toward an Intellectual History of Women.*
29. Cott, *Bonds of Womanhood.*
30. Kerber, *Toward an Intellectual History of Women.*
31. *Ibid.*
32. Hewitt, "Beyond the Search for Sisterhood."

2

NEI AND WAI

The Relevance of Separate Spheres in the History of Women in Traditional China

The theory of separate spheres attempts to explain the construction of arenas of autonomy and influence whereby the public space was open to men and the private to women. In case of the Chinese society, Confucian moralists constructed the norms of gender difference around a bifurcation of spheres into inner (*nei*) and outer (*wai*)—terms which demarcated separate spaces but also claimed a complementarity between them. Charlotte Furth sees the demarcation of inner and outer spheres as an extension of the Chinese cosmological concepts of *yin and yang.*[1] Thus, she argues that traditional Chinese philosophers and moralists used *yin and yang* to give a metaphysical grounding to the gender boundaries demarcating domestic and public space in the social as well as natural world. In the textual tradition of the Inner Canon during the Han dynasty, *yin* was supposed to evoke darkness, cold, moisture, that which was hidden, latent or passive, the moon, night and the feminine. *Yang*, on the other hand symbolized brightness, the sun, fire, warmth, activity and the masculine principle. By analogy, *yin and yang* further regulated the social world and its spatial divisions of upper and lower, inner and outer regions.[2]

However, as Charlotte Furth points out, *yin and yang* were highly ambivalent and relative concepts. Thus, when structuring a binary of complementarity of hierarchy, they established relations of equality or inequality. Furth, further illustrates that in the movement from night to day or from summer to winter, *yin and yang* forces are matched evenly over the longrun, since the rise of one is balanced by the decline of the other. Following from this, latent phases of an aspect was considered— "*yin within yang*" or "*yang within yin.*" Furth says that the second relationship arranged *yin and yang* into a hierarchy.[3] Both models of the relationship between *yin and yang*—(1) the hierarchical, unequal and encompassing, (2) complementary and equivalent, are visible in the gender discourse within the Chinese society.

Hence, just as there could be multiple possible configurations of *yin and yang* within the natural world of the human body, which varied from individual to individual, so too within the context of society, though men were excepted to tilt towards a preponderance of *yang* qualities and women were expected to have an affinity for *yin* qualities, in fact the two were interpenetrable.

A thorough study by historians such as Dorothy Ko and Susan Mann, shows that *nei and wai* were not watertight compartments, but were rather interpenetrable divisions which worked best when they worked in cooperation.[4-5] The strict demarcation of the inner and outer spheres is more of an ideological view which does not always conform to the reality of traditional Chinese society.

Dorothy Ko highlights the two widely held misconceptions regarding the status of Chinese women, firstly, the image of the cloistered woman, crippled by bound feet and imprisoned in her inner chambers. Secondly, that the female domestic sphere is totally separate from the male public sphere and that the family is immune to politics. In order to refute these misconceptions, it is essential to take a brief look at the social construction of gender identities in China.[6]

Right from the time of her birth, a girl was seen as a small happiness while a boy's birth symbolized a big happiness. When they reached seven years of age, girls and boys in elite families were not allowed to sit and eat together on the same mat. At age ten the distinction between *nei and wai* became very specific. Ideally there was to be very little contact between the two. Men were expected to go to *nei* only at night. At fifteen *sui,* the rites of passage for a girl were performed as the hairpinning and at twenty *sui* the boys had their copping ceremony. Both were now considered adults—ready for marriage.[7] Thus, right from childhood the roles of girls and boys were demarcated. The girls were being prepared to follow *San Cong* or three obediences: to their fathers, husbands and sons and *si de* or the four womanly virtues: (1) virtue, (2) handwork, (3) speech and (4) comportment. Thus, as Ann Walters has shown, at each stage a child was expected to assume more of the responsibilities and roles of an adult and those responsibilities and roles were always specific to gender.[8]

Dorothy Ko, in her book *Teachers of the Inner Chambers* clarifies and refutes the two misconceptions about Chinese women and society, discussed earlier in the essay. Firstly, she says that despite the moral precepts saying that women should stay at home, even gentry women travelled a great deal.[9] They accompanied their husbands across long distances on official appointments and also went on excursions for pleasure and pilgrimages with other women. Moreover, as Susan Mann points out, even within the home, women were not confined simply to their inner quarters, she shows by the example of Zhang Xuecheng's mother, that some women did emerge from the women's apartments and mingled with the guests when their husbands entertained.[10]

Dorothy Ko, attacks the second misconception by reflecting on the crucial interaction between family and state on the one hand and between men and women, both inside and outside the family on the other. Susan Mann agrees with Ko and says that women philosophized about their influence in the public sphere during the eighteenth century. She substantiates her view by referring to a highly educated eighteenth century Chinese woman Jiang Lan, who studied the Odes and followed her wifely duties. She said that the "women's quarters" were the place where filial respect and collegial relations began extending outward through those who ruled. She, even went as far as saying that, there was no place which women did not govern. Susan Mann rightly says that, Jiang Lan was a product of eighteenth century classical revival and understood herself to be at the heart of political discourse and knew that her power derived precisely from her cloistered position in the home.[11]

Further on, Susan Mann argues that the history of gender

relations in the High Qing era shows that in Chinese culture at that time, women's homely place in the elite public discourse was recognized and articulated by leading intellectuals. Philosopher Zhang Xuecheng acknowledged the dependence of the public man on cloistered woman, by noting that her words too could be "everyone's" thus, showing a pervasive awareness of the intimate relationship between family life and public politics.[12]

Further, Ko's study of women and culture in the seventeenth century, shows that through reading and writing, elite women developed new spheres of influence and expanded the domain of kinship and friendship beyond the domestic space and mastered the tools of learning that had been the domain of men and articulated notions of talent and beauty in a dialogue with husbands, lovers, fathers and teachers, both male and female.[13] Thus, reading, writing and emergence of talented women in companionate marriages expanded women's sphere into a domain previously dominated by men.[14]

Both Susan Mann and Dorothy Ko question the validity of 'separate spheres' as an analytical tool for the study of women's history.[15] A brief look at the western debate about this issue via means of Joan Kelly's influential essay in 1979, argued that women's history should be approached in rational terms and with a "doubled vision". Kelly says that, women's place is not a 'separate sphere' or domain of existence, a position within social existence generally, she further stresses that relegating men and women to neatly defined spheres often reflects the wishes of the patriarch more than it does social reality.[16] Ko further argues that binaries such as "domestic" and "public" are inadequate because they assume an opposition as a historical given rather than explaining its existence in the first place.[17]

Another major criticism levied against the concept of 'separate spheres' is that it does not take into consideration socio-economic differences. As discussed in the Western debate regarding the relevance of 'separate spheres', elsewhere in the book, feminist Historians like Nancy Hewitt, Gerda Lerner and Elizabeth Fox-Genovese, negate the importance of 'separate spheres' by saying that often society is madeup of class interests and so womanhood is not a unifying experience which cuts across class lines. Thus, there was no homogenous body called Chinese women, since there were differences between elite women, wives of traders and countryside peasant women. And all these groups had different experiences. Susan Mann illustrates this point by showing examples of poor women who were at work breaking up clods of earth with a hoe, some were ploughing in pairs alongside their husbands.[18] In the novel, *Dream of the Red Chamber,* Granny Liu, who was close to Grandmother Jia in age, leads her life in sharp contrast to that of the latter.[19] She doesnot live confined to her own quarters, rather she farms a plot of land and travels all alone with her small grandson all the way from her village to the city. Mann further says that nowhere were the marks of class distinguishing women more clearly visible than in the practice of footbinding. She shows how unbound feet marked the low-born pariah woman and set her apart.[20] So the distinctions between inner and outer spheres were not absolute in themselves, rather they changed with changing socio-economic circumstances.

Ko also follows along similar lines and argues that there was a continuity between inner (*nei*) and outer (*wai*) domains of action that women inhabited. Ko points out that although always rendered in English as "domestic" and "public" or "inner" and "outer", in their Chinese context, these were always relative and relational terms.[21] She elaborates on the point and says that the inner and outer construct does not demarcate mutually exclusive social and symbolic spaces instead the two define and constitute each other according to shifting contexts and perspectives. For example, *Qing* monarchy saw the family as the site where public morality could be exemplified.[22]

Susan Mann also supports this view, saying that in the *High Qing* times the distinction between *nei and wai,* between women's inner sphere and men's outer sphere is quite unlike the western dichotomy separating the "domestic" from the "public" sphere. Instead, the principle of *bie* or 'separate spheres' is invoked to stress that wives and mothers inside the home embody the moral autonomy and authority on which husbands and sons must rely to succeed outside.[23]

As Charlotte Furth asserts that there existed a complementarity between *nei and wai.* Since the family as the 'inner' was seen as a microcosm of the state as the 'outer' responsible for its own sphere of social order.[24] Public functions such as education and learning, often began at home with the mother being expected to perform the role of the instructoress for both boys and girls. Hence, it is appropriate to agree with Dorothy Ko and Francesca Bray that the inner and outer are best imagined as nested and overlapping spheres whose boundaries shifted with circumstances.[25]

Ko stresses that since the borders between inner and outer or between private and public are ambivalent, shifting and open to negotiation, cases of women crossing boundaries are particularly revealing about the nature of those boundaries and the terms of their negotiation. She cites as examples cases of such gender role reversals as girls raised as boys and women as professional writers who were the bread winners of the family.[26] Susan Mann, in her article "Learned Women in the Eighteenth Century", also writes about learned women like Jia Yi who brought inkstones and brushes into her marriage as part of her dowry and "within a few days turned the bedroom into a study". Similarly, in a Ming memoir of their mother, Lady Li, Yuan Biao and his brothers recorded her enterpreneurial skills, including her ability to wring savings out of a Spartan budget and keep the patriline out of debt.[27]

Ko agrees that the rich tradition that the seventeenth century literate women created and celebrated was largely separate from the world of men, although it was definitely not "separatist". She argues that while shared concerns, routines, rituals and emotions distinguished the female world from the male, the very construction of such routines and rituals was a product of interactions with the prerogatives, networks and enterprises of men. She argues that no single word such as "domination" or "subjugation" can adequately describe the nature of relationships between these men and women. Tensions are inherent in the workings of *yin and yang.* However, the situation is not simplified, rather as in the case of other social setups the Chinese concept of separate spheres is also quite complicated.

The inner and outer beings are relative and not absolute, Martin W. Huang establishes an analogy between two marginalized groups within Chinese society, the women on the one hand and the politically distressed male literati on the other. He said, like wives and concubines competed with each other for the husband's favours, so too the ministers competed for the emperor's favours and so both marginalized groups suffered from the so-called 'concubine complex'. Therefore, Huang concludes, femininity is a gender attribute not a fixed identity associated with women alone. Further, he says that women were not necessarily subjugated by men, merely by virtue of their being women.[28]

Hence *yin and yang* are in fact hierarchical and complementary. Had they been purely heirarchical, their relationship would have been separate and unequal. Conversely, had they been purely complementary, the resultant relationships would have been separate and equal. However, the case is not so clear or simple. Both kinds of relationships existed, simultaneously. Since the Chinese society tolerated both these seemingly contradictory kinds of ideas.

Thus, although the use of 'separate spheres' is helpful in shedding light on certain aspects of women's experiences, it fails to take into consideration the whole picture. Women's 'sphere' was in fact a part of and intricately linked to the public 'sphere'. Moreover many women did not confine themselves to the traditional roles within their ascribed 'sphere', rather they ventured into men's sphere of activity. Hence, there was constant interaction and coordination between the two 'spheres' and the success of one depended on the proper and smooth functioning of the other.

REFERENCES

1. Charlotte Furth, *A Flourishing Yin: Gender in China's Medical History.* (Berkeley: University of California Press, 1999), p. 2.
2. *Ibid.*, pp. 6-7.
3. *Ibid.*, pp. 21, 28, 49-50.
4. Dorothy Ko, *Teachers of the Inner Chambers: Women and Culture in Seventeenth Century China* (Stanford: Stanford University Press, 1994).
5. Susan Mann, *Precious Records: Women in China's Long Eighteenth Century* (Stanford: Stanford University Press, 1997).
6. Ko, *Teachers of the Inner Chambers,* pp. 12-14, Passim.
7. *Sui* symbolizes the Chinese version of the age of an individual in years. However, the Chinese count the beginning of every year as a new year in a person's life, so for example, five years in western parlance could be equated to six *sui.*

8. Mann, *Precious Records*, p. 47.
9. Ko, *Teachers of the Inner Chambers*, p. 12.
10. Mann, *Precious Records*, p. 247, n. 37.
11. *Ibid.*, p. 204.
12. *Ibid.*, p. 223.
13. Ko, *Teachers of the Inner Chambers*, p. 12-17. Passim.
14. Mann, *Precious Records*, p. 236, n. 19.
15. *Ibid.*, p. 223.
16. Joan Kelly, *Women, History and Theory: The Essays of Joan Kelly.* (Chicago: University of Chicago Press, 1984).
17. Ko, *Teachers of the Inner Chambers*, p. 12.
18. Mann, *Precious Records*, pp. 163-64, 167-68.
19. David Hawkes, *The Dream of the Red Chamber,* Vols. 1-5. (London: Penguin Books, 1973).
20. Mann, *Precious Records*, p. 55.
21. Ko, *Teachers of the Inner Chambers*, P. 10-13, 115, 133. Passim.
22. *Ibid.*, pp. 140-42.
23. Mann, *Precious Records*, pp. 163-64, 167-68. Passim.
24. Furth, *A Flourishing Yin*, pp. 6-7.
25. Ko, *Teachers of the Inner Chambers*, p. 133-37.
26. *Ibid.*, pp. 10-13, 17, 98, 122, 207-09, 219-24.
27. Susan Mann, "learned Women in the Eighteenth Century," in *Engendering China: Women, Culture and the State*, ed., Christina Gilmartin. (Cambridge: Harvard University Press, 1994).
28. Martin W. Huang, *Literati and Self-Representation: Autobiographical Sensibility in the Eighteenth Century Chinese Novel.* (Stanford: Stanford University Press, 1995).

3

GENDER IN THE IMMIGRANT EXPERIENCE

The Role of Women Migrants in the Process of Immigration and Integration in the American Society

Until recently, the history of immigration suffered from the same gender stereotyping which was characteristic of other social histories, the term 'migrant' carried a masculine connotation, unless otherwise specified. However, the assumption that the 'true' migrant is male, leads to misleading theoretical conclusions regarding the history of immigration. In her essay, "The Role of Gender in the Dominican Settlement in the United States," Patricia Pessar writes that until the late 1970s, most researchers excluded women from the study of migrant populations.[1] She argues that the early immigrant histories often assumed that a dichotomy existed between men and women. Men were allegedly more apt to be risk-takers and achievers, while women were portrayed as guardians of tradition and stability.[2] Based on this premise, women migrants were passive followers of male pioneers. A classic example of this kind of study is Oscar Handlin's *Boston's Immigrants*, published in 1959, which assumed that immigrants were primarily male.[3] This kind of misconception was cleared away by the publication of later works, especially since the late 1970s onwards. Such studies describe patterns of immigration in which women migrate first, and later may be joined by other family members. This approach towards immigrant history is characteristic of Hasia Diner's *Erin's Daughters*, which traces the history of immigration through female lines.[4] This book focuses on Irish women immigrants who represent the only group of immigrants in which women outnumbered men by constituting 52.9 per cent of the total immigrant population. In this case, often daughters were the first members of their families to migrate and then helped others to emigrate.

The second factor that contributed to the disregard for female migrants was the common conflation of the term 'migrant' with 'waged-labour,' and the misapprehension that women do not work. This misconception was reflected in the French Government's classification of Algerians in official statistics, as men, and as women and children under sixteen. The latter group was assumed to be dependent on wage-earning males.[5] However, such a lop-sided view has long been corrected. Women are no longer seen as dependents of men. Patricia Pessar reiterates this point by quoting that 19.5 per cent of all Dominican women surveyed in the New York Metropolitan area in 1981 had been employed at least once since their emigration.[6] Other works such as Hasia Diner's *Erin's Daughters,* Christine Stansell's *City of Women*, Susan Glenn's *Daughters of the Shtetl,* Alice Kessler Harris' *Out To Work*, and various essays on Chinese, Japanese and Mexican immigrants in *Unequal Sisters*, Ellen Du Bois' anthology on women, give detailed accounts of women as factory workers, domestic helpers, nurses and teachers. Even women whose culture did not allow them to work out of the house, such as Italian women, took in lodgers and did their washing and cooking to supplement the household income.[7] Pessar shows that it has been recognised that immigrant women's work in the household can help to stretch the low family income.[8]

Hence, women contribute in various ways to the immigrant experience of the family just as men do, therefore, considering just men would give only half the picture because women also contributed to the income and helped stabilize the home. Similarly, by writing a genderless history, one generalizes the experiences of both sexes into a common one and this amount to negation of gender differences and the resulting distinctiveness of male and female immigrant experiences.

At this juncture, it is essential to briefly understand, why women's immigrant experience is different from that of men. A very significant factor which shapes the experiences of women immigrants differently from men is the fact that women are forced to suffer dual oppression. Asian Indian writer Mina Alexander writes in her book, *The Shock of Arrival*, that while the experience of living within an immigrant household is difficult for every member of the family, it is especially tough for women because they have to contend with both, how they are seen as women, given the harshness and domination of patriarchy, and secondly, how as immigrants they are seen as marginal to the mainstream.[9]

Another significant difference in women's experience as immigrants is rooted in the fact that they often moved around and socialized in their own spheres of activity and daily household chores. As Hasia Diner puts its, "politics and saloon life, clubs and organizations belonged to men, but the home and its purse strings as well as its future belonged to women. The immigrant women knew which sphere was more important."[10] They were very content and secure in the knowledge that they managed the home economy. This is especially true for those immigrants whose ethnic background prescribes women's role to be limited to the household economy, rather than working outside with men. Moreover, even in cases where women did work outside the house, they simultaneously remained much preoccupied with and responsible for running the household and taking care of their families, thus, they develop social relations with neighbours, street vendors and local grocery merchants. Moreover, while on the one hand, men work side by side with men from different ethnic backgrounds, on the other hand, women who are confined to their homes, often located within their own ethnic enclaves such as, ghettos and *shtetls*, consequently the women continue to interact within their own ethno-cultural circle, and thus find it difficult to become part of mainstream America.

Significantly enough the problem of the language barrier also hinders women's assimilation process. Men and children find more opportunities to interact with the mainstream society, at work or at school, as a result, they are more likely to pick up the new language faster than their mothers who spend most of their time at home. Women's inability to learn the new language as fast as their children creates a cultural and linguistic chasm between them and their children and sometimes results in shaking or diminishing the mother's authority.

Finally, another major factor distinguishing women immigrant experiences from those of men is the emotional variable. Writings of Hasia Diner, Christine Stansell, Susan Glenn, and films on immigration such as *Hester Street*, show experiences of western European women immigrants, many of whom were deserted by their fathers or husbands. However, unlike many men who could not cope with the dislocation resulting from migration, and the pressure of maintaining families and ultimately deserted their wives and children, women rarely had this option. The emotional and altruistic nature inherent in most women and their social and cultural conditioning as nurturers and caretakers of the family, bound them to their families. Instead of fleeing, they worked double shifts—at work place and at home, to feed, clothe and shelter their families. In other words, they could not afford to escape the immigrant experience, and could not return home as some of the Irish male immigrants did. These women were forced to face the challenge meted out to them in the new land and culture, and they tried to make the best of it.

The double worked load, and the responsibility of running the household, left the women drained physically, mentally, and even materially. Sometimes, they did not have adequate resources to support themselves. In *City of Women*, Christine Stansell argues that the immigrant women were able to create urban communities in the context of massive transience by drawing on traditions of cooperation and mutual aid.[11] Women formed support groups. These mutual aid societies and support groups could take the form of religious institutions, such as the Irish *Sisters of Service* and *Sisters of Mercy*, where nuns, helped Irish women.[12] They could also take the shape of welfare organizations run by the community, such as *Manushi* and *Shakti*, run by Asian Indian women, these organizations organize cultural festivals and also give shelter to victims of domestic violence. As Hasia Diner says women found aid through the support of female religious orders, and benevolent self-help institutions which emerged from the tradition of gender segregation and from sympathetic bonds that untied women with one another. Hence, through such networks, women formed a sub-culture of their own within the broader mainstream ethnic culture of their community.[13]

Just as the formation of these welfare organizations is common to women immigrants of all ethnicities, their experiences at work are also similar and cut across racial, ethnic and geographical lines, and in some cases they even transcend the boundary of time and place. Work has been common to the experience of most women immigrants to the US from around the world. Even women who came from societies, where women traditionally did not leave the house, for example, in Japan, began joining the ranks of working women once they came to the US. The next section of the essay explores some cross-cultural experiences which working women immigrants had.

One of the most significant avenues of work available to immigrant women in both the nineteenth and the twentieth centuries is constituted by domestic service. Domestic service was initially provided by Chinese girls and thus was looked upon as leading to status degradation, thus, none of the Caucasian women wanted to do such work.[14] The only exception being Irish women who accepted such occupations firstly, due to the sheer excess of their numbers vis-a-vis the number of jobs which were available to them, and secondly, they were victims of discrimination in factories, and so they tried to avoid confrontation with hostility by working as maids. Thirdly, it is essential to note that young Irish girls often came without their families, and hence did not mind residing in their employers' house. In the nineteenth century, Irish girls filled the ranks of domestic servants, in fact as Hasia Diner writes, the image of "Bridget"--the Irish house-maid became almost synonymous to that of an Irish girl.[15] In the twentieth century, on the west coast of America, Japanese women provided similar services. Even though a century, and miles of land separated the two groups of domestic workers, yet, their experiences were not so different from one another. Unlike the European immigrant women, who were young and single, most of the *Issei*, or the first generation-Japanese women domestics were married and had children.[16] However, at work, they both had similar experiences, both had to work long hours, suffer the humiliation of being spied upon and face the menace of the sexual innuendoes of male members of employers' household.[17]

The largest employer of immigrant women was the factory or the mill. While during the nineteenth century, on the east coast of the US, garment or textile factories were the largest employers of European immigrants on the west coast, canneries were the biggest employers of Mexican women immigrants.

In her essay on Mexican cannery workers in Southern California. Vicki L. Ruiz argues that Mexican family and work networks rèsemble those found by historian Thomas Dublin in the Lowell, Massachusetts mills in the antebellum era.[18] Californian canneries and New England cotton mills, though a century apart, contained similar intricate kin and friendship networks. She further says that Dublin's statement, "women recruited one another, secured jobs for each other, and helped newcomers make the numerous adjustments called for in a very new and different setting," can be applied directly to the Mexican experience. Like the Irish women who called over their sisters and nieces to America and found them jobs, Mexican women too not only assisted their relatives and friends in obtaining employment but also initiated *neophytes* into the rigour of cannery routines.[19] She reiterates Dublin's view that factories provide clear evidence of the maintenance of traditional kinds of social relationships in a new setting and serving new purposes. These Mexican women formed friendships across cultural lines, especially with Russian-Jewish women, who also found employment in Southern Californian food processing firms.[20]

Historians Leslie Tentler and Susan Porter Benson studying women workers on the east coast, have also documented the existence of female work cultures. However, a major difference was that, unlike the European immigrant women workers. Mexican women were not waiting for a Prince Charming to take them away from factory labour, rather they realized that they would continue their seasonal labour even after marriage.[21]

The third major means of employment at the disposal of women immigrants was their piece work at home--they took in pieces of clothing to be finished by sewing the seams or buttons etcetera. Stansell points out that such piece work assignments fulfilled the requirements of married women, tied to the demands of children and household, as it provided a means of earning a living without leaving the tenements.[22] These home workers sewed pieces of the garment-cuffs, buttonholes, sleeves, and artificial flowers.[23] Mostly Jewish and Italian women did not traditionally work outside the home, rather they took in boarders and supplemented household income.[24]

The interaction of women with people from different cultures and ethnicities, their experiences at work in a new country and societies inevitably result in changing at least some or many aspects of women's lives. In many cases, the migration to America profoundly altered family relations and affected the status of women within traditionally patriarchal families. Moreover, in the context of migratory groups dominated by women, such as in the case of the Irish, the nature of migration and the high proportion of women, it should not be surprising that the Irish communities in the United States were likewise predominantly female. Moreover, the frequent desertion of the male breadwinners, industrial accidents leading to deaths produced a striking number of female-headed households. Yet, despite all odds, Irish women had a fierce determination to sustain their families and to ensure some degree of upward movement, in fact, Irish women exerted tremendous influence within their families.[25] Diner argues that even some families with fathers present could also have been described as mother-centered. Even though, the tradition of strong, assertive Irish women, which had its roots in Ireland's rural economy, this Irish trait became even more pronounced in America and its urban environment.[26]

The status of the father in the Irish family eroded after migration, since the father no longer exerted the same degree of authority connected with the whole process of transfer of land. Diner argues that, as the male role weakened, the female one, accumulated greater prestige and authority. Much of the Irish popular literature portrayed women as "civilizens" constantly attempting to stop men from drinking.[27] Diner quotes sociologist Andrew Greeley saying that the forceful Irish matriarch "exists in America."[28] Even women who renounced the world and became nuns as *Sister of Service* played important economic roles within the community by donating vast sums of money to their *parishes* and to buy plots of land for church buildings. In *Out to Work*, Alice Kessler Harris writing about Russian Jew said that working girls earned their own room and board and got there own rooms within their houses. Fathers gave such privileges to working daughters.[29]

The migration to America gave greater autonomy and self-reliance even to women who came to America from societies without a legacy of female assertiveness. A classic example of this case being that of the *Issei*--or the first generation Japanese women. In her article on Japanese women, Evelyn Nakano Glenn writes that Japanese women who worked as domestics, despite hardships involved, felt lucky to be in the United States because here they got economic opportunities which they would not have had in Japan. They felt proud to be self-sufficient and could face life even when their husbands died or wasted their earnings in getting drunk. Many women defied their husbands and worked secretly and kept their earnings to spend on themselves or their children.[30]

Besides the economic benefits of being working women, Japanese women also formed relationships outside the family, often when the husband abused them, they found material and emotional comfort in the support offered by their employers.[31] However, the most significant reward was the pride and power to spend, which came from being self-sufficient. Nakano-Glenn argues that far from being passive and expressing the traditional Japanese attitude of bearing hardships, these women actively fought with their husbands.[32]

Immigration to the US provided the gift of modernism and education and proved most valuable to women. This is especially true in the case of Chinese women, their restrictive lives began to change in the twentieth century, a growing number of them began to free themselves of social restrictions by working outside the house and more particularly, by educating their daughters.[33] Judy Yung argues that the contemporary Chinese newspaper *Chung Sai Yat Po*, published in San Francisco's China Town also reported cases of divorce which were definitely an American influence on the response of Chinese women to unjust and unhappy marriages.[34]

Even though the decline of patriarchal authority and family control over the individual had positive effects in the improvement of women's status, nevertheless, this breakdown of the traditional, familial authority had a serious negative consequence in the form of prostitution. Christine Stansell writes that the trans-Atlantic migration separated many daughters from their parents and sent them off on their own, and hence the patriarchal controls over young women's leisure time, earnings and sexuality weakened accordingly.[35] Such freedom could have drastic effects if coupled with what Stansell calls the degrading and impoverished situation of female wage labourers. In City of Eros, Timothy Gilfoyle argues that the major factor inducing women to sell their bodies was the low wages female labour.[36] This situation was further heightened by the great numbers of immigrant women, which led to greater competition for a limited number of jobs. Gilfoyle further says that Federal Immigration Acts of 1921, 1924 and 1929, considerably reduced the number of transient men and women of the streets of New York.[37] Stansell refers to women who engaged in sexual barter in return for food, drink and lodgings. She also points out the fact that incidences of desertion or death of spouse in industrial accidents also forced women, especially mothers with very young children to resort to prostitution. John D' Emilio and Estelle B. Freedman also report such cases. In one such instance, a German woman was robbed of all her money, the very day she reached the shore.[38] The authors of *Intimate Matters* also argue that the immigrant families, especially women were also influenced by the American sexual and commercial culture. They mention the example of Seattle, where Japanese-American families lived alongside burlesque houses whose doors were covered with life-size paintings of half-naked girls, making it hard for girls to grow up into the "refined, young maidens," their parents wished them to be.[39] Similarly, many lodging houses in which single, working men or young women lived were also locales for casual prostitution. Many Chinese girls, who were kidnapped or indentured had to pay their passage to America by working in the lowest form of brothels–the small "cribs," or rooms that lined San Francisco's China Town.[40] However, this dark side of the immigration experience was countered by the presence of reform houses where destitute women could go for shelter. Gilfoyle records that in 1843, Roman Catholics established Sisters of Mercy to dissuade Irish girls from falling into prostitution and Sisters of the Good Shepherd to redeem those who had fallen.[41]

The influence of mainstream American society and social movements is also visible in the influence of the American feminist movements which influenced similar movements among immigrant groups. As discussed briefly, earlier immigrant women have to suffer dual oppression, as women and as immigrants, this oppressive burden is even further heightened in the case of the so-called, "coloured women," mainly from Asia and Latin America.[42] In contrast to the Caucasian women immigrants, Alma M. Garcia, in "The Development of Chicana Feminism and Discourse," says that the nature of social inequality for women of colour was multi-dimensional. Stirred by the Civil Rights movement in the 1970s, these Asian America and *Chicano* women also organized feminist movements and fought for social equality. In fact their feminism involved more than an analysis of gender because as women of colour, they were affected by both gender and colour in their everyday lives. Both Asian American and *Chicano* feminists believed that their movement had both nationalist and feminist components. Asian American women and *Chicanos* were all confronted with the issue of engaging in a feminist struggle to end *sexist* oppression within a broader nationalist struggle to end racist oppression.[43] Both experienced male domination in their own communities as well as in the large society. Ngan-Ling Chow in her work on Asian American women identifies gender stereotyping and patriarchal family structure as the major oppressors of women.[44] They failed to join the general White Women's feminist movement because they believed that it overlooks the crucial question of racial differences.[45] Hence these immigrant women came to America, and inspired by the mainstream feminist movement formed their pawn feminist organizations which were formulated to cater to needs which were specific to their experience of racial and gender discrimination and oppression.

Thus, women play very important role in migrant communities. The character of immigrant groups changes considerably once women are included. They, in fact help make a migrant group into a settlement. Providing male migrants with the anchorage of family and home life. They set up and managed the home economy. Most often Women's aspirations for upward mobility were responsible for pushing the family and motivating the men to work towards a rise from the lower to the middle class. What Diner calls making their way from a "pick and shovel" shanty life to the "lace curtains" of the middle class. Thus, they had a stabilizing influence on the family members.[46]

Another important role played by immigrant women was their role as teachers and guides helping their children to integrate within the mainstream American culture and ideology. Surveys of immigrant mothers, by Indian writers have shown how mothers helped smoothen the process of migration to and assimilation into a new society. The mothers have been reported as explaining concepts of nationalism and multi-religious, and multi-ethnic society.[47] In Hester Street, a film on Jewish immigration, the mother of a young boy insists on using the Americanized version of his name in a bid to acculturate and make assimilation in American society easy for him.

However, while mothers do try to help the children in their integration into the new society, they are at the same time, the main preservers of tradition. As Jewish women in Abraham Cahan's stories compiled by Moses Rischin in *Grandma Never Lived in America*--their most precious possessions, which they had carried across the Atlantic were the traditional candlesticks, which they lit every Sabbath, similarly, these women were most concerned about serving only kosher meat, to procure which, they even took the butchers to court.[48]

Studies in Ellen Dubois' anthology also stresses the role of Japanese mothers as preservers of tradition. The Issei women instilled a sense of great respect for traditional values and authority in their Nisei or the second generation Japanese children.[49] Indian mothers are at the forefront regarding this issue. They insist on repairing and serving the time consuming and laborious Indian style meals. They take their children to celebrations of their community and teach them traditional dances and other aspects of their culture. In her essay on Mexican women immigrants, George J. Sanchez writes that Chicanas in particular have been seen as the "glue" that keeps the *Chicano* family together, and they have been designated as the individual responsible for the maintenance of Mexican tradition.[50]

As Hasia Diner puts it succinctly, the actions of immigrant women stemmed from family loyalties and represented a commitment to "Irish catholic" culture, and their own national heritage and its way of life. She argues rightly that the move to America did not represent a search for a new identity, nor did it constitute a break from the past.[51]

A brief look at the experiences of women immigrants to the US in the nineteenth and the twentieth centuries shows many similarities. Women's still have to encounter occasional racist attitudes at work. In traditional communities such as those from India and Pakistan, women still have to carry the double burden of working outside as well as within the house, though now they are beginning to get some help from their male counterparts. Significantly enough, a comparison of the two centuries also shows a positive trend in various other aspects of the lives of immigrant women in the twentieth century. Today women have much easier access to educational opportunities, which form an important tool in their development and provide them opportunity for rise in occupational and professional hierarchy, so that they can create better lives for themselves and their family. The Silicon Valley in California provides one such example, where women have managed to raise the status of living by undergoing training in computer technology.

Greater acceptance of immigrants and a gradual erosion of sentiments of racial prejudice within mainstream American society creates environment, which facilitates women's adjustment into the new society. Moreover, women today are more aware of their rights and they cannot be exploited by their employers. The presence of support groups and women's bureaus and anti-domestic violence cells has also deterred husbands from physically abusing their wives. Women's legal position has also improved by the enactment of laws safeguarding their rights. Victims of physical and mental abuse can now also secure psychiatric help. Revolution in mass media, communications and information technology has linked the world better. Thus, women immigrant from different cultural and ethnic backgrounds do not suffer from cultural shock, thus, easing their assimilation into American mainstream society. Hence, the immigrant experience is much less painful today than it might have been in the nineteenth century.

In conclusion, this survey of the histories of women immigrants to the US from around the world, demonstrates the necessity of including gender as a key variable in accounting for features of the migration experience. As preservers of tradition, women pass down a unique cultural heritage to their daughters. Hence, not just immigrant women but even women who are daughters of immigrants play a crucial role in assimilating what Moses Rischin calls "Two Worlds and Two Souls."[52] Hence, women immigrant are responsible for helping the male immigrants in coping with dualism and biculturalism--the natural by-products of immigrant experience. The process of bequeathing values and beliefs of the old country strengthens bonds between first and second generation immigrants, and from unique blend of the two cultures which goes beyond generational differences.

REFERENCES

1. Patricia Pessar, "the Role of Gender in Dominican Settlements in the United States," in *Women and Change in Latin America*, ed. June Nash and Helen Safa. (Massachusetts: Bergin and Garvey Publishers, Inc., 1985), pp. 273-74.
2. *Ibid.*, p. 273.
3. Oscar Handlin, *Boston's Immigrants* (Cambridge: the Belknop Press of Harvard University Press, 1959).
4. Hasia R. Diner, *Erin's Daughters in America: Irish Immigrant Women in the Nineteenth Century* (London: The John Hopkins University Press, 1983).
5. Pessar, "Gender in Dominican Settlements," p. 274.
6. *Ibid.*
7. Christine Stansell, *City of Women: Sex and Class in New York, 1789-1860* (Chicago: University of Illinois Press, 1987); Susan A. Glenn, *Daughters of the Shtetl* (Ithaca: Cornell University Press, 1990); Alice Kessler Harris, *Out To Work* (New York: Oxford University Press, 1982); Ellen Carol Du Bois and Vicki L. Ruiz ed., *Unequal Sisters: A Multicultural Reader in U.S. Women's History* (New York: Routledge, 1990).
8. Pessar, "Gender in Dominican Settlements," p. 286.
9. Mina Alexander, *The Shock of Arrival: Reflections on Postcolonial Experience* (Boston: South End Press, 1996), p. 155.
10. Diner, *Erin's Daughters,* p. xiv.
11. Stansell, *City of Women*, p. 56.
12. Diner, *Erin's Daughters*, pp. 57-59.
13. *Ibid.*, p. 138.
14. Stansell, *City of Women*, pp. 11-12.
15. Roger Daniels, *Coming to America: A History of Immigration and Ethnicity in American Life* (Princeton: Harper Collins Publishers, 1990), p. 131.

16. Evelyn Nakano Glenn, "The Dialectics of Wage Work: Japanese American Women and Domestic Service, 1905-1940," in *Unequal Sisters*, p. 365.
17. *Ibid.*, pp. 357-63, Passim.
18. Vicki L. Ruiz, "A Promise Fulfilled: Mexican Cannery Workers in Southern California," in *Unequal Sisters*, p. 265.
19. *Ibid.*
20. *Ibid.*, p. 266.
21. *Ibid.*
22. Stansell, *City of Women*, p. 106.
23. Kessler Harris, *Out To Work*, pp. 127, 138.
24. Stansell, *City of Women*, p. 53.
25. Diner, *Erin's Daughters,* p. 65.
26. *Ibid.*, pp. 66-67.
27. *Ibid.*
28. *Ibid.*, p. 68.
29. Kessler Harris, *Out To Work*, p. 126.
30. Nakano Glenn, "Dialectics of Wage Work," pp. 355-57.
31. *Ibid.*, p. 361.
32. *Ibid.*, pp. 36-67.
33. Judy Yung, "The Social Awakening of Chinese American Women as Reported in Chung Sai Yat Po, 1900-1911," in *Unequal Sisters*, pp. 196, 201.
34. *Ibid.*, p. 199.
35. Stansell, *City of Women*, pp. 83-84.
36. Timothy Gilfoyle, *City of Eros: New York City Prostitution and the Commercialization of Sex, 1790-1820* (New York: W.W. Norton, 1992).
37. *Ibid.*, p. 309.
38. John D'Emilio and Estelle B. Freedman ed., *Intimate Matters: A History of Sexuality in America* (Chicago; University of Chicago Press, 1997), p. 136.
39. *Ibid.*, p. 199.
40. *Ibid.*, p. 135.
41. Gilfoyle, *City of Eros*, p. 183.
42. Alma M. Garcia, "The Development of Chicana Feminist Discourse," in *Unequal Sisters,* p. 419.

43. *Ibid.*, pp. 419-20.
44. *Ibid.*
45. *Ibid.*, p. 426
46. Diner, *Erin's Daughters,* p. xiii.
47. The women of the South Asian Descent Collective, *Our Feet Walk the Sky: Women of the South Asian Diaspora* (San Francisco: Aunt Lute Books, 1993).
48. Moses Rischin, ed., *Grandma Never Lived in America: The New Journalism of Abraham Cahan* (Bloomington: Indiana University Press, 1985).
49. Valerie Matsumoto, "Japanese American Women during World War II," in *Unequal Sisters,* p. 374.
50. George J. Sanchez, "'Go after the Women:' Americanization and the Mexican Immigrant Woman, 1915-1929," in *Unequal Sisters*, p. 251.
51. Diner, *Erin's Daughters,* p. xiv.
52. Rischin, *Grandma Never Lived in America.*

4

THE SUBVERSION OF GENDER IN EIGHTEENTH CENTURY CHINA

As Portrayed in the *Dream of the Red Chamber*

The novel stands at the point where social history and the human soul intersect.

-Yi-tse Mei Feuerwerker[1]

In recent years, many historical and sociological studies have been carried out, using literature as an illuminating source material. Although, every kind of literary works makes a unique contribution in its own way, the expanse and variety provided by the novel, makes works belonging to this literary genre particularly notable in their contribution. Historians are increasingly using the novel to map a broad range of social behaviour.[2] Feuerwerker believes that the Chinese novel, allows us to understand the conscious and unconscious assumptions of a society and indicates what has happened to religious and ethical ideals after they have been popularized and diluted by the common people. He further says that novels bring out the imperfect ways in which social institutions operate within ambiguous and refractory human situations.[3]

In cases where the author and the historian are separated by a vast gulf in space and time, the latter might digress from the original authorial intent, and this might result in a misreading of the text. However, in spite of this pitfall, this spatial and temporal distance also affords the historian a broader advantage in historical perspective, which as Paul S. Ropp says is an advantage denied even to the author's closest friends and contemporaries for whose readership the text was originally written.[4]

Robert Ruhlman believes that, Chinese literature provides those details of social history and insights into popular attitudes which were systematically excluded from orthodox Confucian inspired histories.[5] Historians, in general, and social historians in particular have increasingly begun to realize this unique character of the works of fiction which renders them as useful sources in reconstructing the history of traditionally marginalised groups, especially that of women. When researching women's lives, the works of literature become particularly important because non-official documents such as diaries, stories, novels and folk songs portray a realistic picture of the life of the people. The official documents such as gazettes were written in order to reinforce the traditional gender hierarchy and not to subvert it. Stemming from this, Paul S. Ropp has noted: "In a sense, literature can be a more reliable guide to China's past than both private and official histories."[6]

In this light, the eighteenth century Chinese novel, *Honglou Meng*, translated as the *Dream of the Red Chamber*, written by Cao Xueqin, proves to be a very vivid account of the life of an upper class scholar official's family and clan. This is a study of the subversion of gender roles, as represented, in the *Dream of the Red Chamber*, it argues that the division of social roles between men and women was not definite or irreversible. The literature reveals that the gender roles were, in fact, not water tight compartments but rather fluid categories which were often submerged by individual personalities and changing household situations and power equations. The paper presents a brief overview of gender roles as prescribed by the Neo-Confucian orthodoxy and the state policy for women and contrasts it with evidences of gender subversion such as the superiority of talented women and the crossing of gender characteristics between Jia Baoyu's bisexuality and Wang Xifeng's quest for power.

The Chinese society is known for its practice of subordination of women, a process which allegedly began during the Sung dynasty. This change has been explained as a consequence of the adoption of Neo-Confucianism, a doctrine which was systematized by the scholar Chu Hsi.[7] Chu Hsi's ideas were a product of the society he lived in. China, like many other societies, had a long tradition of subordination of women. *The Book of Songs*, a Confucian classic, contained admonitions like, "A wise man builds up a city but a wise woman overthrows it,....Disorder does not come from Heaven, it is produced by a women."[8]

The other notable Neo-Confucian Ch'eng I, also maintained that women were inferior to men. Chu Hsi quotes him in *Reflections on Things at Hand* saying that, "Between man and woman, there is an order of superiority and inferiority...there is the principle of who leads and who follows. This is a constant principle."[9] Intellect was considered to be only within the grasp of men. Chu Hsi refused to believe that women had the same intellectual capabilities as men. He believed women to be incapable of understanding the higher metaphysical principles he himself propounded.[10] Hence even though, Chu Hsi did not create the tradition of subordination, he did indeed revive and strengthen certain gender distinctions found in the classical teachings.

Since the Neo-Confucian doctrine continued to be the state orthodoxy under the Qing dynasty during the eighteenth century, all these ideals were applied to the Chinese women via the medium of state policy. Many of the Manchu policies focused specifically on women. These policies promoted female chastity and sharply curtailed public displays by female entertainers.[11] Even the local officials who reported to the Manchu emperors regarding their plans for ensuring the welfare of peasant families focused their writings on "two key gender issues: women's work and women's religious practice."[12]

Various distinguished local administrators wrote texts explicitly addressing women's behaviour and female morality. These didactic works included: *Record of Four Mirrors*, which gave moral instruction to women, regardless of their class, *Biographies of Exemplary Women*, recorded the lives of women who were judged worthy, pure, wise, virtuous or heroic by their deeds. Other works such as, *Bequeathed Guidelines for Instructing Women* and *Women's Learning* were written to emphasize the role of women in the smooth functioning of the house and thereby eventually of the state.[13] All these advice books laid down the ground rules for women's conduct that the High Qing government idealized: Women must show chastity in their words and conduct, and take primary responsibility in caring for children and the elders as well. These official records were equally outspoken in censuring female behaviour which was considered heterodox or threatening to the generally accepted and state prescribed Neo-Confucian family and political order.

The description of these official accounts reveals their orthodox nature. They were written with a view of reinforcing and preserving the traditional gender hierarchy. The main objective of these state endorsed writings was to maintain the social order and discourage any attempts to upset it. However, the society cannot be expected to follow the rigid rules of social hierarchy prescribed by official texts in a strict manner. This was particularly true regarding the rules determining the position of women in the society. The proof for this contention lies in the discrepancy, which exists between the position of women canonized in Neo-Confucian and other official texts, on the one hand, and the literature depicting the everyday life of the people, especially women, on the other.

Contrary to persistent gender stereotypes that relegated females to the position assigned to people of low birth, and considered them incapable of intellectual appreciation, the women, in fact, often showed intellectual brilliance.[14-15] Similarly, even men digressed from their prescribed roles. The Neo-Confucian texts emphasize the separation of spheres saying that the observances of propriety begin by, "distinguishing between exterior and interior parts. The men occupied the exterior; the women the interior."[16] However, the literature written during the time reveals contradictory evidence. While the Chinese households mostly conformed to the Neo-Confucian rules, however, they also aberrated from the traditional path in many ways.

The *Dream of the Red Chamber* is known for its brilliant portrayal of female characters and for its surprisingly liberal outlook towards women. Thus, it has justifiably been judged as being "*almost* feminist even ...by modern standards" and has received the title of being a "novel fundamentally about women."[17] In a similar vein, Keith McMahon has suggested that the novel contains, "a critique of patriarchy."[18] The representation of women's superiority vis a vis men's inferiority forms one of the central themes of the novel.

According to Keith McMahon, the *Dream of the Red Chamber* is "a 'shrew's' novel in which,..women are superior while men are weak and venal."[19] The novel often contrasts the poetic world of the feminine with the vulgar world of the masculine, as represented by Xue Pan, Jia Zhen, and Jia Lian.[20] McMahon further substantiates this view by writing that, "even the finest men in *Honglou meng*, such as Liu Xianglian or Baoyu, fail to live up to the more loyal and heroically self-sacrificing women such as You Sanjie, Daiyu...., all of whom die for the sake of their one love."[21] McMahon says that *Honglou meng*, "stands out with its pronounced sympathy for women's suffering and its elevation of women over men."[22]

The novel emphasizes the fact that the young girls are far more superior to their male counterparts in a variety of different fields, such as, managerial responsibilities, poetry writing, literary knowledge, musical talent, philosophical understanding and morality. Jia Tanchun displayed both literary talent as well as managerial abilities. She not only organized a literary society in the form of a poetry club but later on also acted on Wang Xifeng's behalf to run the Jia family, she also introduced a series of fiscal reforms.[23] The stories of Wang Xifeng's and Jia Tanchun's managerial resourcefulness and effective household organization is a portrayal which testifies to the efficiency of women, vis-a-vis the mismanagement of affairs displayed by Jia She and Jia Rong.

It is essential to note that, in this respect, the women of the Jia household conform to the Neo-Confucian ideals. The spatial separation within Neo-Confucian rules guiding women prohibits men from speaking of what was inside the house, this implied that the women were in charge of the house and were thus responsible for the budget, expenditure, savings, and controlling the servants of the household.[24] In this respect, Xifeng conformed with Neo-Confucian ideals in their entirety. Even though she occasionally showed a tendency of thinking like her male counterparts, Xifeng managed the household very efficiently and thus wholly conformed to the Neo-Confucian ideas regarding the role of a wife and the duty of a daughter-in-law. In fact, the primary goal of education for women was not to increase their learning, but to facilitate their role as managers of households.

The insignificance of such learning is evident in the fact that though Xifeng was not educated, she nevertheless, was the most efficient administrator of the inner sphere.

Although the Jia household was ordinary as far as the conduct of the married women and their respective roles within the household were concerned, but it proved to be an extraordinary household when it came to the education and literary talent of the young, unmarried girls living within the household. Daiyu and Xiangyun's poetic talent are a part of the celebration of female talents in the novel. The superiority and versatility of Daiyu's talent is also displayed by her knowledge of the Qin, a musical instrument for which the artist has to acquire considerable skill (ch. 86, 152). Hereafter I will be citing the exact reference for quotes from the *Dream of the Red Chamber* within parentheses. Baoyu's teacher and the other literary gentlemen believed that Baoyu had, "a certain meretricious talent for versification not undeserving of commendation" (ch. 17, 326). However, Baoyu was the object of the young girls' mirth during the poetry club's meetings for his slow and clumsy poetic skills.[25] Indeed, Louise, P. Edwards points out that, "in almost all matters of scholarly or cultural knowledge Baoyu shows less aptitude than his female peers."[26]

Apart from emphasizing the superiority of women, Cao Xueqin, has also highlighted the "crossing of gender characteristics" by creating parallels between two central characters: Baoyu and Xifeng, both of whom display reverse gender tendencies.[27-28] Just as Baoyu was characterized by his femininity, Xifeng exhibited marked tendencies, generally associated with masculinity, at the time.

Louise P. Edwards argues that Jia Baoyu becomes "the site of conflict between masculine and feminine gender prescriptions through a manifestation of a metaphoric bisexuality."[29] This argument is substantiated throughout the novel, where, Jia Zheng and the rest of the family see Baoyu as the eldest son and expect him to excel in his studies and become a scholar-official; but Baoyu on the other hand is happy writing poetry and playing with the girls in the garden. Thus, the essentially male expectations of his parents clash with his own feminine desires. The First Twelve-Month ceremony, held during the infancy of Baoyu, itself revealed his feminine interests. Of all the objects placed before him, he picked up combs, bracelets and powder, and ever since, Jia Zheng did not feel much affection for the child (ch. 2, 76.) Jia Baoyu's 'confused' gender preferences keep emerging from within the text. His earliest description called him an exceptional young boy who was gentle, beautiful, and considerate and loved poetry deeply. Baoyu rejected the correct social behaviour, by eating the girls' cosmetics and thus, represented a symbolic explosion of gender boundaries.

Martin W. Huang regards the portrayal of Baoyu as the most successful in the long gallery of effeminate male characters in late Ming and Qing fiction.[30] Baoyu's femininity is expressed throughout the novel in his mannerisms, likes and dislikes. His favourite company is that of girls. In fact, Grandmother Jia even mistakes him for a girl. She observes his habits and concludes that perhaps he was born in the wrong sex. She says, "Perhaps he was a maid himself in some past life. Perhaps he ought to have been a girl" (ch. 78, 556). Baoyu's page, Tealeaf, also prays for his master's rebirth as a girl (ch. 30, 104).

Interestingly enough, not only Baoyu's personal disposition, but even the treatment he receives from his family resembles one which is usually reserved for girls. While lamenting his lack of opportunity to visit Qin Zhong's grave, Baoyu describes how he is powerless to leave the 'inner quarters' freely. He complains to Liu Xianglian, "I wish I weren't so cooped up all the time at home.... The slightest move I make is sure to be seen and reported, and...I'm physically prevented from going where I want to" (ch. 47, 439). This type of restriction of movement is usually applied to women of aristocratic households and not to the young men. Thus, this detail in the novel exposes another aspect of the feminization of Baoyu, this time facilitated by the family, the supposed upholders of the Neo-Confucian gender rules. However, Edwards, points out that though, ordinarily, feminization might imply a loss of sexual power, such is not the case with Baoyu. Edwards argues that Baoyu's social position as a young gentleman ensures that the loss of sexual power resulting from his adoption of feminine traits is balanced by a general social power.[31]

Cao Xueqin has not only portrayed Baoyu as an effeminate character, but has also presented him as the most outstanding advocate of female superiority. Thus, while it is difficult for a girl to express the superiority of her gender, for this would be regarded as immodesty and lack of virtue, the advocacy of female superiority through Baoyu, the central male figure of the novel, lends weightage to the author's view in this regard. Baoyu shows a marked affinity for the company of girls and thus he becomes the channel of the actual articulation of the inferiority of men and the superiority of women. At the tender age of seven or eight, he defined men, "as essentially base, like 'mud,' and women as pure, like clear 'water.'"[32] Baoyu believed that, women made him feel, "clean and refreshed," while men were, "dirty and smelly to the utmost degree," (ch. 2, 28-29). And consequently, he believed that contact with men through marriage, contaminated the women. Therefore, the "priceless pearl...loses its lustre and develops...flaws and becomes a mere boiled fish's eye" (ch. 59, 138-139). Reflecting on such views expostulated by the main protagonist of the novel, McMahon, observes that, women are assumed to be better than men because until they are infected by male influence, they remain untouched by base instincts.[33]

In sharp contrast to Baoyu, Wang Xifeng is seen as a character, "who negotiated her position in reference to the parameters set by her status as a young married woman, which meant sometimes stretching the boundaries and at others complying with them."[34] According to Louise P. Edwards, one of the boundaries which she did stretch was that of "perceived appropriate gender relations."[35] The most shrewish of all the characters in the *Dream of the Red Chamber*, Xifeng was said to have been brought up like a boy. Even her name, which was acquired in the schoolroom was somewhat boyish, the word *feng*, in Chinese implying the male phoenix (ch. 3, 91-92).

She plays the role of a tough, sharp-tongued, but effective manager of the Jia household. She can be as usurious as hard-core misers.[36] When the polygynous and lustful world of the men invades the peace of the women, some oversensitive, like Daiyu weep, others become nuns or commit suicide, but Xifeng fights back and emerges the winner in most cases. She, thus, provides a counter-model to the Neo-Confucian paragon of passivity and submission.[37] C.T. Hsia rationalizes her power with her womanhood by arguing that, "women were driven by their subordination to protect their interests by cunning manipulation."[38] Hsia believes that, "it was her (Xifeng's) tragedy that she had to become mean and cunning in order to cope with male domination."[39]

While Baoyu is often mistaken for a girl, and himself desires to be reborn as one, Wang Xifeng, consciously or unconsciously tends to look at things from a male perspective. In chapter 46, she jokes with grandmother Jia and says that, if she had been a grandson, she would have asked for Faithful, and if her good deeds enabled her to be a man in her next birth, she would certainly ask grandmother to give Faithful to her (ch. 46, 643-644). Xifeng is considered to be, "more than a match for most men" (ch. 2, 83). Qin Keqing praises her for being, "such a paragon among women that even strong men find more than their match in her" (ch. 13, 255). Xifeng has even been compared to the "Tyrant King of Chu," Xiang Yu (232-202 BC), who is regarded as the conventional symbol of male physical strength.[40] She even tries to act in a masculine fashion, for instance, she tries to put the boat on the lake at Prospect Garden and boasts to Youshi that she can let firecrackers off better than boys (ch. 54, 32, 42).

Martin W. Huang believes that the gender reversal between Baoyu and Xifeng becomes more stark because they are often presented in a careful juxtaposition to each other.[41] Huang cites examples such as chapter 15, where Baoyu is pursuing his friendship with Qin Zhong, an act characterized by feminine tenderness, and Xifeng is busy pursuing profit and money, an act characterized by traditionally male attributes of power and aggressiveness.[42]

The most striking gender reversal between the two can be seen in their responses to unwanted sexual advances. Xifeng ruthlessly punishes Jia Rui, who dares to lust after her. She disrupts the, "passive/active gender role pattern by assuming the role of an aggressive seductress and emerges as a triumphant conqueror" (ch. 12, 243-253). In sharp contrast, "Baoyu is forced to assume the feminine/passive role when he is approached by Skybright's aggressive sister-in-law," who pulled Baoyu on top of her and gripped him tightly between her legs (ch. 77, 546-47). This picture of the male Baoyu, being raped by a female, is seen by Huang as a complete reversal of gender roles and so he concludes that the juxtaposition evident in these two very different sexual encounters reveals a "fascinating switch in gender as Baoyu and Xifeng move towards the opposite gender roles."[43]

Apart from the gender reversal between Baoyu and Xifeng, the novel also showed instances of the crossing of male and female characteristics between Baoyu and girls such as Daiyu and Shi Xiangyun. The visiting Granny Liu and a doctor mistake Baoyu's residence in the garden for that of a girl because of its special arrangement and decoration (ch. 51, 718). While visiting the Naiad's House, Granny Liu noticed the inkstone and brushes on the table and books lining the bookshelf and mistakenly concluded that, "this must be 'the young gentleman's study" (ch. 40, 282). The second character which displays the crossing of a woman into a man is that of Shi Xiangyun. Shi's masculine bearing is evident when she puts on an attire which is jokingly compared by Daiyu to that of a "saucy Tartar boy." Everyone laughs at that the fact that she is more handsome as a boy than as a girl (ch. 49, 679-680). Thus, these young girls defied the traditional gender roles by excelling in their literary and artistic talents, while Baoyu whom everyone expected to excel in the civil service examination, tried to avoid going to school and studying the classics.

Such increase in the presence and importance of women is quite representative of the literature of the late Ming and the early Qing periods. Correspondingly, many male figures in this kind of fiction became increasingly effeminate. Most scholars associate this trend of feminizing the traditional Chinese literature with the liberal influence of the radical Taizhou School of Neo-Confucinism.[44] The iconoclast philosopher, Li Zhi showed an unconventional view regarding female talent and education. He thus, signified the emergence of a more liberal and sensitive attitude towards women.[45] However, Martin W. Huang studies this trend of general feminization in relation to the anxiety experienced by the male literati writers and interprets it within the general historical framework of allegorical conventions.[46] He believes that the *Dream of the Red Chamber* is an example of male literati frustrations being released through female personalities.[47] Huang establishes the analogy between two marginalized groups within the Chinese society, the women on the one hand and the male literati in political distress on the other. Huang asserts that as the wife/concubine had to compete for her husband's attention, similarly, the ministers had to compete with each other for the emperor's favour. Thus, both the wife and the minister represented marginalized groups suffering from the "concubine complex."[48] Some feminists who believe that femininity is a gender attribute and not a fixed identity associated with women only, agree with Huang in view that, "what makes one feminine is the position of marginality."[49] This theory divorces literature from its historical context.

While this view can be convincing to some extent, however, it cannot fully explain the feminization of male characters and the prominent role played by women in the Qing fiction. The gender roles represented in the *Dream of the Red Chamber* are not purely symbolic or allegorical. The male "concubine complex" is not one universal theory applicable to male anxiety all over the world; rather, it needs to be contextualized within a specific historical space and time.

Susan Mann has studied the position of women during the High Qing era, based on women's writings. She cites Yun Zhu's *Correct Beginnings*, an anthology of women's poetry, and brings out the fact that Yun Zhu marks the achievement of learned women as one of the hallmarks of High Qing rule.[50] Stemming from this, Mann argues that the power of women's writing meant that women themselves were participating in the reconstruction of gender relations.[51] According to Mann, the history of gender relations in China shows that within the culture prevalent during the High Qing era, "women's homely place in elite public discourse was recognized and articulated by leading intellectuals, as when the philosopher Zhang Xuecheng acknowledged the dependence of public man on cloistered woman by noting that her words, too, could be "everyone's."[52]

Women as writers and artists were part of the socio-cultural process that re-shaped gender relations in High Qing times. Elite women, such as the young managers, poets and artists of the Jia household, "embraced the spirit of the age in their own terms and used their talents to empower themselves, especially within the family."[53] Hence, Mann, rightly asserts that, during the eighteenth century, women's accomplishments were being recognized. Thus, the *Dream of the Red Chamber* cannot be studied in isolation from its period of composition. It is essential to place the novel within its historical context of the society's rising awareness of female intelligence and the fact that women had achieved recognition. In the eighteenth century, many women had already acquired fame as poets. Hence, Mann points out that this kind of feminized literature should not be seen in allegorical terms because at this stage in the Chinese history, women were earning acknowledgement in their own right. Thus, the women in *Dream of the Red Chamber* were not personifying the frustrated male literati, but rather they were representative of the Chinese literary women as well as the unsung heroines, who managed large households daily and worked much harder than the men--the housewives and managers of the inner quarters.

In this manner an in-depth study of the novel reveals that the eighteenth century Chinese society was indeed one where the notion of 'honouring men and disdaining women' was upheld, and very remarkably, Cao Xueqin proposed, 'honouring women and disdaining men.'[54] The novel has thereby attempted to reverse the traditional proverb, 'lack of virtue is a talent in women.'[55] Society cannot be compartmentalized into watertight divisions and therefore, the ideologies of femininity and masculinity did not form rigid or closed structures. They were in fact, fought with internal contradictions and ambiguities which, "functioned simultaneously and seemingly abrasively to establish a patriarchal gender order."[56]

Hence, indeed, part of the superbness of Cao Xueqin's literary talent lies in his ability to recreate these ambiguities and contradictions within his fictional account. These roles were not rigidly compartmentalized and the lines of division often blurred under the influence of individual personalities and temperaments of the participants within the society. Therefore, even though, the *Dream of the Red Chamber* was a work created in the writer's imagination and idealized the position of women, it nevertheless, portrayed the reality associated with gender roles. Thus, this eighteenth century literary work of creativity will continue to provide interesting insights, and serve as a useful link in the reconstruction of the history of women and gender relations in China, for years to come.

REFERENCES

1. Yi tse Mei Feuerwerker, "The Chinese Novel," in *Approaches to the Oriental Classics*, ed. Wm. Theodore de Bary (New York, 1959): 172, quoted in Paul S. Ropp, *Dissent in Early Modern China: Ju-lin wai-shih and Ch'ing Social Criticism* (Ann Arbor: The University of Michigan Press, 1981), p. 5.
2. Keith McMahon, *Misers, Shrews, and Polygamists: Sexuality and Male-Female Relations in Eighteenth Century Chinese Fiction* (London: Duke University Press, 1995), p. ix.
3. Ropp, *Dissent in Early Modern China,* p. 5.
4. *Ibid.*, p. 4, 6.
5. *Ibid.*, p. 4.
6. *Ibid.*
7. John W. Chaffee and Wm. Theodore de Bary, eds., *Neo-Confucian Education: The Formative Stage* (Berkeley: University of California Press, 1989), p. 325.
8. *Ibid.*, p. 329.
9. *Ibid.*, p. 331.
10. *Ibid.*
11. Susan Mann, *Precious Records: Women in China's Long Eighteenth Century* (Stanford: Stanford University Press, 1997), p. 21.
12. *Ibid.*
13. *Ibid.*, p. 28-29.
14. Dorothy Ko, *Teachers of the Inner Chambers: Women and Culture in Seventeenth Century China* (Stanford: Stanford University Press, 1994), p. 68.
15. Chaffee, *Neo-Confucian Education*, p. 329-31.
16. *Ibid.*, p. 332.
17. Martin w. Huang, *Literati and Self-Representation: Autobiographical Sensibility in the Eighteenth Century Chinese Novel* (Stanford: Stanford University Press, 1995), p. 76.
18. Keith McMahon, "A Case for Confucian Sexuality: The Eighteenth Century Novel 'Yesou puyan'," *Late Imperial China*, 9, No. 2 (December 1988): 47, quoted in Louise P. Edwards, *Men and Women in Qing China: Gender in The Red Chamber Dream* (New York: E. J. Brill, 1994), p. 4.
19. McMahon, *Misers, Shrews and Polygamists,* p. 177.

20. Huang, *Men and Women in Qing China*, p. 88.
21. McMahon, *Misers, Shrews and Polygamists*, p. 178.
22. *Ibid.*, p. 202.
23. Clara Wing-Chung Ho, "The Cultivation of Female Talent: Views on Women's Education in China During the Early and High Qing Periods," *Journal of the Economic and Social History of the Orient*, 38, no. 2 (May 1995): p. 214-15.
24. Chaffee, *Neo-Confucian Education*, p. 345.
25. Edwards, *Men and Women in Qing China*, p. 51.
26. *Ibid.*
27. McMahon, *Misers, Shrews and Polygamists*, p. 182.
28. Huang, *Literati and Self-Representation*, p. 90.
29. Edwards, *Men and Women in Qing China*, p. 37.
30. Huang, *Literati and Self-Representation*, p. 89.
31. Edwards, *Men and Women in Qing China*, p. 42.
32. McMahon, *Misers, Shrews, and Polygamists*, p. 184.
33. *Ibid.*, p. 203.
34. Edwards, *Men and Women in Qing China*, p. 71.
35. *Ibid.*
36. McMahon, *Misers, Shrews, and Polygamists,* p. 189.
37. Anne E. McLaren, trans., *The Chinese Femme Fatale: Stories from the Ming Period* (Sydney: Wild Peony, 1994), p. 2.
38. Edwards, *Men and Women in Qing China*, p. 70.
39. C.T. Hsia, *The Classic Chinese Novel*, 26, quoted in Edwards, *Men and Women in Qing China*, p. 70.
40. Huang, *Literati and Self-Representation*, p. 92.
41. *Ibid.*
42. *Ibid.*
43. *Ibid.*, p. 93.
44. *Ibid.*, p. 82.
45. *Ibid.*
46. *Ibid.*
47. *Ibid.*, p. 83.
48. *Ibid.*, p. 79.
49. *Ibid.*

50. Mann, *Precious Records*, p. 214.
51. *Ibid.*, p. 222.
52. *Ibid.*, p. 223.
53. *Ibid.*, p. 225.
54. Edwards, *Men and Women in Qing China*, p. 51.
55. Ho, "The Cultivation of Female Talent," p. 191.
56. Edwards, *Men and Women in Qing China*, p. 51.

5

WERE VICTORIANS PRUDES AND PURITANS REALLY PURITANICAL?

A Review of Puritan and Victorian Attitudes Towards Sexuality

A proper analysis of the usage of the terms "Puritan," "Victorian" and "Prudery" as interchangeable synonyms deems it necessary to understand what these terms usually connote. The Oxford English Encyclopedic Dictionary defines "Puritan" as practising or affecting extreme strictness in religion or morals (including morality regulating sexuality).[1] "Victorian" is described as the age or society characterized by improved standards of decency and morality.[2] Finally "Prudery" is defined as having or affecting an attitude of extreme propriety or modesty, especially in sexual matters.[3] On the surface, all three definitions seem to be describing a common code of conduct. However, a thorough study of the sources of the period reveals that though somewhat similar in their outlook towards sexuality, owing to their common root in "Protestantism," these terms in fact denote different characteristics, pertaining to different historical periods and societies and hence their use as interchangeable synonyms is inappropriate as it does not do justice to the individual traits pertaining to each of these periods.

Puritanism

Central to any study of sexuality, is the role played by the agents of sexual regulation. During the early American period, from the colonial through the Seventeenth Century, the Puritanical hold over individual sexuality was primarily in the hands of the State and the Church. Puritanical clergy and laymen schooled under the tenets of the Protestant Reformation hoped to establish close knit, "Godly" communities, centered upon family and Church. It was this belief which shaped the Puritan ideology towards sexuality. While on the one hand, economic and geographical mobility formed the backdrop of the Victorian sexual ideology, on the other, the challenge of establishing settlements in a new country inhabited by a different race and society was responsible for shaping the Puritan views on sexuality which aimed at creating stable family life and implementing the values of moral and reproductive sexuality.[4]

Puritan views on marriage and sexuality upheld the idea that marriage was acceptable primarily as a way to channel lust and sexual sin." Consequently, marital love and more importantly the need to reproduce children justified sexual intercourse. The most well known of the colonial authorities, the New England Puritan clergy had extremist Protestant views on issues of Church Doctrine and sexual morality, and emphasized marriage as the only suitable outlet for sexual desire. They warned their congregations against both masturbation and pre-marital sex. In Conjunction with this, colonial statutes in both New England, and Chesapeake Bay outlawed[5] fornication, rape, sodomy, adultery and incest, sometimes going as far as prescribing Capital punishment, fine or banishment for sexual transgressors.[6]

Since marriage was the only legal and moral outlet for sexual desires, New England Puritans held conjugal union as a duty the spouses owed each other and the absence of which could be treated as grounds for divorce. However, even within marriage, moderation and fruitfulness were the key words. Thus, sexual activity had to be moderated and was aimed at resulting in the propagation of the species. The Puritans followed the Biblical injunction-"Be fruitful and multiply." Emanating from this, they rejected the practice of contraception, not only because of the Biblical injunction but also as a strategy to increase the population of their Church. (Though women spaced their pregnancies by breast feeding their children for a year and maintaining a low rate of sexual intercourse during this period.) For most Puritans however, sexuality was not really a private matter, for family and community draw few boundaries between sexual concerns of individuals and those of the group.[7]

Victorian Era

The transition from the Puritanical to the Victorian era spanning across the mid-eighteenth century to the late nineteenth century was marked by extensive economic progress, entailing tremendous economic and geographical mobility. Post-Revolution formation of local and state governments, led to the separation of Church and Civil Authority, and also resulted in the abolition of most church courts. Consequently, the role of the Church and the State in sexual regulation diminished, as opposed to the era of Puritanism where, these two institutions were the main agencies of regulation.

The vacuum left by the absence of these agencies of regulation left the family, which increasingly meant women in their roles as mothers and wives with the task of creating self-regulating sexual beings, both male and female. Thus, women formed a specialized female model authority. Elaine May also emphasizes that Victorianism was a moral code which found its expressions within the walls of the home. She also emphasizes women's role by saying that Victorian women were expected to maintain a home environment free from sensuality, to help protect husbands and sons from dissipation. Hence, a woman's effectiveness at home was vital to the nation's future.[8]

Another agent of regulation which came to the forefront at this time was the medical profession which played an important role in fostering the objective of sexual self-control. Similarly, various voluntary associations were created to help reduce and correct sexual deviance in society. In *City of Eros,* Timothy Gilfoyle argues that "purity reform" was not born full-grown in the post-bellum era, rather it had its roots in America as early as the seventeenth century.[9] Gilfoyle further argues that seventeenth century Boston housed "The society for Suppression of Disorder," the first known anti-vice organization in North America.[10] This "society" aimed at shutting down Boston's brothels. Similarly, in the eighteenth and the nineteenth centuries, numerous reform organizations had sprung up with a view to end sexual crimes. Gilfoyle's study reveals that in 1835, New York saw the growth of a variety of anti-prostitution organizations such as, "The American Society for Promoting Observance of the Seventh Commandment," and "The American Purity Alliance," which emerged in post-bellum 1890s.[11] During the nineteenth century, all these three agencies argued unanimously that the state ought to play a larger role in regulating personal morality.

A brief look at the methods which these agencies employed to regulate sexuality reveals that nineteenth century Victorian women led movements such as, the "American Female Guardian Society." This movement blamed lustful men for social subordination and sexual victimization of young women. Movements like the "New York Female Moral Reform Society" show nineteenth century Victorian women's efforts for moral reform and social purity, and their desire to impose a single code of morality that of-chastity before marriage and fidelity within it, upon both men and women.[12] Doctors criminalized abortion. Opposing anarchist, free-lovers and couples opting for birth control, Censors like Anthony Comstock proposed laws to limit materials and information regarding birth control.

John D' Emilio and Estelle B. Freedman study the evidence from harmonious spouses, divorcing couples and adulterous lovers and arrive at the conclusion that despite the concept of strict, sexual morality, traditionally regarded as being characteristic of the Victorian period, the ideal of sexual pleasure coexisted with the search for sexual control. Stemming from this, D' Emilio and Freedmen delineate three important points of the departure of Victorian sexual morality from the Puritan ideology.[13]

Firstly both men and women became self-conscious about sexuality as a personal choice no longer limited to merely a reproductive responsibility. By mid-nineteenth century port towns like Boston and Charleston had a bustling maritime trade and comprised of more heterogeneous and highly stratified. All these factors undermined the patterns of stable community which had earlier largely regulated sexual morality. Even within the agricultural sector, young couples established households in outlying areas beyond the reach of family, Church and traditional community surveillance. Consequently individual choice rather than parental or state control gained precedence in matters of courtship, marriage and the treatment of sexual deviance.[14]

The second change highlighted by D'Emilio and Freedman was noticeable especially among the middle class where sexual desires became increasingly fused with a romantic quest for emotional intimacy, departing from the earlier frankly physical and reproductive terms in which earlier Americans spoke of sexuality. Later, new terminology such as spiritual joy and blending of heats was introduced.[15]

Thirdly, while sexual relations under the earlier ideology was marked by an equality between the two sexes, the influence of the Enligntenment gave more sexual freedom to men.[16] Although both men and women shared in both the intensification of sexuality as a form of interpersonal intimacy and the separation of sexuality from reproduction, gender differences dictated how men and women experienced these changes. The separate spheres of the middle class and the emphasis on purity of women created double standards which made the transformation of sexuality more problematic for women. Elaine May substantiates this argument by pointing to the fact that a certain amount of indulgence was condoned for men, while a woman appearing just once in a vice zone, ruined her reputation permanently.[17]

In *Powers of desire,* Barbara Epstein refers to late-Victorian formulation of new sexual desires to have sex without having children.[18] However, Epstien asserts, women found it difficult to fulfil this desire because while birth control meant greater freedom for men, on the other hand, a highly controlled access to contraceptives tended to restrain female sexuality. Women were not too free to decide what portions of their lives they wanted to devote to motherhood and what portion to other pursuits. Male attitudes in this regard were not very cooperative. Epstein cites evidence that the medical campaign against abortion in the 1860s and 1870s was composed of overwhelmingly male, white, upper-class, native-born and Protestant physicians. However, despite such limitations and obstacles, historian Linda Gordon describes the late Victorian age as the age of voluntary motherhood which symbolized a woman's right to refuse her husband's demands when she did not want to have children.[19]

These changes are starkly evident in the transition from Laurel Thatcher Ulrich's description of the Puritan ideology regulating the life and times of Martha Ballard in contrast to the Victorian poems quoted by D'Emilio and Freedman–which reveal open sexuality and commercial transaction in sexuality. Evidently as young men began to leave their homes in search of livelihood in the cities supervision of sexuality by community so characteristic of Martha Ballard's time was lost now.

New research on the history of sexuality has made the distinguishing features of Puritans and Victorians more clear and has challenged the older, stereotypical views regarding these concepts. Contrary to previous thought, Edmund Morgan has pointed out that the Puritans were more interested in sex and more egalitarian about male and female sexual expression. Older pictures regarding the Victorians have also been revised. One school argues that though the official ideology was characterized by repression, just below the surface of the society, lay a sexually active underground. Other views regarding the issue deny the existence of repression even at the level of the ideology. Rather, scholars like Carl Degler and Peter Gay propound that middle class Victorians accepted sexual pleasures as long as they occurred within the sanctuary of marriage.[22]

Thus, the old misconception regarding the central commonality of characteristics between Prudery, Puritanism and Victorianism has failed to hold its might before the strength of recent research. The distinctions between these three terms becomes even more stark when one considers Michel Foucault's view which rejects the traditional "repressive hypothesis' as the hallmark of sexual relations during the Puritan and Victorian ages. Instead, Foucault views sex as an expression of complex, dynamic power relations in the society. He goes so far as saying that the Victorians were actually obsessed with sexuality, an argument which is supported by the fact to the Victorians' to elaborate on the meanings of sex and their creation of new categories of sexual deviance and identity.[23] While on the one hand, the whole Puritan ideology of sex revolved around an emphasis on marriage, reproduction and the fruitfulness of sexuality, the Victorians on the other hand, were not 'puritanical' in the sense that, though they were trying to repress sexuality, especially in the middle class respectable families, they were in fact talking about sexuality during their discussion regarding its repression. Further on, Victorians were not really prudes. Hence the Victorian view of sexuality exposes a double standard looming large over it, since their talk about sexuality was also accompanied by their thoughts about preserving purity within the society.

Such views are further supported by Carroll Smith-Rosenberg's study about the existence of same-sex relationships between women in the Victorian era. Even though, the Anglo-American culture in the period influenced a new ideal of female "passionlessness," however, incidences of "Boston Marriages," or same sex relationships between women were visible to the outside world and acceptable to the "Victorian society," which described these female lovers euphemistically as close friends and devoted companions. Moreover, the laxity of sexual morals displayed by unmarried men, and the fact that despite a seeming public distaste, pornography and prostitution both had gained a foothold in nineteenth century cities, coupled with incidences of "Boston marriages," would hardly credit the validity of using "prudery" as a synonym for Victorian.[24]

Just as the Victorians were not 'puritanical' in their approach to sexuality, similarly, the Puritans were not necessarily 'puritanical' in their sexual beliefs and practices either, thus the dictionary definition of the term "Puritan" is not a sound description of their actual behaviour. Martha Ballard's diary reveals numerous cases of pre-marital pregnancies and various methods which women used in their attempts to terminate their unwanted pregnancies.[25] Moreover, during both the Puritan and the Victorian periods, there never existed a single unifying or universal value system regarding sexuality as it was practised in day to day life of the people.

Echoing similar views, Elaine May argues that the notions of 'prudery' and 'pure womanhood' have blinded our vision of the totality of nineteenth century life, with its intricate ideological and institutional framework.[26] As discussed earlier, the same can be asserted regarding the misconceptions concerning Puritanism. Thus, to see Puritanism and 'prudery' as interchangeable synonyms is to oversimplify the significance and broader ramifications of the puritanical way of life. This is so because such a simplifying generalization of the terms Puritan and Victorian ignores the fact that even within these movements, sexuality exhibited more complexity and heterogeneity than modern assumptions about their repressiveness suggest.

REFERENCES

1. Joyce M. Hawkins and Robert Allen, ed., *The Oxford Encyclopedic Dictionary* (Oxford: Clarendon Press, 1991), p. 1174.
2. *Ibid.*, p. 1611.
3. *Ibid.*, p. 1165.
4. John D'Emilio and Estelle B. Freedoman, ed., *Intimate Matters; A History of Sexuality in America* (Chicago: University of Chicago Press, 1997).
5. *Ibid.*
6. *Ibid.*
7. *Ibid.*
8. Elaine May, *Great Expectations: Marriage and Divorce in Post Victorian America* (Chicago: University of Chicago Press, 1980).
9. Timothy Gilfoyle, *City of Eros:* New York City, Prostitution, and the Commercialization of Sex, 1790-1920 (New York: W.W. Norton, 1992).
10. *Ibid.*, p. 182.
11. *Ibid.*
12. *Ibid.*
13. D'Emilio, *Intimate Matters.*
14. *Ibid.*
15. *Ibid.*
16. *Ibid.*
17. May, *Great Expectations.*
18. Anne Snitow, Christine Stansell, Sharon Thompson, eds., *The Powers of Desire* (New York: Monthly Review Press, 1983).
19. D'Emilio, *Intimate Matters.*
20. *Ibid.*
21. Laurel Thatcher Ulrich, ed., *A Midwife's Tale: The Life of Martha Ballard Based on her Diary-1785-1812* (New York: Vintage Books, 1990).
22. D'Emilio, *Intimate Matters.*
23. *Ibid.*
24. Carroll Smith-Rosenberg, *Disorderly Conduct: Visions of Gender in Victorian America* (New York: A.A. Knopf, 1985).
25. Thatcher Ulrich, *A Midwife's Tale.*
26. May, *Great Expectations.*

SECTION 2
WOMEN AND MARRIAGE

6

WOMEN IN ROMAN SOCIETY, LAW AND LITERATURE

The literature of a period often provides vivid accounts of its social customs, values and norms, thus acting as the mirror of the society. This certainly holds true in case of Roman society during the first and the second centuries AD. Ranging from historical annals, poems and novels to seduction manuals and medical treatises, the literary sources of this period shed light on a myriad of social aspects such as love, sexuality, marriage and religion. One such aspect of society which has a bearing on all the others is the demarcation of stereotypical gender roles for men and women. The writings of this period provide a deep insight into the functioning of these gender roles and show that there was a definite inequality between the two sexes. This paper attempts to study the essentially patriarchal Roman society towards women by describing the social and legal position granted to women and by tracing the reasons for the inequality of relations, which lay in the erroneous belief that women were physically, morally and intellectually inferior to men.

The Roman polity was an imperial one and so the tradition of authoritarianism passed down from the level of the emperor as the head of the state to the *pater* [father] as the head of the patriarchal family system. Since, there were not many laws or decrees which demarcated the legal role of a woman in legally defined terms, such gender stereotypes were often fashioned by the family and the clan. As the head of the family, the father controlled the daughters and under the system of *conubium* or the lawful marriage, as the girl was transferred to the husband's family, this control passed from the hands of the father to those of the husband. Apart from such control which was more symbolic in nature, even in financial matters the wife was subject to the husband's authority. At the time of her marriage, the wife received a dowry for her protection and maintenance, but it was under the control of her husband and she could get it back only in case of a divorce or widowhood. A woman was also not entitled to any inheritance from her husband, since the children and not the wife were the beneficiaries after the death of a man.

Such inequality also extended itself to the legal codes governing marriage and adultery. *Lex Julia de adulteris*, the Julian law on adultery made adultery a public concern and regarded it as crime. However, the crime had different implications for men and women. According to this law if well summarized, a married woman indulged in extra-marital sex it was regarded as adultery and if an unmarried woman committed this crime it was considered as committing *stupro* or a publicly outrageous act and implied that the future husbands would not trust the fidelity of that woman. While on the other hand, the same acts when committed by men with slaves, tavern waitresses, actresses and prostitutes were not regarded as adultery but as *concubina* or concubinage. Under this system, a married man could engage in sexual relations with a woman, he could not marry due to the inter-class barriers laid down by the *Lex Julia....demaritandis ordinibus* or the Julian law on marriage. And if a man entered into physical relations with a married woman it was regarded not so much as an adulterous act as an immoral and a scandalous one. Since, later adultery was made a public concern, if a husband found his wife in an adulterous situation, he was forced to prosecute her; if he failed to do so, he was regarded as a pimp, aiding and abetting his wife's extra-marital affair. Thus, the legal codes and social norms pressurised men to punish their wives for crimes they themselves were allowed to commit without fear of severe penalty. In addition an 'adulterous' wife also lost some of her civic rights.

Such discrepancy between the codes regulating adultery by men and women existed because the Romans gave great importance to the question of paternity. Paternity was important for deciding inheritance. Therefore, while on the one hand men could have sexual relations with women of inferior classes because these women could not legally produce heirs, on the other hand women were forbidden to engage in such relations because it would lead to questioning of the paternity of the children reproduced by the women. Hence very often, it was deciding the paternity of the child and not preserving the chastity of the women which was the main motive behind the enforcement of strict laws for women. It, therefore, seems that women were less regarded as individuals and more as child-bearing machines. And this was the major reason which often led men to keep their women under lock and key. The supervision of women by guards appointed by the fathers and husbands seems to be common in the Roman society. Ovid, a poet of the Roman period composed *Amores*, a collection of poems and oftens referred to such arrangements of guardian-ship several times.[1]

> Love at first sight. I dashed off a note....
>
> and got the nervous answer: It's not allowed.
>
> Why not?... It turned out that you were the trouble,
>
> An over-strict guardian...
>
> *guard dog... just allow your mistress her freedom..."*
>
> (*Amores,* Book 2:2)

Referring to a guard who was a eunuch, Ovid wrote:

> Bad luck that your mistress should have a keeper who is neither
>
> Male nor female, who can't enjoy true sex!
>
> (*Amores,* Book 2:3)

Eunuchs were often employed as guards because the Romans believed that they were not manly and not upto the mark to be attractive to the women and even if they were, they were not capable of producing children. Both these above excerpts show that often women were treated as prisoners in their own houses. They were guarded like common criminals while the men could freely commit adulterous crimes.

Women were forced into adulterous situations because they were often unhappy with their marriages and had not married the men they loved. Such situations arose because the girl did not have much of a say in her marriage since the minimum age for the marriage of girls was twelve and the typical marrying age was sometime in their later teens while the husband was in his late twenties or early thirties. Such a big difference between the ages of the bride and groom led to an authoritative relationship in which the latter dominated over the former. Moreover, the marriage matches were fixed by the parents and grandparents of the girl and they gave little consideration to the preference of the girl. Concerns of property, good alliances, social status, political connections and procreation were primary in making the decision.

Women thus often found themselves bound by a sense of obligation towards their family's status and reputation. One of the poems, which are ascribed to a Roman noblewoman Sulpicia, expresses such a concern on the part of the girl as she shares her fears with her lover saying,

> But some are anxious for me; their greatest cause for worry
>
> Is that I may lose to a vulgar couch.
>
> (Sulpicia: 3.16)

Evidently this noblewoman's love transcended the barriers of class and so she was worried about the outcome of such an alliance. Somehow she felt responsible for letting down her family which felt that she would lose face if she chose someone inferior to her. Hence a sense of duty restrained women from marrying for love, this factor coupled with the legally weak position of women in a marriage led to the possibility of desertion by the husband. Such sorry plight of women was reflected in the Roman senator Seneca's plays. In *Medea*, a play based upon an earlier Greek play, the princess Medea betrayed her father and her country for her love.[2] However, Jason, her husband married her in order to get her help in finding the golden fleece and after having two children, Jason desired to further realize his ambitions and decided to marry a politically well-connected woman. Medea could not bear this news. She could not even return to her father, and so in her desperation she killed herself and her children. Such examples of desertion and extramarital relations must have been very common since Ovid also referred to the phenomenon in his book. *The Art of Love*. He wrote:

> No bride can expect That degree of devotion...
>
> (*The Art of Love*, Book 2:388)

This maxim clearly outlines the helpless situation of women. The society expected them to give their full devotion to their husbands, but in return, the women themselves could never be sure of such single-minded love.

In this backdrop of stringent and unfair rules of conduct laid down for the women by the Roman society, it is not surprising to see the image of women created by the poets and writers. Not only were the imperial laws and decrees unfavourable to women but even the works of literature and medicine emphasized the physical, intellectual and moral inferiority of women.

Being a conservative society, the Romans often kept their women segregated, hence in case of illness they were mostly treated by midwives. As a result, doctors who were typically male, had hardly any opportunity to study and learn about the female anatomy. This lack of knowledge, however, did not deter them from formulating ill-found notions in medical trèatises. Galen, the physician to the emperor Marcus Aurelius, wrote a medical textbook in the second century AD. (Galen, *On the Usefulness of the Parts of the Body WIV 6-7*) in which he tried to explain the human anatomy in terms of the four elements: earth, water, fire and air and their physical attributes: dryness, wetness, heat and coldness respectively. In order to explain the female anatomy, Galen transferred his social observations to the reproductive organs. Thus, he believed that since socially men were superior to women they were so even physically. He firmly believed that the male and female bodies possessed the same reproductive organs, the only difference being their location in the body. According to Galen, since men were hot and dry, their genitals lay external to the body while the converse being true for women, their genitals lay internally. Such erroneous notions must have gone a long way in strengthening the popular social beliefs that women were inferior because nature itself made them so.[3]

Women not only found themselves in disfavour with the medical writers but even the poets and novelists regarded women with a cynical eye, doubting their moral integrity. Such an attitude is reflected in the works of Seneca. In *Phaedra*, he portrays a woman as being sexually dangerous to man. She is a lustful creature who seduces her stepson and makes him break his vow of celibacy.[4] While Medea, (referred to earlier) is portrayed as a woman who betrays her father and her country for her love and desire for a man. Both these plays paint images of women as being driven by sexual desires, possessing no strength of character and leading to the degeneration of the virtues of men as well. Thus, in a way such literature warned men to beware of women and resist sexual desires since they led to unhappiness and death.

In a similar vein, Apuleius, a novelist belonging to the Roman period projected women as being moral degenerates. In *The Golden Ass*, he presented character sketches of various women and showed that they were wanting in character.[5] His tales involved women who were witches, women who killed their husbands to be with their lovers and women who seduced their stepsons and then murdered them. (Apuleius, *The Golden Ass:* 65-69, 212-220). Such images of women being seductresses and murderesses being projected by popular fiction must have found ready acceptance amongst the Roman readers. They probably found it in consonance with their own views thus, it is evident that women were not regarded with much respect. They were considered to be lacking in morals and capable of committing evil deeds to satisfy their lust.

Poets such as Catullus and Ovid include similar reflections in their poems concerning matters of the heart. Adding to the list of physical and moral weaknesses, these poets label women as being intellectually inferior too. Catullus lamented:

> I can remember Lesbia when you swore you were mine and mine only,...
>
> Now that I know, you're much cheaper, lighter,..
>
> (Catullus, *Love Poems from a Man to a Woman:* 72)

These lines are a clear evidence of how fickle-minded and untrustworthy the poets considered women to be. Ovid, who wrote the seduction manual, *The Art of Love* also spoke of women in similar terms. Guiding men on how to woo women, Ovid said, "Light minds are captivated by trifles" (Ovid, *The Art of Love:* Book One: 159) thus implying that women had poor intellectual qualities and their minds are not concerned with matters deeper and more thoughtful than being fanned and getting their cushions plumped. Women were considered as being immature and full of vanity and men were advised to praise them even if it was not a genuine praise. This was considered to be a definite way of winning the heart of their lady love. The fact that the leading seduction manual of the time which suggests such methods for beginning relationships, is in itself an evidence of degree of respect the Roman men had for the women and amount of trust or rather distrust with which they viewed the intellectual capacity of their female counterparts.

A study of the mosaic of Roman literature clearly brings out in rich hues the tribulations and injustices which women had to face in those times. The society, the lawmakers and the literary class all joined hands in restricting and regulating the freedom, liberty and the growth of women. This coalition gave men the right to have sexual relations without marriage and gave women the duty of remaining faithful to their husbands. The pressure of the family and clan, the authority of imperial decrees and the erroneous and provocative ideas propagated in the popular literature of the time all worked together as interactive forces setting the mould for the stereotypical position of women in the western society in the centuries to follow.

REFERENCES

1. Ovid, *Amores: Text, Prolegomena, and Commentary*, ed. , J.C. McKeown (Liverpool: F. Cairns, 1987.)
2. Euripides, *Medea; Hippolytus; Electra; Helen,* trans. James Morwood (Oxford: Oxford University Press, 1998.)
3. Galen, *Three Treatises on the Nature of Science,* trans. Richard Walzer and Michael Frede (Indiannapolis: Hacket Pub. Co. , 1985.)
4. Seneca, *Phaedra*, ed. , Michael Coffey and Roland Mayer (Cambridge: Cambridge University Press, 1990.)
5. Apuleius, *The Golden Ass, or, Metamorphoses*, trans. E.J. Kenney (London: Penguin Books, 1998.)

7

EXPRESSIONS OF WOMEN'S POWER AND THEIR RESPONSES TO MALE

Domination the Heian and the Kamakura Periods

Like in most other early and medieval societies, men dominated the political, economic and social life in the Japanese scenario as well. Such male dominance over most aspects of life was further accentuated by the prevalence of the custom of polygamy. Although Japanese women were culturally conditioned to suffer neglect on the part of their husbands and endure the ensuing loss of pride, nevertheless, these women were often afflicted with a troubled psyche and as a result experienced the very natural emotions of jealousy and anger. These emotions inevitably evoked a response from the agonizing women. However, this response differed depending on the degree of power and rights which the women held at a particular time during the course of Japanese history. These responses can be classified into two categories: personal and public. The personal responses included firstly, poems or entries in a diary and secondly, renunciation of the world in pursuance of spiritual attainment. The public response took the highly dramatic form of spirit possession. The concept of female bonding was constant in both forms of response. The main source of information regarding the life of Japanese women during this period is women's writing itself and since the upper class women were the only educated women at the time, hence, here the focus is only on these elite upper class women.

The essay will follow the chronological pattern by discussing two major forms of female responses during the Heian period: spirit possession and women's personal writings. It will then go on to explain the reasons for the decline of these outlets of response in the Kamakura period and their replacement by a more spiritual course inspired by Buddhism. Within this broad framework of discussion the essay will also highlight the role of the first two responses as being women's expressions of power. And finally the paper will also paper special emphasis on the significance of female bonding as expressed both in case of the spirit possession of Aoi in *The Tale of Genji*[1] and the story of renunciation by the four women in *The Tale of the Heike.*[2]

As the number of ladies favoured by him grows, Genji tries to divide his time between them and this leaves two women disgruntled: his principal wife Aoi and Lady Rokujo.[3] On the Day of Lustration before the Kamo Festival, a pregnant Aoi is persuaded to attend the festival and Lady Rokujo is also there to see and be herself seen. Her carriage becomes trapped behind Aoi's carriage and Genji acknowledges only his wife's presence. Lady Rokujo feels defeated and a carriage fight ensues. Genji wishes that both these women should have been less proud and obstinate but he does not try to mediate between the two rivals. The two women compete for Genji's attentions and Aoi experiences a seizure which is interpreted as spirit possession.[4]

Observing that anthropological studies, particularly ones focusing on polygamous societies show that it is usually women who became victims of spirit possession, Doris Bargen[5] argues that this supposedly "supernatural event of spirit possession momentarily reverses traditional roles and upsets the normal order of values so that victimized women temporarily rule over men."[6] Traditionally jealousy of the *possessor* has been regarded as the major force behind the spirit possession in *Genji monogatari,* however, Bargen adds a new perspective, that of the emotions experienced by the *possessed.* Aoi is not simply jealous of Genji's other women but rather her pride is hurt. Unlike Rokujo's jealousy,

Aoi's is not so much a result of sexual possessiveness but rather of "status anxiety."[7]

Bargen believes that Rokujo and Aoi are united in spirit possession by their aggression: revengeful and defensive respectively.[8] Hence a physically violent women's quarrel is "transformed into an esoteric spiritual rite in which the psychologically allied women vent their repressed anger at a third party—Genji— and the polygynous society that allows men to neglect their women with near impunity."[9] Even if outwardly the possessing spirit is hostile to the victim, it actually functions to express female grievances. Thus, their "oblique aggressive strategy"[10] succeed because Genji stands in awe of the spectacle and intuitively feels that it is a sort of a revolt against male predominance.

Bargen is thus alluding to the concept of female bonding in the face of masculine oppression. Aoi and Rokujo, the worst rivals in love became the best allies in revenge.[11] Thus, they displayed a strong sense of female bonding at the level of the sub-conscious. One can, thus, safely conclude that spirit possession in the Heian times was an expression of sublimated social conflict.[12] It signified a temporary release for the Heian women who were immobilized in layers upon layers of robes and were dimly visible through the manifold enclosures of screens. The Heian code of behaviour forbade women to directly criticize men and so one of the few means of protest at the women's disposal was the oblique aggressive strategy. It would not be impossible to believe that perhaps Murasaki Shikibu was hinting at an ideal that men and women will not reach happiness as long as their relationship is based on inequality.

Apart from this public demonstration of emotions, Doris Bargen also talks about a very "private form"[13] of emotional expression in the form of women's writing which often included entries which were a direct outcome of the women's feelings of jealousy and anger in the face of a polygamous society. The tenth through fourteenth centuries in Japan are marked by a dense proliferation of consciously female creativity expressed in the form of memoirs and diaries (*nikki*) composed in the "woman's hand" (*onna-de*).[14] This trend began in the Heian period, reached its zenith in the mid-Heian period and then began to taper with the onset of the

Kamakura period. Hino Meishi's memoir, the *Takemukigaki* from the mid-fourteenth century is the last piece in the stream of aristocratic women's personal voices.[15] Education was deemed necessary for both boys and girls and comprised instruction in literature, calligraphy and music. However, as opposed to boys, girls studieds Japanese poetry instead of Chinese poetry.[16] This poetry was, thus, composed in *hirakana,* the Japanese syllabry and gave the women's work authorial subjectivity in writing far more than did men's work written mostly in Chinese.

Truly women often used their writing as a means of giving vent to their feelings. The *Gossamer Years*[17] is an account of twenty years in the life of Kagero during which she was a secondary wife of Fujiwara no Kaneie, one of the most politically powerful men of his times who served both as chancellor and regent. Kagero's entries in her diary concern her relationship or rather the lack of it with Kaneie. She expresses her jealousy and anger resulting from Kaneie's attention to his other women. She was also enraged by his numerous casual affairs. There are references to "counting the nights"[18] and many poems addressed to Kaneie who had failed to visit her for quite some time, thus, indicating the plight of women suffering under the usual practice of men dividing their time between their numerous wives in an essentially polygamous marriage culture.[19]

Educated women were highly valued in the marriage market. Women of the mid-Heian period, writing during the ascendancy of the Fujiwara regency around the year 1000, were enabled to write partly because they lived in a community of women who wrote.[20] Heian women's autobiographical wirtings were expressions of power in the sense that they were a way of defining oneself, discovering an identity in oneself and becoming an autonomous person by oneself. Very often these diaries show women acting autonomously.[21] Kagero, left the veranda despite her husband's contrary instructions, on another occasion, she went to a mountain temple and remained there for several weeks despite her husband Kaneie's attempts to bring her back home. On yet another occasion, she refused to do his laundry and sewing or to have intercourse with him.[22] Sarashina, another diarist confides in her diary, that "having firmly made up her mind" she planned to leave Kyoto and go on a pilgrimage alone barring for a few servants.

Hence these diaries were like confidantes of the women, sharing their desires and plans, in addition these writings played the very crucial role of being safety valves which gave an easy release to the feelings of the women.

Although abundance of leisure and membership in the ruling class were important factors in the development of women's writing in Heian Japan, there were several other factors instrumental in giving women the freedom to engage in the socially valued deed of writing, especially autobiographical writing. According to Denise O'brien, "Heian women's autonomy had an economic and legal basis in residence rules and inheritance codes. Women's ownership of property, particularly of family residences and rural income-producing estates gave them economic independence. Uxorilocal or duolocal residence created households with a stable core of female members—a community of women at the family level mirrored in a larger community, the salon, at the imperial court."[23]

Such a hypothesis expressing a causal relationship between residence rules, household structure, inheritance patterns, and women's writing is further strengthened by the historical evidence from the post-Heian period. Takamure Itsue, a pioneering women's historian charts the development of the Japanese marriage pattern passing through the phases of : tsumadoi (visiting a wife), mukotori (taking a groom or son-in-law) and finally reaching the phase called yometori (taking a bride or daughter-in-law).[24] Takamure further argues that, "the new marriage system accommodated the intensified need on the part of the patriarchal institution to maintain private property along the patrilineal line of descent and inheritance."[25] Thus, the inheritance of the matrilineal residence shifted to the patrilineal line. Women now moved from a situation where they lived with their sisters and their respective offspring to one in which homes were owned by men and a wife lived in her husband's home. Denise O'Brien emphasizes that this shift in household structure and a decrease in women's economic independence occurred at the same time as a decline in women's writing or, "at least an absence of writing entering the public cannon."[26] Scholars are in agreement regarding the absence of women writers of any note in Japan from the mid-fourteenth to the nineteenth century.

The slow transformation of marriage practice paralleled the gradual diminution of property rights of women. Female property-holding deteriorated steadily after the fourteenth century and Takamure points out that aristocratic women post-Kamakura period faced personal and economic conditions markedly different from those experienced by most of their female forebears in the earlier three centuries. Women now experienced an economic dependency that further weakened the already vulnerable position of women associated with patrilocal marriage.

This downward slide in the women's position had already begun at the beginning of the thirteenth century. By the Kamakura period, women had declined in social status and were less free to create a stir. Hence, they took up a much quieter and personal path in tune with the more gloomier aspects of Buddhism, they frequently renounced the world and the men who ruled it.[27]

In their response to the men's world and their ensuing decision to stay away from it, many women chose the path of celibacy. The thirteenth century saw the establishment of many institutions created to accommodate women who intended to stay celibate either by avoiding marriage or after widowhood. The Zen and Ritsu Schools of Buddhism established nunneries alongside monasteries.[28] These institutions served both religious and social functions. They served to absorb surplus aristocratic females, sometimes in their infancy. Since women were prohibited from ascending Mount Koya, they sought alternative religious sites such as Zenkoji, an important pilgrimage site in the (modern) city of Nagano.[29] According to Hitomi Tonomura, the demand for nunneries increased from the thirteenth century onwards.[30] She quotes Taira Masayuki who believes that, "the new demand reflected the growing belief that access to the woman's body should remain solely with the husband during and after his lifetime."[31] However, Hitomi Tonomura counters this argument by saying that it does not explain renunciation by unmarried women. Stemming from this she argues that the rising instances of retiring to a nunnery may have been caused by a general trend towards attenuation of property rights among aristocratic women.[32]

Renouncing one's sexuality was, however, not always voluntary. After the death of Prince Ogawamiya, his sixteen year old concubine was forced to shave her hair and thus become ineligible for marriage by her father-in-law, the retired Emperor Go-Komatsu. Nunneries also provided a shelter for women who remained single and childless as was the case with many palace attendants.

Sometimes, lack of protectors also left a woman no choice except renunciation.[33] Nowhere is this phenomenon more visible than in the episode of Gio in the Tale of the Heike. Taira Kiyomori, the head of the Taira clan had a "famous and accomplished *shirabyoshi* dancer"[34] named Gio living in his house. Kiyomori bestowed generous gifts on her mother Toji and sister Ginyo. He was so taken in by Gio's beauty and talent that he refused admission to any other dancer in his palace. Once a dancer named Hotoke decided to try her luck but was harshly dismissed. It was only on the intervention of Gio that Kiyomori agreed to see Hotoke's performance. He was dazzled by Hotoke's charm and ordered Gio to leave the house. The auther of the tale says that, "Gio had resigned herself to this possibility long ago.... with regret and grief....she bid farewell to her house of three years,"[35] because she was familiar with the ways of a society which treated women as men's playthings, to be taken up and discarded on a whim. Weeping, she scribbled a poem on a sliding door:

Since both are grasses
of the field, how may be either spared by autumn-
the young shoot blossoming forth
and the herb fading from view?[36]

Her response in the form of poetry may be reminiscent of the Rokujo Lady in the Tale of Genji, however, Gio's ensuing actions are a world apart from those of the Rokujo Lady. While Rokujo Lady's emotions led her to unknowingly enter the world of spirit possession, Gio on the other hand chose a much quieter and pious path. In these two tales, both Lady Rokujo as well as Gio were humiliated. The former in the carriage parking incident during the Day of Lustration[37] and the latter by Kiyomori's threats and her treatment at Kiyomori's house.[38] Gio, however, was compelled by her economic conditions and concern for her mother and sister to chose a different path. She was bound by lack of economic means and independence and so she could not give her emotions a dramatic vent as Rokujo Lady did (as discussed earlier in the essay). So, at the tender age of twenty one, Gio became a nun living "in a brush-thatched hermitage" her mother and sister joined her soon afterwards. Finally, one day even Hotoke joined them in the hermitage. She described a woman's lot to be sorrowful and said that, "A woman is a poor, weak creature who can't control her destiny."[39] Hotoke read Gio's poem on the sliding door and decided to follow her footsteps. While Gio renounced the world because of her jealousy and resentment towards the male world, Hotoke was inspired only by true piety. Thus, these four women display a form of defiance against the men's world. They invoked a sense of female bonding and sought salvation from the evil realm of men's greed and lust by living in seclusion and chanting the name of Amida Buddha.[40]

In her collection of medieval revelatory tales, called *Rethinking Sorrow*, Margaret Helen Childs has presented the tale of *The Seven Nuns.*[41] This tale describes seven women's journey to renunciation. Of these seven women, five were driven to this path because of parting from a loved one either because of the man's death or by his infidelity. In the first instance Shiragiku's two lovers leave her alone due to the sympathy and deference they feel for each other. Thus, their respect for each other outweighs any practical regard for the women's welfare.[42] Another woman Hanakazura takes the tonsure because she loses her husband to his first love: warfare.[43] A third woman, Lord Kikui's wife learns to meditate and thus conquer her emotions of jealousy and hostility when her husband takes up a mistress.[44] The narrator in the fourth instance is Lady Miike's maid, who describes how Lord Miike took up a mistress and neglected his wife. The distressed wife then committed suicide and her maid took to the spiritual path in order to pray for the salvation of her employer.[45] The fifth woman became a nun after witnessing the murder of her lover, and stabbing an innkeeper to save herself from being raped.[46] Since literature is considered to be the mirror of society, these tales reflect the prevalence of the practice of women taking tonsure as a respite from emotional and physical injuries inflicted upon them by men.

The discussion of the varied reactions of women in response to the injustices of a polygamous society and the men who created and perpetuated such a society shows a distinct pattern. When the rules of marriage and residence and the economic structure accompanying them secured a favourable position for the female members of the society, the women indulged in self-expressions of power either through their writings or created a public stir by esoteric tactics. However, when the residence rules made women subject to direct male authority, in a house owned by a man who was also responsible for the upkeep and welfare of the woman who lacked any independent source of income, the women felt much more restricted and in their frustration chose to renounce their submissive life altogether by not only leaving the man but also all the other pleasures and luxuries which were a part of the man-created and man-dominated world.

REFERENCES

1. Helen Craig McCullough, trans., *Genji and Heike: Selections from The Tale of Genji and The Tale of the Heike* (Stanford: Stanford University Press, 1994), pp. 20-242.
2. *Ibid.*, pp. 244-58.
3. *Ibid.*, pp. 131-59.
4. The large number of deaths during pregnancy and childbirth were attributed to the supernatural and therefore possession during childbirth was considered to be a common phenomenon.
5. Doris A. Bargen, "Spirit Possession in the Context of Dramatic Expression of Gender Conflict: The Aoi Episode of the Genji Monogatari," *Harvard Journal of Asiatic Studies* 48 (June 1988): pp. 95-130.
6. *Ibid.*, p. 95.
7. *Ibid.*, p. 101.
8. *Ibid.*
9. *Ibid.*
10. *Ibid.*
11. *Ibid.*, p. 110.
12. *Ibid.*, p. 127.
13. *Ibid.*, p. 103.
14. Hitomi Tonomura, "Re-envisioning Women in the Post-Kamakura Age," in *The Origins of Japan's Medieval World,* ed. Jeffrey P. Mass (Stanford: Stanford University Press, 1997), p. 139.
15. *Ibid.*

16. Denise O'Brien, "Women's Writing in Heian Japan: Expressions of Power," in *Configurations of Power: Holistic Anthropology in Theory and Practice*, ed. John S. Henderson and Patricia J. Netherly (London: Cornell University Press, 1993), p. 211.
17. Edward Seidensticker, trans., *The Gossamer Years: A Diary by a Noble woman in Heian Japan* (Tokyo: Charles E. Tuttle Company, 1973).
18. *Ibid.*, pp. 35, 132.
19. *Ibid.*, pp. 39, 41.
20. O'Brien, Women's Writing in Heian Japan, p. 212.
21. *Ibid.*, p. 219.
22. Seidensticker, *Gossamer Years,* pp. 65, 100-101, 105-110.
23. O'Brien, Women's Writing in Heian Japan, p. 223.
24. Tonomura, Re-evisioning Women, p. 146.
25. *Ibid.*
26. O'Brien, Women's Writing in Heian Japan, p. 223.
27. Bargen, Spirit Possession, p. 103.
28. Tonomura, Re-envisioning Women, p. 165.
29. Margaret Helen Childs, trans., *Rethinking Sorrow* (Ann Arbor: Center for Japanese Studies, 1991), p. 6.
30. Tonomura, Re-envisioning Women, p. 166.
31. *Ibid.*
32. *Ibid.*
33. *Ibid.*
34. McCullough, Genji and Heike, p. 266.
35. *Ibid.*, p. 268.
36. *Ibid.*
37. *Ibid.*, pp. 133-34.
38. *Ibid.*, pp. 268-70.
39. *Ibid.*, p. 271.
40. *Ibid.*, p. 272.
41. Childs, *Rethinking Sorrow,* pp. 91-140.
42. *Ibid.*, pp. 95-99.
43. *Ibid.*, pp. 102-106.
44. *Ibid.*, pp. 114-19.
45. *Ibid.*, pp. 119-28.
46. *Ibid.*, pp. 128-40.

8

THE POSITION OF WOMEN WITHIN THE INSTITUTION OF MARRIAGE IN EIGHTEENTH CENTURY ENGLAND

The Eighteenth century was the century of enlightenment. It was an age when secular power rather than theological dictates remained supreme. The period produced thinkers like V.A. Smitth, David Hume, Imanuel Kant and Rousseau. Ideas of observation, rationalization, natural deduction and individualism became the hallmarks of the age. However, social developments and new found knowledge was centered around men and the masculine world, notions of democracy and individualism catered only to men, women were left out of the realm of these high-sounding, noble and moralistic values. This isolation of women from the new kind of thinking is most starkly evident in the institution of marriage. This chapter aims at bringing to light the nature of the arrangement of marriage in Enlightenment England the motives behind such an arrangement and its adverse implications for women, as revealed by the literature and art of the period.

During the seventeenth, eighteenth and nineteenth centuries, the system of marriage prevalent in England was the one handed down by previous centuries, namely that of arranged marriages. This arrangement had its roots in the social and economic system of England. Among the elite or the aristocracy, it was essential for a match to be socially acceptable and it was preferable if the bride brought dowry with her. Since 1700 onwards, the wealth of the aristocracy was diminishing and as a result, sons of peers began looking for heiresses outside the aristocracy and found their answer in the noveau riche trading class of England. This kind of arrangement is vividly portrayed in the first plate of William Hogarth's (1697-1764) series of engravings called "Arranged Marriage."[1] The scene described in this plate consisted of the fathers of the bride and groom to be. The father of the boy was shown to have an unfinished house which he wanted to complete with the funds he hoped to get from his prospective daughter-in-law. He was shown bargaining with the father of the girl. The father had a long list of aristocratic lineage and the latter was probably a textile merchant who was ready to pay in cash. While these negotiations were going on, the girl and the boy sat with their backs to each other, representing the general unwillingness and unhappiness experienced by couples under such arrangements. Moreover, Lord Hardwick's Marriage Act of 1753 made the consent of parents essential if the boy and girl were under 21. Thus, this clause also played a role in thwarting the dreams and aspirations of young lovers.

However, statistics show that from 1800 onwards many sons of peers were marrying for other reasons also. This could be so because, now they were marrying at a later age, hence they were not only more mature, but in most of the cases their parents had already died and so they were free to choose their own mate rather than accept one which was forced upon them. Moreover, this period saw the development of the idea of 'companionate marriage' which meant that there was a positive affection between the bride and groom. Such relationships were based on active acceptance rather than a passive tolerance. Such views were also echoed in the literature of the times. The novels by Jane Austen (1775-1817) such as *Pride and Prejudice, Sense and Sensibility* and *Mansfield Park* emphasized that love was an important force in shaping one's life and finding one's sexual partner.[2 3]

Thus, men often allowed themselves to be guided by the idea of love rather than wealth and social status. The writers of the period fully endorsed such ideas. In Samuel Richardson's (1689-1761) novel *Pamela*, published in 1740, the employer falls in love with the righteousness and beauty of a female servant. And he marries her for her qualities as a person, rather than because of the considerations of wealth.[4] Thus, men often were in a position where they could defy social conventions and break the taboos impased by class hierarchy.

However, for a woman such expressions of personal preference and desire were not possible. Social conventions stood in the way of her being able to find a mate whom she found companionable and her family found respectable. Letters written by Lady Mary Wortley Montagu (1689-1762) to her cousin Philipe Munday discuss the problem of finding a suitable life partner. In their private correspondence, the two girls code worded 'hell' as marrying a person one hated, 'purgatory' as marrying a person one merely tolerated or was indifferent to and 'paradice' meant marrying the person one loathed.[4] In her letter dated September 25, 1711, Mary wrote, "I have that aversion to hell, I shall resist it all my life, though without hope of paradise, and I am very well convinced I shall never go to hell". And within less than a year this young girl was forced to change her views. However, less than a year later, in April, 1712. She wrote, "I see no probable prospect of my ever entering paradise. This is the real state of my heart, which is now so much perplexd and divided. The apparent impossibility of dear paradise often makes me resolve to plunge to hell and lose the thought for ever." The contrast which the two statements produce is very stark indeed. In the first letter, the fantasies, dreams and desires of a young girl are still alive, and then she faced the harsh reality of her cousin being jilted for an heiress of a wealthy fellow. Thus, social reality stood in the path of her dreams and in fact even forced her to accept 'hell', a notion she was so averse to earlier. Later in her life, she went on to have an unhappy marriage with long periods of separation from her husband. The second plate of the series *Arranged Marriage* by Hogarth also shows the young bride trying to allure her husband, who is disinterested in her.[6] Similarly, Arthur Denis' painting of the Rookleeds family portrays a husband and wife standing or among from each other and separated by a daughter. The man is standing aloof, away from the world of the mother and the daughter. his posture authoritative and gives no visible sign of affection between him cap his wife, rather he appears to be, giving the impression that he considers himself to be the possessor or owner of his wife and daughter.

It was while reflecting on such loveless relationships that Mary Astell (1668-1731) wrote-*Reflections Upon Marriage*.[7] She asked that age had executed a monarch and established the system of the distribution of power between the monarch and the parliament, then, why was it so that there was no distribution of power within the family. She questioned the social system of the period saying, if all men were born free, then why was it so that all women were born slaves, women despised men, and yet had to serve them. Such views reveal the fact that there was such social inequality between men and women in that society that it forced women thinkers such as Mary Astell, Lady Mary Wortley Montagu and Mary Wollstonecraft (1759-97) to raise a cry against the unjust social system.

This injustice stemmed from the fact that while both men and women entered into an arranged marriage, such an arrangement had different implications for both the genders. Men had means of escape and could look for and find affection elsewhere. Having mistresses for pleasure was socially acceptable. The third plate of Hogarth's engraving showed the young man with his mistress whom he shamelessly maintained on by squandering away his wife's wealth.[9] While there were religions taboos and legal penalty for adultery, the society accepted it as a matter of fact. Thomas Turner, (1729-93) a Justice of Peace, recorded the case of a still bonn illegitimate child of a women called Elizabeth Elless.[10] Instead of taking the illegitimate fathar to law, Turner, symphathised with Peter Adams the man and justified his position saying, "And for a great while past they have been as conversant and familiar as if they were lovers though he was a married man. To do him justice, he has had one child before by another woman, and his wife, poor woman is now busy with child."[11] Thus, he regards the whole fact of Mr. Adam's adultery and production of illegitimate children with a casual complacency. Hence men justified other men's actions and having mistresses was considered to be common practice.

Similarly, James Boswell (1740-95) had affairs with fifteen women, liaisons with four actresses, and had three mistresses.[12] Thus, not surprisingly he had 20 different outbreaks of gonorrhea and finally, he even infected his poor and dutiful wife Margaret. Even thinkers of the time such as the utilitarian, Jeremy Bentham

(1748-1832) believed that heterosexuality was natural. According to him the ascetic condemnation of sex outside marriage was unnatural.[13] He further said that if sex outside marriage gave pleasure, it was justified. Such views further reinforced the practice of adultery by men. However, women were not free to do so, because men were always apprehensive about the question of paternity. As Hogarth's engraving in plate IV showed that while it was fine for the husband to have a mistress and impregnate her too, such was not the case with women.[14] If the wife ventured to look elsewhere for affection, her lover had to be fought in order to settle the question of paternity if the wife become pregnant. Thus, all these instances show that the disastrous effects which such heterosexual relations of the husband had were extremely painful for the wife, not just psychologically, mentally, emotionally, but as in the case of Margaret Boswell, even physically.

The existence of such conditions induced women thinkers such as Lady Mary Wortley Montagu, when she was reflecting on the death of a young women called Eleanor Bowe, a few months after her marriage. Lady Montagu wrote that it was good that she died when she was in love and being dearly loved by her husband, before she faced the reality and found out that her husband was faithless, indifferent and domineering and so she was lucky to get love without the tribulations of marriage because after the high bliss of the early months, it was all the way down hill.

Thus, the literature and art of Enlightenment England reveal that the institution of marriage was an unfair one and had unjust implications for women. They were subject to the whims and fancies of their husbands and were given hardly any choice in the matter. They were seen merely as procurers of dowry or as ladders to upward social mobility. The system of marriages which were arranged to fit within the choices of wealth, class status and social respectability left little room for affection and mutual understanding. While on the one hand this arrangement suited the men who could seek pleasure outside marriage, it had left few means of escape for the women for whom heterosexual relations were impractical becuase of the fear of pregnancy and the question of determination of paternity. Hence, even in the eighteenth century when England replaced absolute monarchy by the parliamentary system and limited monarchy, thinkers like Mary

Astell were forced to ask, "If absolute power is bad, then why is it so in every household?"[15]

REFERENCES

1 Sean Shesgreen, ed., *Engravings by Hogarth* (New York: Dover, 1973).

2. Jane Austen, *Pride and Prejudice* (London: Octopus Books, 1987), *Sense and Sensibility* (London: The Zodiac Press, 1956).

3. Jane Austen, *Mansfield Park,* ed. James Kinsley (Oxford: Oxford University Press, 1998).

4. T.C. Duncan Eaves and Ben D. Kimpel, ed., *Pamela; or, Virtue Rewarded* (Boston: Houghton Mifflin, 1971).

5. Robert Halsband, ed., *The Complete Letters of Lady Mary Wortley Montagu* (Oxford: Clarendon Press, 1965-1967).

6. Shesgreen, *Engravings.*

7. Bridget Hill, ed., *The First English Feminist: Reflections upon Marriage and Other Writings by Mary Astell* (Aldershot: Gower/ Maurice Temple Smith, 1986).

8. Sylvana Tomaselli, ed., *A Vindication of the Rights of Men: With, A Vindication of the Rights of Woman, and Hints by Mary Wollstonecraft* (Cambridge: Cambridge University Press, 1995).

9. Shesgreen, *Engravings.*

10. David Vaisey, ed., *The Diary of Thomas Turner, 1754-1765* (Oxford: Oxford University Press, 1984).

11. *Ibid.*, 52.

12. Richard C. Cole, ed., *The General Correspondence of James Boswell, 1766-1769* (Edinburgh: Edinburgh University Press, 1993).

13. Timothy L. S. Sprigge, ed., *The Correspondence of Jeremy Bentham* (London: Athlone Press, 1968).

14. Shesgreen, *Engravings.*

15. Hill, *The First English Feminist.*

SECTION 3

WOMEN AND FAMILY

9

CORRECT BEGINNINGS

The Role of the Chinese Mother as the Moral Guide and the First Teacher of the Child

In 1831 Wanyan Yun Zhu compiled an anthology of women's poetry and called it *Correct beginnings* because she believed that goodness begins in the women's inner quarters. If a family wants to successfully follow the virtuous path, the education of its members must be initiated in the inner quarters. This traditional Chinese belief indicates the importance of women in the society and the influence they had on the family. Women exercised this influence as mothers, wives, writers and courtesans. This study focuses on the Chinese mothers of the eighteenth, the nineteenth, and the twentieth centuries, who had to be extremely pure, moral and virtuous women in order to give birth to healthy children and subsequently to raise those children to be virtuous and intelligent members of the Chinese society.

The Chinese Classics as well as the subsequent texts laid great premium on the purity and virtuousness of a mother. The role of the mother as the first informal tutor or educator of the child began when he or she was three or four years old. However, her responsibility for the good health and correct moral conduct of the child began even before the child's birth. To ensure the fetus' and later the infant's health and morality the expecting mother was expected to be the paragon of virtue right from the time of conception. Likewise this paper studies two periods of women's role as moral guides and educators--the pre-natal and the post-natal.

Like most other spheres of Chinese society, women were subordinated even within the sphere of reproduction. In this case the subordination was reinforced through medical norms.[2] Essentially male medical authorities taught: "Successful childbearing, like successful wifehood, was a matter of moral discipline and restraint. Maternal and child health depended on the same virtues of passionless calm that served the patriarchal family well in the social regulation of its wives."[3] Moreover, these texts alleged that female vices such as, "resentment and anger, lust and passion, indulgence and immoderate desires—all were implicated in the pathological disorders of pregnancy and neo-natal disease."[4]

The pro-natalist Chinese society regarded childbirth as socially esteemed labour and laid an immense responsibility on the pregnant mother's shoulders. To ensure that expectant mothers carry out their role properly, the medical authorities gave advice on pre-natal care. As a means of scaring the expectant women into behaving as the society desired, this advice on pre-natal care was disguised as seven means by which women could lead themselves into a difficult delivery. "During gestation women were warned against (1) physical inactivity, (2) overeating, (3) anxiety, and (4) lust. During parturition they were to guard against (5) weakness and cowardice, (6) premature and excessive 'labour' (li), and (7) exhaustion of vital energy."[5]

These medical men also kept in mind the Chinese emphasis on the importance of diet for health and gave advice such as, "Eat bird-meat and the child will be lustful."[6] However, "fetal education"[7] focussed more on the emotional than the physical aspect. The gestating mother's most important responsibility was "to regulate emotions: the internal 'heat' of anger and lust were sure causes of miscarriage. Lust or sexual desire was associated with the pollution of the birth process and the new born child's propensity for illness and therefore sexual abstinence was stressed for both maternal and child health. "Hence the best mother is a person of 'virtuous nature and retiring disposition, having little fire in her vital organs."[8] Such admonitions against a woman's excessive desires made "fetal education" recover some of its classical moral force. It is not surprising, therefore, to find some medical authorities advising a woman to consider her preparation for childbirth ultimately as "spiritual self-cultivation."[9] Hence by avoiding meddling into other people's affairs, staying away from envy and passionate emotions will keep one's vital energy intact, one's blood ample in quantity and one's essences sufficient.[10] Thus, by their physicians' advice, the pregnant women were guided towards a meditative ideal of self-cultivation like that enjoined on men by Neo Confucian teachers. And finally at the actual time of child birth, a woman's virtue not only became her vehicle to a safe delivery but conversely a safe delivery and the birth of a healthy child became a proof of her womanly virtue.

After the birth of the child, the duties of a teacher were added to the mother's duty as a moral guide. Even though a woman's contribution to the Confucian scholastic tradition was subsidiary and indirect, it was however indispensable. As a mother, she was expected to give birth to children, preferably sons, supervise their early education and if the financial situation of the family demanded it, to work incessantly at the spinning wheel and loom to support their studies. Thus, "the glorification of moral motherhood, especially motherhood, endowed private responsibilities with public and political significance."[11] Wang Huizu, a distinguished legal expert of the Qing period wrote an advice book, named in honour of the two women who raised him. He said that continuing the family line requires the guidance of mothers, hence they are crucial to the governance of the state and the management of the home.[12]

The performance of these roles required that women themselves be educated. Many Chinese texts were written around the theme of women's education, the prominent ones being the ones written by Pan Chao and Ch'en Hung-mou. These writers usually believed that since a girl went on to become a wife and a mother, therefore a family's future and purity is tied to the education of its women. This education included training in the arts of needle-work, poetry, painting, calligraphy and music-making; the women of the upper class received in addition "moral instruction: education in the *tai*, or 'ultimate significance,' of Classical texts."[13]

In addition to having received such an education there is

another characteristic of model moral motherhood. Most of the model mothers in Chinese history were widows. Thus, the Chinese society and the literati propagated the cult of the virtuous mother and the chaste mother simultaneously. The most famous examples were Mencius' mother and Zhang Zao. They were widowed mothers who did not remarry but assumed the responsibility of their sons' support and education.

Another characteristic of such mother-educators was their lenient attitude towards their children. "The mother-as-teacher is most often marked by the adjective *ci*, 'kindly' or 'nurturant'." For instance a daughter and a son studying at their mother's feet are described by Wanyan Yun Zhu as *tong cheng ci xun* (together receiving "the maternal instructions"), "using the word *ci*, 'nurturant,' as a synecdoche for mother." The phrase *yan fu ci mu* ("stern father and indulgent mother") brings out the contrast between the role of the two parents.[14] But this did not mean that the mother could not enforce discipline. In fact, of the two parents, she was the one in charge of disciplining the children and ill-disciplined children reflected more on the mother than on themselves. Thus, a mother could correct her son without suffering embarrassment. Sons endured criticism openly—even sentimentally, as is revealed in a poem by a high official Xie Daocheng. Referring to a time when he hesitated in replying to his mother's question, Xie wrote:

> *My mother's face changed colour and flared up in anger:*
>
> *To spread out a book with a humble heart, this is a student's responsibility;*
>
> *In studying the ancient ways, are you no better than a woman?'*
>
> *Alas!*
>
> *My mother's words are still in my ear,*
>
> *My face still gleams with perspiration...*
>
> *Would that she could ever be angry, and I ever anxious!*
>
> *Now I hear no one urging me to study.*[15]

The above poem reflects on the nature of the teacher-student relationship between mother and son. By the eighteenth century, a boy's formal classical education began as he reached four sui (three years in Western parlance) under the tutelage of a family member, usually his mother, particularly if his father was away from home or deceased. Mothers were often portrayed as reeling thread in their chambers while tutoring their sons in the Classics. Later on, after the son grew up, the mother was still the guiding force. Mothers wrote poems expressing their anguish as their sons went through the gruelling competition for degrees and office, it was the mother again who faced the challenge to keep her son from giving up the struggle for a degree. The famous story of Mencius' mother epitomizes the importance of a mother's morality in her son's scholastic success. She was said to have moved three times to shield Mencius from the bad influences in the neighbourhood. When he still ran off from school, she cut the web of her loom to teach him the perils of abandoning one's vocation halfway. Apart from imparting moral virtues, it was widely recognized that a mother well-versed in the Classics could enhance her son's examination success. The Ming state formally recognized women's contribution to men's education by conferring honourary titles on the mothers of scholar-officials.[16]

Even more intimate than the relationship between mother and son was the relationship between mother and daughter, probably because she spent more time with her mother in the inner chambers as compared to her brothers. For a daughter, "mother's effort and example lay at the heart of powerful emotional bonds."[17] Yun Zhu emphasized the intellectual ties between mother and daughter and frequently referred to a daughter inheriting her mother's teaching.[18] "The job of educating girls was a natural extension of the sacrosanct duties of mothers in the domestic realm."[19] This education included, "pleasing speech and manners, to be docile and obedient, to handle hempen fibers, to deal with the cocoons, to weave silk... to be present at the sacrifices...and assisting in setting out the appurtenances for the ceremonies."[20]

According to Susan Mann, some women found the act of instructing their daughter to be an act of "love and joy that produced in time a female companion with whom one could exchange poems and, through them feelings and thoughts." While on the other hand, teaching a daughter brought back memories of youthful talents and hopes that were never realized. Even if the mother wanted to teach her daughter along the lines of her son's education, she knew it was useless because of the society's constraints as she herself had very well learnt when her dreams and ambitions were thwarted during her youth. As Liang Lan'e wrote:

Meekly obey and practice wifely conduct-

As for everything else-its beyond your reach.[21]

This tradition of the mother's role as the guide, mentor and teacher of the sons and daughters of the family, continued even into the early twentieth century, when China was undergoing tremendous transformation. Yu-I, the first woman in Republican China to get a divorce, recalls her growing up years in a traditional Chinese household and testifies to the tremendous hold which the mother exercised over the children in the family.

When Yu-I's mother caught her brothers gambling at dice while they waited for their tutor to return from the toilet, she scolded them saying, "What a disgrace! Return to your studies at once!"[22] The boys stood before their mother with their heads hung in shame. Later on when their father threatened to punish them with the memorization of fifty chanted verses each by the following morning, it was their grandmother who intervened timely and stopped him from doing so. This incident reveals the role of the mother in disciplining the children. And, the children in turn did not turn mutinous but listened in silence and obeyed the wishes of their mother even when they themselves had become fathers.

Similarly, when Yu-I got married, her mother instructed her to "never say no, only yes."[23] As a result even when Yu-I wanted to take care of her child instead of relying on the servants, she did not object to the ways of her in-laws. Thus, she placed her mother's teaching before her maternal desire to care for her son. These examples show that the mother-as-teacher role was not just a part of the Classical literature but was very much extant even in the twentieth century China.

Hence, a survey of the indispensable role which the mother played in the life of the sons and daughters of China starting from even before the birth of the children and continuing till even when the children themselves had become parents, shows how the women formed the central pillar of the society and polity in China.

On the one hand the Confucian tradition sanctioned "the cultural education of the women in preparation to become the son's first teacher and the mother's role in the oral transmission of the Classics won her niche, albeit indirect, in the Confucian canonical tradition."[24] On the other hand the literati also invoked images of the model mother inspired by the ancient myth of a powerful goddess who was the "perfect mother, perfect lover, and perfect teacher."[25]

However, inspite of such a high status of women they were still regarded as inferiors of men. Women could prepare their sons for the Civil Service Examination but they could never themselves take the exam, nor could their daughters. Rather, as one poem indicates, mothers dissuaded their daughters from aspiring to anything other than being a filial daughter and an obedient wife since it would only lead to disillusionment. Hence, even though mothers had authority over their sons, they had little authority over their own lives. Their role in life was charted out for them by the men--their fathers, husbands and sons. Hence in spite of their crucial role in the Chinese society and the high regard which the society accorded them, the image of their power in the society was in fact just like the images created by the literati--perfect but mere myths.

REFERENCES

1. Susan Mann, *Precious Records: Women in China's Long Eighteenth Century* (Stanford: Stanford University Press, 1997), p. 76.
2. Charlotte Furth, "Concepts of pregnancy, Childbirth, and Infancy in Ch'ing Dynasty China," *Journal of Asian Studies* 46, no. 1 (February 1987): p. 9.
3. *Ibid.*
4. *Ibid.*
5. *Ibid.*, p. 14.
6. *Ibid.*
7. *Ibid.*
8. *Ibid.*, p. 15.
9. *Ibid.*
10. *Ibid.*

11. Dorothy Ko, *Teachers of the Inner Chambers* (Stanford: Stanford University Press, 1994), p. 165.
12. Mann, *Precious Records*, p. 28.
13. Rubie S. Watson, *Marriage and Inequality in Chinese Society* (Berkeley: California University Press, 1991), p. 214.
14. Mann, *Precious Records*, p. 102.
15. *Ibid.*, p. 105.
16. Dorothy Ko, *Teachers of the Inner Chambers* (Stanford: Stanford University Press, 1994), pp. 158-59.
17. Mann, *Precious Records*, p. 105.
18. *Ibid.*
19. Ko, *Teachers of the Inner Chambers*, p. 128.
20. Susan Mann, "Grooming a Daughter for Marriage: Brides and Wives in the Mid-Ch'ing Period," in *Marriage and Inequality in Chinese Society*, ed. Rubie S. Watson (Berkeley: University of California Press, 1991), pp. 207-208.
21. Mann, *Precious Records*, p. 106.
22. Pang-Mei Natasha Chang, *Bound Feet and Western Dress* (New York: Doubleday, 1996), p. 48.
23. *Ibid.*, p. 97.
24. Ko, *Teachers of the Inner Chambers*, p. 159.
25. Mann, *Precious Records*, p. 76.

10

THEIR MOTHERS' DAUGHTERS

The Mother-daughter Relationship in Asian Indian Immigrant Households in the US

"Two souls, two thoughts...in one dark body."

—W.E.B. Dubois.[1]

These simple words invoke a meaning which is beyond the realm of any particular race or ethnicity. They represent a universal feeling which is experienced by immigrants all over the world. Yet they are also uniquely suited to the experience of the Asian Indian immigrants in the United States. The Indian and the American cultural values are so far apart that every Indian American indeed carries within herself two souls, belonging to two different worlds, two diverse cultures: one belonging to the parents and the other to the children, one representative of the first generation Indian-Americans and the other representing the second generation, one transported from India and the other born in America. While the experience of living within an immigrant household is difficult for every member of the family, it is especially tough for the women because they,"have had to contend both with how they are seen as women given the harshness of patriarchy and how as Asian-Americans they are considered as marginal to the mainstream."[2]

While the second generation might find it easier to identify with the American society, such is not the case with the first generation immigrants.

Whether your father and mother like it or not
you are American and want to be part of the Melting Pot.
For now we can only keep on loving you
and hope for the best.
The situation is out of our hands.[3]

These lines, from a poem written by a first generation Asian-Indian mother in the US, could reflect on the experiences of immigrant mothers from any part of the world. Still, the phrases also seem uniquely Indian in their silent plea for a closer bond and identification between the mother and the daughter. Mothers and daughters belonging to two different generations and representing two different worlds, often find themselves polarized. Even though the poem above portrays an extreme case of estrangement between the mother and the daughter, a deeper study of the Indian immigrant literature shows that, despite their different outlooks, these mothers and daughters overcome the generational gap and identify with each other as women. The writings of the Asian Indian women in America reveal that gender takes precedence over generation.

In a statement issued by the US Congressional Caucus on India and the Asian Indians on October 24, 1994, Indians have been called the "model minority" because most of the Indian immigrants since the late nineteen seventies are highly educated and financially secure professionals.[4] They belong to the upper and middle class of the Indian society. Most of the recent Indian immigrant women are wives of these professionals and are therefore, themselves well-educated. Almost all of them are at least college graduates, while some have joined American universities to earn their Masters and Doctorate degrees. While the earlier wave of women immigrants also experienced the emotional upheaval normally associated with the ordeal accompanying immigration, the recent women immigrants have been more successful in giving words to their feelings. The educational and literary qualifications of these women have enabled them to produce a plethora of writings on diverse aspects of the immigrant experience. These writings which include poetry, essays and short stories might have an element of fiction in them, but are nevertheless inspired by the real life experiences of the authors. Hence they manage to provide a fairly accurate picture of the day to day lives of the immigrant women, a subject which would be hard to find in the official accounts on the Indian immigrant experience. Some of the images thus suggested by the literature have been corroborated by secondary writings based on interviews of Asian Indian women.

Indian women in America have to carry the dual burden of struggling against the pressures of conflicting cultures, as immigrants, and of struggling against the bonds of patriarchy and male domination, as women. According to Lorna Gonsalves-Pinto, the identities of these Asian Indian women in the US emanate from their personal histories which are rooted in the two countries as well as in familial and societal expectations of them. As a result, Asian Indian American women have to battle all the endemic pressures and prejudices of mainstream American culture and at the same time they have to bear the burden of the yoke of patriarchy in their communities and household situations.[5]

The experience of moving from one culture to another has been much written about in the Indian American women's writings. Indu Krishnan, the director of *Knowing her Place*, a film based on the life of Vasu, an Asian Indian immigrant women, commented: "Growing up in two cultures, or coming from one to live in another, is like moving in two directions at once, or like being in two places at once."[6] Vasu was raised in the US and at age twelve, she was sent back to her grandparents in India to ensure that she spent her teen years in a protected environment, safe from the influence of the dangerous notion of dating. At sixteen she married and joined her husband in the US. As a result of all these relocations, Vasu experienced a sense of dualism. She described this duality in terms of a conflict between America and India, and concluded that, "it takes a long time to figure out where you belong. That's the pain of being, sort of, a second generation immigrant child."[7] As a mother of two sons, Vasu struggled between her parental desire to conform to the cultural norms which were contrary to those of her peers while at the same time she was trying to cope with her uneasy integration into the American society. She was expected to play different roles, that of an Indian daughter when she visited her parents, and that of a dutiful Indian wife when she was with her husband and all this while she was also struggling to be an American mother to her children.

In their day today interaction with their children, these first generation Indian mothers of second generation Indian children are repeatedly reminded of the fact that they are Indian and their offspring, despite their Indian blood are American in their beliefs, outlook and lifestyle. One of the first signs of the children's rapid integration into the American mainstream is reflected in their use of the English language. In families where mothers are not highly educated, they often face the language barrier. While the mothers stay at home, the immigrant children go to school and interact with English speaking teachers and classmates. Moreover, language skills are sharper at a younger age and so these children very quickly develop their English language skills.

In most cases the children speak English both at home and outside. If the mother has a very limited knowledge of the language, she finds it difficult to communicate with the children. Chitra Bannerjee Divakaruni's poem "Yuba City School" describes the dilemma of a non-English speaking mother, who felt that her tongue was, "a stiff embarrassment in (her) mouth" because she knew only, "a few English phrases" and consequently would find it hard to interact with her child.[8] Similarly, the language barrier can also pose as an embarrassment for the children as well. In a story by Amita Vasudev the narrator confessed to her journal that when her mother spoke to her in Hindi--the Indian national language, in the Indian grocery store, she hated it. She froze with tensed embarrassment and pretended not to hear.[9] One's own language is referred to as the mother tongue, thus awarding it the revered status which one associates with one's mother. Hence, Indian mothers view the rejection of the mother tongue as a personal insult and a rejection of the values they uphold.

Even if in most cases the language barrier has been overcome, there are indeed unsurmountable differences which result from the difference between the upbringing of the mother and the daughter. Although many Indian women are well educated and hold professional qualifications, they are less likely to join the labour force, as compared to other Asian American women.[10] Consequently, they are less in tune with the mainstream American culture and tend to get even more distanced from their children's culture and way of life. The sad feeling of helplessness which this generational conflict brings, about is very movingly expressed by Lalita Gandbhir in a poignant poem "To My Beloved Teenager":

I realized that you think your mother
has no manners whatsoever.
From your point of view I am
'Hopelessly'...'ancient,'...'oldfashioned,' ...'lousy,'
...my knowledge ...'worthless.'
you hate to go out with me and your father
Because we might run into one of your friends,
And to be seen in public with your parents
Would surely ruin your reputation.
...you wonder why I am upset
When you claim home-cooked Indian food is fattening
And then go out for french fries, hot fudge sundaes and double
cheeseburgers.
You don't seem to understand why I interfere
With your life though I am your mother

The mother then went on to describe her own childhood and drew out the stark contrast between the two scenarios;

My childhood was so different. I could never have put on
an act like yours.
My family would never have tolerated such disrespectful behaviour.

She analyzed the situation, trying to find out where had she gone wrong and how could she remedy the situation.

If our move to a different culture was an error,
I would gladly return home now,
But I realize the move will not help you.
For I know despite trips to India, cultural school,
association with other Indians
you have imbibed a heavy dose of Western culture.
Moving will not erase the western influence.[11]

This poem describes the wide chasm which exists between

the mother and the child as a consequence of their contrasting cultural upbringing. The situation was painful not only for the mother but also for the daughter who was unable to communicate with her mother and had apparently given up on the possibility of any such exchange. Each generation found the other lacking in respect and each failed to measure up to the other's expectations. The mother blamed her decision to emigrate, meanwhile the daughter might have wondered, if Indian culture was indeed so glorious, why did her parents, at all, decide to move? They chose America over India, however, when their daughter decided to make the same choice, the parents, at all felt cheated and betrayed both by this country as well as their own offspring.

Many mothers are fearful of an invasion by the western culture and respond by suppressing the desires of their daughters in the hope of nipping the problem in the bud itself. However, such a policy can often backfire. Though the rebel could either be a son or a daughter, greater societal pressure and control over girls pose bigger problems for them than for their male counterparts and they respond by rebelling against their parents' wishes.

A classic example of such rebellious reaction in the face of extreme parental control can be found in "Leaving Yuba City,"[12] a moving a account of a twenty year old woman, Sushma, who, "hate(d) the old ways (her family was) always pushing (her) into." She felt "suffocated" and wanted to live on her own for a while.[13] She remembered all the years of parental restrictions and repression of her simple, girlish desires, such as wanting to wear make-up. Finally, one day she bought a fuchsia coloured nail polish and that simple act had magnified ramifications. This small act of defiance of her parents' old-fashioned rules symbolized her liberation from parental repression and control; she decided to leave home and go out in the world just to be on her own in a free, open world without any restrictions.

This story brings out the feeling of frustration which unnecessary repression might give birth to. The Indian immigrant daughters have to face dual hardships because of their status as a minority in an alien country and as women in a world dominated by patriarchs. In this case Sushma's rebellion was particularly directed against her mother, and her mother undoubtedly felt it intensely. Since the mothers also suffer from the same dual hardships, they are, therefore, more caught up in this emotional conflict than fathers. Evidently, the emotional division of labour in Asian Indian families is not always equitable.[14]

In the Asian Indian mind, the family is given paramount importance and motherhood is glorified. In turn, children are a source of joy and hope to the mother. However, sometimes India-born mothers feel alienated from their American-born children since the children's rejection of their views is seen to be an entire cultural heritage in danger of extinction. And sadly, the more uncompromisingly the mother responded against such rebelliousness, the more pain and isolation resulted for her. As in the case of Sushma, often cracking the whip might mean more open rebellion, in the form of delinquencies, desertion, or even suicide.

According to the literary evidence, a major issue on which mothers and daughters usually do not see eye to eye concerns dating. Studies based on interviews with Asian Indian mothers and daughters show that the fear of dating which consumes Asian Indian families is primarily a fear of women dating. Although many parents do worry about interracial marriage and its implications during their old age, there is little attempt to control men's sexuality. *India West,* the Asian Indian weekly in the Bay Area published a rap song which captured the essence of life as a second-generation Asian Indian including the double standards applied to the concept of dating:

Dad, oh Dad, may I please go out on a date?
Yes, dear son, but don't be out too late.
Mom, dear mom, may I please go out on a date?
Sorry, dear daughter, but such is not your fate.[15]

While this song may seem to make light of the issue, secondary writings based on interviews prove that such discriminatory behaviour is a recurrent theme of mother-daughter confrontation in many Asian Indian families. Daughters are more strictly policed with the stick of tradition because they are burdened with the responsibility of continuing the traditions and ways of the old country. Interviews with second-generation women show that despite the prevalence of strongly patriarchal attitudes in the Asian Indian society, mothers rather than fathers were more opposed to dating. Mothers believe that their views are based on life-long experiences which tell them that teenage infatuations do not last. However, daughters born and raised in the US, do not see much sense in clinging to the traditions of some distant exotic land, as one interviewee stated, "I'm American. I was born in America. My parents were not, but I don't care about India."[16]

The gravity of arguments which usually results from differences of views regarding dating is visible from the fact that it has been a recurrent theme of Indian immigrant poetry and short stories. Divakaruni has captured the thoughts of Asian Indian mothers in her poem "Indian Movie, New Jersey". The poem described a theater which featured Indian films where Asian Indian people could go and try to connect with their old country at least for the duration of the film. Mothers watching the movie felt that,

"The flickering movie light

wipes from our faces, years of America,

...daughters who date on the sly."[17]

According to the poet, the mothers associated their children with "years of America", even though they had given birth to these children yet, they were not fully their own because the children's souls were owned by America. Still, the daughters too seemed to be cut off from the mainstream American culture because of parental pressure. The poem suggests that these young, bicultural women rebelled against their parent's culture in their quest to be "American" and be accepted by their peers. These women remain in a state of flux during their growing years but finally most of them realize that in fact they are not as "American" as their American friends. They try to wholly identify with the American society but discover that their Indian heritage will always be a part of their bicultural experience.[18]

Marriage is almost as full of problems as dating according to the literature. The issue of marriage is a battlefield where the east and the west, tradition and modernity, love and arrangement stand opposed to each other. Indian arranged marriages are based on the premise that a person's family is most familiar with her likes, dislikes, tastes, temperament and habits, and would, therefore be in a suitable position for the task of finding a mate. In "Doors," a story by Divakaruni, Preeti, a second-generation Asian Indian is in love with an engineer freshly arrived from India. While parents would ordinarily be overjoyed to find their daughter in love with a man from the old country, such was not the case in this story. Preeti's mother was raised in India and was well-versed in Indian ways; she was equally familiar with her daughter's temperament and could foresee disaster in this match. However, she was not overbearing enough to stand in the way of her daughter's wishes. And, soon enough, Preeti who was raised with American values and prized her privacy, felt her husband and his Indian friend intruding upon her private world. The couple ended up separating, just as the mother had predicted.[19]

While the issues of race, religion and nationality are regarded as important factors to be considered while giving one's approval to a child's choice of a partner, parents also see class as a crucial determinant. In the Indian society children are considered to be the responsibility of the parents. The education of Indian children in most cases is sponsored by the parents, thus making the children even more dependent on their parents. Since parents look after the needs of the children, they try to ensure that their children, especially their daughters, marry in a household which is at par with their own so that the daughters can continue to enjoy all luxuries and are able to keep up the lifestyle they have been used to since they were born. Naturally, mothers are stricter than fathers regarding this issue since mothers are more concerned and well versed with the kind of lifestyle their daughters are used to and the various luxuries which are taken for granted by their children.

A mate who satisfies the racial, ethnic and religious requirement is often rejected due to his class background. There are many girls like Meera, the protagonist in Aarti Kohli's "Thrka" who have failed to understand why their growing friendship with Indian immigrant boys became the target of their mother's hostility.[20] The main objection raised by Meera's parents was one of a class difference between the two families. Her mother who was shocked by her revelation of this clandestine relationship, forbade Meera to see the boy and threatened to put her out on the street if she failed to comply with the orders. She objected to Meera's friendship with Anil saying that it would ruin the good name of the family. She tried to make Meera feel guilty by asking her, "Do you know what his parents do?" and remarking that, they run a liquor store! They're not even metric passed. He doesn't come from a good family...They're just not our kind of people. Do you want to be associated with illiterates?"[21] The mother's position is justified if one keeps in mind the fact that she was the product of a society where social relations are based on class affiliations.

Indians believe that marrying someone with the same economic and social standing is a pre-requisite to a successful marriage. As a result, Asian Indian marriages are marriages between two families and not just two individuals, whereas American marriages follow the direct path from love to the altar. Indian immigrant women, both mothers and daughters find themselves at crossroads. Mothers often face the choice of complying with tradition or accepting their children's happiness; the daughters too face the dilemma of fulfilling their own desires or acceding to their parent's choice.

With changing times, mothers are becoming more liberal and broadminded. They are trying to reconcile the fact that they are in a society different from the one they or their mothers had grown up and married in. Immigrant Indian mothers are now open to the idea of their daughters' inter-regional marriages to men from a part of India other than theirs, inter-rligious marriages to men outside their faith but Indian in ethnicity, and finally intere-racial marriages in that order respectively.[22] On their part, even the young women are growing more receptive to their parents' suggestions. According to Nita Shah, "The close family ties of (the Asian Indian community) have provided an anchor of gratitude to the younger generation growing up here."[23] The absence of a large number of broken homes and an extremely low divorce rate has made the young people aware of the merits of an arranged marriage. Most of them consider marriage a lifelong institution. Since society cannot be compartmentalized into black and white, so there is no fixed rule of marriage; both the Indian and the western styles of marriage continue to exist within the Asian Indian social scenario.

While parents might compromise on the kind of marriage chosen by their children, they, however, do not approve of contractual relationship and live-in arrangements. Hence, the latter are pretty uncommon among the members of the Asian Indian community. Single motherhood is even less frequent. The idea of being a single mother as a result of premarital sexual relations is unacceptable to the parents. Moreover, the parents are also opposed to premarital pregnancy resulting from modern scientific methods such as artificial insemination. However, conception in this manner is permissible for the daughter within marriage.

Parental opposition to premarital pregnancy is aptly described in Bharati Mukherjee's story, "A Father."[24] This story revolved around an immigrant couple, and their daughter, who was raised in the United States.[25] One day, their daughter, an electrical engineer dropped a bombshell by announcing her pregnancy. The mother who was known for her "wild and progressive" ideas[26] suddenly metamorphosed into a conventional Asian Indian mother. During the confrontation the mother attacked the daughter with a rolling pin in her hand while the daughter threatened to call the police. The mother was shocked at the knowledge of pregnancy out of wedlock but was even further appalled at the knowledge of how Babli got pregnant. She was horrified because in her mind artificial insemination was only used for perpetrating species of livestock and was inappropriate for humans.[27]

Another allegation which immigrant mothers have to face is that of favouritism. In households where there are siblings of both sexes, daughters often feel that their brothers' wishes are given preference over their own. In "Viewpoint from a female," Sajani Patel wrote about this kind of discrimination.[28] While weeding the backyard, a son got exemption from the arduous chore while the daughter had to put in extra effort. The girl also questioned the norm of allowing the brother to go out whenever he wanted to, even on school nights while she had to stay home. She tried to predict the future and saw herself and her friends earning degrees and having careers, but at the same time she could foresee that they would be held responsible for managing the household and rearing their children. She concluded by saying, "Sometimes I feel as if women are imprisoned in this world for men."[29]

While this accusation might be true for some households, it is not a general rule followed in all Asian Indian families. In fact, within Indian families residing in the US, there are ample educational and career opportunities for both girls and boys. Traditionally, boys might have received preferential treatment in farming households in rural India where the sons would inherit everything and the daughter would be considered as a member of the husband's family. In their old age the parents expected to live with their sons, thus explaining the superior status which the sons enjoyed. However, in modern Indian families, much less in the immigrant families, where girls are at par with their brothers or even superior to them in terms of education and professions, a discrimination between the two is highly unlikely. Moreover, many Indian women in the US are known financially to support their parents and many parents are, in fact, residing with their daughters and are a part of their families.

Besides major issues of dating, marriage and relationships, Indian American kids often find that the everyday rules of the house restrict and are contrary to their American way of thinking. Indira Ganesan has pointed out a few of these rules in her article "Food and the Immigrant."[30] Ganesan explained the general rules of pollution by *etchel* (saliva) and menstruation. The former forbade sharing food from another's plate since it was tainted with etchel and was therefore unclean and the latter referred to the uncleanliness which occurred by coming in contact with menstruating women. Ganesan believed that such rules had led her to develop two sets of behaviour. With American friends she shared food and utensils freely while with conservative Indian friends she was more reserved. Regarding menstruation rules, she wrote that in her own house she disregarded those taboos, but in her parents' house she never entered the shrine room during her periods. She said that, "such schizophrenic behaviour is essential to biculturalism" and was similar to owning two sets of silverware.[31]

She added a hilarious yet realistic touch by reminiscing about some embarrassing situations with which lots of Indian Americans could identify, such as an American striding with her shoes on into an Indian kitchen or the time when the author unthinkingly tasted from a pot in front of her mother's Indian friends and put the spoon back in.[32] Although daughters anywhere in the world might have to tolerate some or other idiosyncracy of their mothers, the gap between the thinking pattern of Indian mothers and their American born children further accentuates the significance of these traditional rules and taboos. Although Ganesan accepted all these regulations in her stride and showed her respect for her mother's beliefs by accommodating them within her own behavioural pattern, not all daughters are this understanding. Even though at the first glance these might seem to be trivial issues, encountering them on a daily basis might irritate the second generation Indian girls who label these rules as superstitious and sometimes rebel against these so-called daily irritants.

However, the literature reveals that often, in spite of such differences in outlook, the woman in the mother and the daughter surfaces, submerging the generational gap between them. The relationship between an immigrant Indian mother and her American-born daughter is like a mirror with two faces, while there is friction between the two, there is also a bond which stems from their desire to protect each other in an environment which might occasionally become a hostile and discriminatory one. Immigrant kids from any part of the world have initial difficulties in adjusting to the new ways of an entirely different country. This problem becomes a bit more exacting for Indian kids because of the wide chasm between traditional Indian upbringing and the peer pressure and demands of a western country. However, mothers soothe away the pain of emotional wounds which might be part of a young Indian child's introductory experiences in an American classroom.

Mothers act as guides and teachers leading the children through their transition from an Indian environment at home to an American one in the outside world such as the school. Writer Zainab Ali, wrote of her experience in the fourth grade, when she refused to say the Pledge of Allegiance because she was a Muslim.[33] Ali was determined not to commit a sin simply because she attended an American school. However, Ali's mother took on the role of a cultural teacher and explained the concepts of religion and nationality to her daughter. The mother first praised the daughter for standing up for something she believed in. However, she then explained that religion and nationality were two different things and that saying the pledge only affirmed her devotion to this country without her citizenship infringing on her religious life. Ali eagerly said the Pledge from then on.[34] This incident points out to the healthy relationship between an immigrant mother and her daughter. Hence a mother's advice acted as a lubricant, smoothing the child's transition from an Indian to an American way of life.

Interestingly enough, this caring attitude is not one-sided but is reciprocated with equal love on the part of the daughters who watch out for their mothers and try to relieve their pain. There are times when the daughters feel a strong identification with their mothers as women belonging to an immigrant community and the years separating them simply wash away. Since both mothers and daughters are living, studying and working within a bicultural and multi-racial society both are equally susceptible to racial discrimination. Daughters feel enraged at the injustice meted out to their mothers. "Thrka", describes the feelings of the young protagonist, Meera, who sympathized with her mother whose boss (whom Meera privately calls 'the bitch from hell') gave her a difficult time at work.[35] Meera's attitude took on a particularly protective colouring whenever she thought about her mother. She was especially enraged and anguished over the fact that her mother received an evaluation which said that she lacked business skills. Meera could not believe the injustice of such an evaluation and tried to justify her mother's position by saying, "What does a woman who sits in front of a screen all the day have to know about business?"[36] Moreover, in order to compensate for the strain her mother had to undergo at work, Meera tried to help out at home by preparing dinner few times a week.

This kind of sympathy is based on the daughter's identification with her mother's ethnicity in a multi-racial society and her struggle to cope up with the realities of a bicultural way of life. Many daughters of immigrant mothers also identify with their mothers purely in terms of the common denominations of gender. These young women understand the travails which their mothers undergo by virtue of being women. In India, as in other societies where separate male and female spheres are the norm, women usually have a support group consisting of other women whose help she can rally in times of crisis. If the husband beats the wife, he is often taken to task by the females of the house, his mother, sisters and sisters-in-law. Moreover, a women can always count on her natal family for protection and support. However, when the woman comes to America, she loses this female support system and often finds herself all alone in an alien country, where her husband is at full liberty to mistreat her.

At such times, the mother finds her only friend in her daughter. In "Daddy", a story by Zainab Ali, Nadia the young protagonist cried out for her mother who was abused by her husband.[37] Nadia loved her mother a lot and therefore she tried to protect her from getting hurt. When the father dragged the mother into a fight, Nadia tried to warn her mother just to leave him alone so as not to allow him to disturb her peace of mind. The heightened pain which the daughter felt for her mother, in spite of their generational difference was visible from the fact that every time her father started fighting, Nadia's "fingers instinctively go for (her) mouth and (she) start(s) biting the skin around (her) nails."[38] She had maternal feelings for her mother and wanted to ease her pain by gently rocking her in her arms all night and soothing her fears by singing her a lullaby and telling her that she was indeed the most beautiful woman in the world.

The mother, in turn, tried to protect her children from her pain by telling them that she did not care any longer as long as her children were happy. Nadia, however, felt otherwise. She knew that her mother cared. She called it a "women's intuition (and) a daughter's insight. I know she cares. I think that she visits India so frequently just to escape this hell-hole called a home."[39] Her mental conditioning as a girl, and the sense of identification with her mother is also evident in the fact that she always envied her brothers because of their carefree manner and their ability to laugh and play, while she herself always felt burdened by her mother's pain which always troubled her everywhere, each time she looked at her mother's face carrying dark circles under the eyes.[40]

An even stronger feeling of a shared identity was expressed by another daughter in a story called "Home" by Preety.[41] The feeling of female bonding was so intense that the daughter felt related to her mother not only at an emotional and psychological level but also at the physical level. She felt herself to be a part of her mother's body and believed what her mother did to herself, she did to her daughter as well. And the pain her father inflicted on her mother, was also inflicted on her.[42] Even when forced by her father, she refused to leave her mother. The bond which united the mother and daughter together in an alien country with no one to shelter and support them was so compelling that the daughter felt, "...as though I am still in you." The danger of facing the wrath of a brutal father did not shake her confidence as she resolved, "I'll save you Mumi. I'll save you."[43] Even though Indian women in America are deprived of their support group of female relatives and friends, the presence of such caring and understanding daughters more than compensates for this loss. The daughters act as the protectors and champions of their mothers.

Apart from sympathizing with the lot of their mothers and crying for them, these young American daughters also celebrate the joys and take delight in the happiness of their Indian mothers. Describing her mother's pleasure while wading in the ocean at Maui, Hawaii, Divakaruni wrote:

I persuaded you to the deserted
ocean, fully clothed,
even your glasses, you hesitated
at the water's edge, then plunged in
you...dived in to chase the foam.
Mother, on your face a look I had not seen
even before father left,
as though a child, long drowned,
had struggled up...and breathed...
you...returned to shore,
shivering a little. I wrapped
the towel around your shoulders.
We walked back, silent, your hand
light as a nesting bird
in the oval of my arm.[44]

This poem symbolizes the depth of feeling which a daughter felt when she saw her mother playing like a child. She did not laugh at her mother nor was she ashamed of her mother going into the water fully clad in a sari. She understood the height of exhilaration which the older woman felt as she ran after the retreating waves. And after the mother returned to the shore, her daughter treated her tenderly as a 'nesting bird' symbolizing the reversal of roles. The daughter now cared for her mother and took delight in her games as the mother had once done for her little daughter.

This reciprocal relationship has a second aspect which alludes to a common need felt by resident minorities in any country of the world: the need to remember one's own nation and its heritage and to keep a part of it alive in oneself. This desire is a potent force behind the organization of India day and the celebration of other cultural festivals in which women are at the vanguard of the organization and management responsibilities. Young Asian Indian girls dressed in traditional Indian attire egerly participate in these events which include classical and folk singing and dancing. While the mothers' dance to the rhythm of the music they have preserved in their memories, the daughters' steps try to follow their mothers' in an attempt to connect with the land of their mothers and grandmothers. Divakaruni has movingly captured the feelings of these second generation Indian girls as they danced to the traditional music of the *Garba*, a folk dance from the west Indian state of Gujarat.

The nine sacred nights of Navaratri
we dance the Garba...
...the old women singing...
Their high keening is an electric net
pulling us in, girls who have never seen
the old land. This October night
we have shed our jeans
for long red skirts, pulled back
permed hair in plaits...
We ignore the men...for now
the women dance alone,
...Our feet glide on smooth wood...

The poet then expresses the change in the scenario as the girls get lost in the steps. They not only believe themselves to be village belles but imagine the transformation of the venue from an auditorium in an American city to a courtyard in a distant Indian village where their mothers and grandmothers had once danced the Garba.

We clap hot palms like thunder. And
the mango branches grow into trees.
Under our flashing feet,
the floor is packed black soil.
Damp faces gleam and flicker in the torchlight.
The smell of harvest hay
is thick...
...We spin and spin
back to the villages of our mothers.[45]

Such longing for the homeland is also the driving force behind the elaborate ethnic meals which Indian mothers prepare in their American households. (As an immigrant, I can identify with the feeling of nostalgia which homestyle cooked Indian meals bring as their aroma wafts through the house). Asian Indian mothers painstakingly cook the highly time consuming Indian meals in their attempt to counter the onslaught of American fast food which has tempted the palate of every Indian child. This effort of relating to India and its culture through culinary means is not restricted just to mothers, but even daughters who were raised in America on grilled cheese and Oreo cookies try to evoke their dim memories of India with food.

Describing her experience on growing up in a bicultural environment, Ganesan wrote that she ate in order to compensate for her loss of growing up away from the land of her parents. She tried to hold on India via its cuisine so that, "America can't claim me, despite my US citizenship."[46] She believed that by consuming Indian food, she ensured that India would not reject her for her American accent, her foreign outlook and her leaving the country at the tender age of six, thirty years ago. She asserted, "My taste buds aren't traitorous; my loyalty lies within my tongue."[47]

The dualism and biculturalism which are natural bi-products of the immigrant experience affect both mothers and daughters equally and often find them at the opposite ends of many an argument. However, the literary works of the Asian Indian women show that, as preservers of traditions, women pass down a unique cultural heritage to their daughters. This process of bequeathing values and beliefs also nurtures and strengthens the bond between the first and the second generation of Asian Indian women in the US. This strengthening of bonds further leads to a unity which in fact transcends generational differences. The writings reveal the reality, that beneath the differences between mothers and daughter lies the bond of common identity which leads the woman in them to take precedence over their generational status. Whether by standing up for their mothers, or by filling the house with the aroma of *sambar*—a South Indian lentil soup, flavoured with spices, or by dancing to the steps of the *garba,* the Indian women will always continue to be their mothers' daughters.

REFERENCES

1. Meena Alexander, *The Shock of Arrival: Reflections on Postcolonial Experience* (Boston: South End Press, 1996), p. 2.
2. *Ibid.*, p. 155.
3. Lalita Gandbhir, "To My Beloved Teenager," in *Our Feet Walk the Sky: Women of the South Asian Diaspora,* ed. The Women of the South Asian Descent Collective (San Francisco: Aunt Lute Books, 1993), p. 23.
4. Manju Seth, "The Immigrants from India: Who Are They?," in *Asian Indian Immigrants: Motifs on Ethnicity and Gender,* ed. B.B. Khare (Dubuque: Kendall/Hunt Publishing Company, 1997), p. 46.
5. Lorna Gonsalves-Pinto, "Breaking Through the Borderlands on the U.S. Ethnoscape," in *Asian Indian Immigrants: Motifs on Ethnicity and Gender,* ed. B.B. Khare (Dubuque: Kendall/Hunt Publishing Company, 1997), p. 165.
6. Lata Mani, "Gender Class and Cultural Conflict: Indu Krishnan's *Knowing Her Place,"* in *Our Feet Walk the Sky: Women of the South Asian Diaspora,* ed. The Women of South Asian Descent Collective (San Francisco: Aunt Lute Books, 1993), p. 32.
7. *Ibid.*
8. Chitra Bannerjee Divakaruni, "Yuba City School," in *Leaving Yuba City: New and Selected Poems.* (New York Doubleday, 1997), p. 106.
9. Amita Vasudev, "Journal Entry," in *Our Feet Walk the Sky:*

Women of the South Asian Diaspora ed. The Women of South Asian Descent Collective (San Francisco: Aunt Lute Books, 1993), p. 132.

10. Roger Daniels, *The History of Immigration to the United States* (New York: The Asia Society, 1989), p. 364.
11. Gandbhir, "To My Beloved Teenager", pp. 23-24.
12. Chitra Bannerjee Divakaruni, "Leaving Yuba City," in *Leaving Yuba City: New and Selected Poems* (New York: Doubleday, 1997), pp. 107-110.
13. *Ibid.*, 109.
14. Nita Shah, *The Ethnic Strife: The Study of Asian Indian Women in the United States* (New York: Pinkerton and Thomas Publications, 1993), p. 59.
15. *India West* (San Francisco), 7 June 1990.
16. Shah, *Ethnic Strife*, p. 64.
17. Chitra Bannerjee Divakaruni, "Indian Movie, New Jersey," in *Leaving Yuba City: New and Selected Poems* (New York: Doubleday, 1997), p. 113.
18. Shah, *Ethnic Strife*, pp. 57-65.
19. Chitra Bannerjee Divakaruni, "Doors," in *Arranged Marriage* (New York: Doubleday, 1995), pp. 183-202.
20. Aarti Kohli, "Thrka," in *Our Feet Walk the Sky: Women of the South Asian Diaspora,* ed. The Women of South Asian Descent Collective, (San Francisco: Aunt Lute Books, 1993), pp. 220-25.
21. *Ibid.*, pp. 223-24.
22. Although none of the writers has presented this view, still, it is common knowledge among Indians.
23. Shah, *Ethnic Strife*, pp. 66-67.
24. Bharati Mukherjee, "A Father," in *Charlie Chan is Dead: An Anthropology of Contemporary Asian American Fiction,* ed. Jessica Hagedorn (New York: Penguin, 1993), pp. 338-49.
25. *Ibid.*, p. 339.
26. *Ibid.*, p. 345.
27. *Ibid.*, p. 349.
28. Sajani Patel, "Viewpoint From a Female," in *Our Feet Walk The Sky: Women of the South Asian Diaspora,* ed. The Women of South Asian Descent Collective (San Francisco: Aunt Lute Books, 1993), p. 98.

29. *Ibid.*, p. 98.

30. Indira Ganesan, "Food and the Immigrant," in *Half and Half: Writers on Growing up Biracial and Bicultural,* ed. C.C. O'Hearn (New York: Pantheon Books, 1998), pp. 170-80.

31. *Ibid.*, 173-74.

32. *Ibid.*

33. Zainab Ali, "Becoming Agents of Our Identity," in *Our Feet Walk the Sky: Women of South Asian Diaspora,* ed. The Women of South Asian Descent Collective (San Francisco: Aunt Lute Books, 1993), pp. 237-41.

34. *Ibid.*, pp. 237-38.

35. Kohli, "Thrka," p. 220.

36. *Ibid.*

37. Zainab Ali, "Daddy," in *Our Feet Walk the Sky: Women of the South Asian Diaspora,* ed. The Women of South Asian Descent Collective (San Francisco: Aunt Lute Books, 1993), pp. 4-11.

38. *Ibid.*, p. 5.

39. *Ibid.*, p. 7.

40. *Ibid.*, p. 8.

41. Preety, "Home," in *Our Feet Walk the Sky: Women of the South Asian Diaspora,* ed. The Women of the South Asian Descent Collective (San Francisco: Aunt Lute Books, 1993), p. 37.

42. *Ibid.*

43. *Ibid.*

44. Chitra Bannerjee Divakaruni, "My Mother at Maui," in *Black Candle: Poems About Women from India, Pakistan and Bangladesh* (Corvallis: CALYX Books, 1991), p. 79-80.

45. Chitra Bannerjee Divakaruni, "The Garba," in *Black Candle: Poems About Women from India, Pakistan and Bangladesh* (Corvallis: CALYX Books, 1991), p. 43-44.

46. Ganesan, "Food and the Immigrant," p. 179.

47. *Ibid.*

SECTION 4

WOMEN AND RELIGION

11

CHINESE BUDDHIST NUNS

The Institution of the Buddhist Convent During the Six Dynasties Period

Buddhism was officially introduced to China in AD 65 during the reign of the Han dynasty. At the time, the national creed was Confucianism which propagated a rigidly hierarchical social system. Confucian ideology was complemented by the Taoist philosophy which guided the Chinese view of the cosmos. However, despite the existence of these philosophical schools, Buddhism gained a stronghold on the Chinese soil mainly because it was successful in adapting itself to the Chinese needs. The downfall of the Han dynasty led to a state of political disintegration in China. This period of disintegration continued for approximately four centuries, from the second to the sixth. During this long period Buddhism offered refuge to various destitute people as well as to individuals who were disillusioned with the existing state of chaos and the political and social instability. One such section of society which was salvaged by Buddhism consisted of women who were very often driven by circumstances to give up the pleasures of worldly life. Such women filled the ranks of the Buddhist monasteries as nuns dedicated to a life of charity, service and devotion to the Buddha.

Here we intend to study the life of such Chinese Buddhist nuns who lived during the Six Dynasties period. This study is based on a compilation of biographies written by Shih Pao-ch'ang during the sixth century along with a variety of secondary sources. The focal point is the discussion about the formal ordination and the reasons for joining the convent, to the life and the intellectual, religious and spiritual activities of the nuns within the convent and the conclusion with a brief summary of the convent's contribution to the life of the nuns.

Like every other religious order, Buddhist nunneries also required their members to go through a formal ordination ceremony. The Chinese Buddhist canons include a text called *Pi-ch'iu-ni chuan (Lives of the Nuns,* hereafter abbreviated as PCNC).[1] This text is a collection of the biographies of sixty-five Buddhist nuns (Each number in parenthese denotes the particular nun's order of appearance in the PCNC). According to the PCNC, for an initiation to be fully orthodox a female candidate must receive the rules not only from ten monks of at least ten years seniority as fully ordained monks, but also from ten such nuns. Hence according to Kathryn A. Tsai, the most serious obstacle to a woman's entering an assembly of nuns was men rather than doctrine. The monastic order of nuns was dependent on the monastic order of monks for several of their required rites and rituals. The reverse was not the case.[2] As a result Ching-chien, the first nun, received merely the precepts of a novice, as she received them only from the monks as there were no nuns in China at the time. Later Ching-chien and twenty-four other women set up the Chu-lin convent at the Western Gate of the Palace District in Lo-yang. However, in the absence of an *acarya* or an instructor, Ching-chien was consulted in matters of doctrine. Later four members of this convent including Chien received full ordination from the order of monks on the basis of the *Mahasanghika-Bhiksuni* (nun) *Rites and Rule Book.*[3]

Apart from the ceremonial initiation into the order, the other important element required for becoming a nun was the desire or will to give up worldly concerns and embrace the other worldly ones. There are several reasons which influenced a woman's decision to join the formal religious order of Buddhism. Most of the biographies in the PCNC explain the causes and conditions which led a woman to become a nun. Not surprisingly, faith and religious aspiration are frequently cited; however, these feelings usually derive from other conditions. Many were driven by family problems, particularly impending marriage to an undesirable suitor, or a widow's refusal to remarry. The most spectacular example of a woman fleeing marriage is T'an-hui. She took a secret vow under a nun, Fa-yu, that if she could not carry out her intentions of leading a religious life and was instead compelled to marry, then she would burn herself to death.[4]

Periods such as that of the Six Dynasties were characterized by frequent and violent political and social disturbances wherein families were uprooted and dispersed and many women had been abandoned and orphaned. Such circumstances sent women on the monastic path and the convent thus became a haven for such refugees.[5] The most poignant case is that of Fa-sheng, who became a nun when she was seventy years old. She longed for her old home and she could overcome her loss and sorrow only by devoting herself to Buddhism.[6]

Very often personal tragedies such as illness or grief over the loss of a parent were also responsible for leading women into the Buddhist religious order.[7] Parents sometimes dedicated a sick child to celibate life as the price of its recovery.[8] The social as well as personal usefulness of the institution made the convent a fairly safe place for an unprotected woman to find protection, in other words, "women could find a home in a 'homeless' life." Therefore, it is not surprising to find that many rich widows, little girls who had run away from brothels and worn-out prostitutes offered themselves to a nunnery and sought peace within temple walls.[9]

According to the records offered by the PCNC religious aspirations often appeared at a very tender age and were especially highlighted as the result of good *Karmas* or deeds done in one's previous birth. The PCNC lists two nuns joining the nunnery at the ages of six and eight, eleven nuns entering the order when they were young (shao) or as a child (yu) though the usual age for leaving the secular life was between seventeen and twenty two.[10] As a result most of the women who entered the religious orders had not yet fulfilled their filial and Confucian duty of marrying and producing an heir to carry on the husband's family line. Therefore, the element of conflict between Chinese social morality and the ethics of Buddhism arose often enough to form a fairly consistent part of many of the biographies. The Confucian scholars often claimed that by asking the monks and nuns to renounce their family life and to give up the worldly pursuits of wealth and fame, Buddhism proved itself to be antithetical to the Confucian way of life. Hence the nuns and monks were regarded unfilial since they could not provide their parents with an heir or bring them honour through the pursuit of wealth or fame. However, much of Buddhism's success lay in adapting itself to the Chinese needs. This adaptation is very much visible in the biography of a nun called An-Ling-Shou. Her Confucian upbringing came in conflict with her Buddhist sacred vow of renouncing the world. When her father objected to her joining the clerical life, An-Ling-Shou replied that her act of renunciation was an act of piety performed for the salvation of all living beings, especially her parents and grandparents.[11]

Moreover, the Buddhist monastic order wanted to avoid coming into direct conflict with Confucianism and therefore it laid down the rule that any woman desiring to enter the monastic order had to have permission from the person who had authority over her, whether father, husband, or son. Sometimes, permission was also given by the local governor.[12] Hence the Buddhist monastic orders tried to prevent their being labelled as anti-Confucian and unfilial.

Once they managed to procure the permission of their guardians and received the formal ordination, the nuns usually enjoyed a healthy life, most of them living past the age of sixty. The PCNC does not identify the secular families from which the nuns came; however, seven of the sixty five nuns stated that a father or a male ancestor held an official position of some kind. Kathryn A. Tsai,[13] believes that it is perhaps not unreasonable to conjecture the upper-class urban background for many nuns recorded in the PCNC because they all appear to be quite familiar with famous monks, secular literati, members of the court, and the royal family including emperors and their consorts.

Moreover, strikingly the PCNC records a literacy rate of as high as eighty per cent. Many of the nuns were described as being educated in both secular and sacred literature, that is, in both the Confucian classics as well as the Buddhist scriptures. Other fairly common accomplishments were the rapid chanting of scriptures, writing commentaries on the scriptures and engaging in debate with the famous monks of the time.

Kathryn A. Tsai analyses the association of literacy with the monastic order for nuns and comes up with a few conjectures among which three seem most plausible: "(1) Literate women joined the order, being already unusual in their literacy;" As was the case with Tao-ch'iung (no. 17)[14] who had received her education at home and when she was about eleven years old, she was already well versed in the classics and history.[15]" (2) Women received their education after joining the order; and related to this, (3) Some women joined the order to be able to pursue literary studies-- in other words, to become scholars."[16] If the last two conjectures have any foundation then they bring forth the importance of the Chinese Buddhist convent for the women of the time since there were no indigenous institutions providing formal literary education for women.

In her research about the education of women during the Southern Dynasties period, Beatrice Spade[17] has reflected on the role of the Buddhist religious order in the spread of literacy among the nuns. She sees the nunneries as playing the role of schools and theological centers which gave women a chance to receive education outside the family environment. Referring to the PCNC, Spade says that even though the nuns who came from higher social and intellectual backgrounds had a much better chance of pursuing their education within the nunneries, nevertheless women with less distinguished social and educational backgrounds also had a chance to work in intellectual fields.[18] The author cites the example of Chih Miao-yin, a nun who lived in the latter half of the fourth century and possessed learning in Buddhist and non-Buddhist subjects. She also excelled in literary composition and held intellectual and theological discussions with the emperor and court officials.[19] This example suggests that in the nunneries the nuns were exposed to a variety of intellectual currents, regardless of their family background. Many nuns often in the company of their teacher travelled from one Buddhist institution to another for purposes of study. The nuns held discussions with other nuns, monks, officials and laymen of both Chinese and foreign origin. As a result the Buddhist orders provided women with a fairly wide education extending beyond the confines of religious matters alone.

Some nuns such as Fa-yuan (no. 37) apparently even learnt some foreign languages.[20] As mentioned earlier, apart from studying and discussing the Buddhist scriptures, the nuns also elucidated upon them in their public lectures which often drew vast audiences. Such lectures not only gave the nuns an opportunity to learn but also gave them a chance to teach. Regularly ordained nuns actively engaged in lecturing on various sutras[21] especially the *Lotus Sutra*, particularly popular was the Kuan-yin chapter in the *Lotus Sutra*, the *Mahaparinirvana*, the *Vilmalakirtinirdesa* and the *Srimaladevi.*[22]

Kuan-yin also featured prominently in the cult practices performed by the nuns. The effectiveness of these cult practices lay in the sincerity of the faith and attitude of the nuns. According to the PCNC Kuan-yin responded to Hui-chan (no. 7), a nun in distress, by staying the knives of the thieves who were trying to attack her.[23] Thus, the goddess confirmed both the worth and her promises stated in the Kuan-yin chapter of the *Lotus Sutra*. Kuan-yin also rescued the nuns from illness. The nuns also called upon Amitabha or Maitreya in order to be granted rebirth in the appropriate paradise. The Pindola cult "proved" both the promises of the scriptures and the holiness of the nun involved in the cult.[24] Apart from such cult practices, meditation was an integral part of the every day life of a nun in a Chinese Buddhist convent. Nuns practised under the tutelage of famous Buddhist meditation masters such as Kalayasas who apparently willingly took on female disciples, one of whom, a nun called T'an-hui (no. 54), is said to have realized her Buddha nature through the medium of meditation.[25]

Hence in conclusion, apart from such spiritual attainments, the Chinese Buddhist convents also served as a place where women could practice religion in which their achievements were not considered inferior to those of men. The nunneries also fulfilled several other important needs in the lives of the Chinese women who became nuns. As discussed earlier the convent acted as a refuge for many destitute women driven by dire circumstances. Hence it was a respectable institution where a woman might find a home. Further on, the order was also a place where the women could exercise their talents, especially scholarly ones. Hence on the whole, while the order of nuns was not particularly influential in the Chinese society in general, it was essential for the survival and well-being of some individual women since it not only provided them the means of survival but also created outlets for their cultural pursuits which otherwise would not have been possible.[26]

Works Cited

Ayscough, F. 1937. *Chinese Women: Yesterday and Today.* Boston: The Riverside Press Cambridge.

Spade, B. 1979. The Education of Women During the Southern Dynasties. *Journal of Asian History* 13: 15-41.

Tsai, K.A. 1994, *Lives of the Nuns.* Honolulu: University of Hawaii Press.

Tsai, K.A. 1981. The Chinese Buddhist Monastic Order for Women: The First Two Centuries. In *Women in China*, ed. R.W. Guisso and S. Johannesen. Philo Press.

Wright, A.F. 1990. *Studies in Chinese Buddhism.* London: Yale University Press.

References

1. Kathryn A. Tsai, "The Chinese Buddhist Monastic Order for Women: The First Two Centuries," *Women in China*, eds. Richard W. Guisso and Stanley Johannesen (Philo Press, 1981), p. 1.
2. Kathryn A. Tsai, *Lives of the Nuns* (Honolulu: University of Hawaii Press, 1994), p. 1.
3. Tsai, "Chinese Buddhist Monastic Order," pp. 6-7.
4. Tsai, *Lives of the Nuns*, p. 92.
5. Guisso, *Women in China*, p. 9.
6. Tsai, *Lives of the Nuns*, p. 7.
7. Guisso, *Women in China*, p. 9.
8. Florence Ayscough, *Chinese Women: Yesterday and Today* (Boston: The Riverside Press Cambridge, 1937), p. 88.
9. Ibid., pp. 88-89.
10. Guisso, *Women in China*, pp. 9-10.
11. Arthur F. Wright, *Studies in Chinese Buddhism* (London: Yale University Press, 1990), p. 70.
12. Tsai, *Lives of the Nuns*, p. 7.
13. Guisso, *Women in China*.

14. Tsai, *Lives of the Nuns,* pp. 40-41.
15. Ibid., p. 8.
16. Guisso, *Women in China*, 13.
17. Beatrice Spade, "The Education of Women in China During the Southern Dynasties," *Journal of Asian History* 13, no. 1 (1990): pp. 15-41.
18. Spade, "The Education of Women," p. 21.
19. Ibid., p. 22.
20. Ibid., Tsai, *Lives of the Nuns*, pp. 67-68.
21. Spade, "The Education of Women," pp. 25-26.
22. Guisso, *Women in China*, pp. 11-12.
23. Tsai, *Lives of the Nuns*, p. 27.
24. Guisso, *Women in China*, pp. 14-15.
25. Guisso, *Women in China*, p. 17; Tsai, *Lives of the Nuns*, pp. 92-95.
26. Guisso, *Women in China*, pp. 19-20.

SECTION 5

GENDER AND THE STATE

12

FEMINISM: YESTERDAY AND TODAY

It is often said that the edifice of today is built on the foundation stone of yesterday. This age-old adage certainly holds true for the women's rights movement in America which began in the nineteenth century and continued into the next one. The degree of success which the latest feminist movement of the 1960s and 1970s achieved, owed a lot to the successes and failures of the previous generation of 'feminists'. The pioneers in the sphere of women's rights, Elizabeth Cady Stanton, Susan B. Anthony and others struggled against a male dominated, conservative society in order to win rights as basic as the right to vote and the right to own property, among many others. The next generation of activists fighting for women's rights took up issues like abortion and child care because they already had the basic legal and property rights. Since they were already equipped with the vote, the most powerful weapon in a democracy, the recent feminists could go a step further and work on many other issues of growing importance to women.

Every century in the past saw a few intellectually minded women who refused to accept the fate of being the inferior sex and fought hard to win privileges such as access to schools and education which their brothers and husbands enjoyed simply by virtue of being men. But such cases of women's defiance of the rules of the conservative society were rare and scattered. The first organized movement of women demanding one of the basic rights which one half of the nation kept the other half from having, began over a hundred and fifty years ago in a Methodist church in Seneca Falls, New York. At that time and place when women did not even have the right of custody of their own children, let alone the right to own property, these 300 women who were working under the leadership of Elizabeth Cady Stanton, the author of the *Declaration of Sentiments,* were definitely breaking new ground[1].

Elizabeth Cady Stanton was joined by the radical and hardworking Susan B. Anthony and together they publicly denounced the constitutional amendment of 1869 which gave Negro men the right to vote but still denied this right to all women. These crusaders of the suffrage movement faced tremendous opposition. Susan B. Anthony's demand for the right to vote earned for her the title of a "culprit who pretends to be a martyr." These early activists of women's rights also took up the cause of the African-American population—almost a hundred years before the rise of the civil rights movement of the 1960s[2].

While veterans like Elizabeth Cady Stanton and Susan B. Anthony were still the guiding lights of the suffrage movement, another generation of women leaders was developing and one of the shining names of this wave of suffragists was Carrie Chapman Catt. Carrie Chapman Catt became the president of the National American Woman Suffrage Association in 1900, thus ushering the Suffrage Movement into the twentieth century. It was Ms. Catt who devised the "winning plan" for the achievement of the federal amendment giving all American women the right to vote.

In *Century of Struggle*, Eleanor Flexor very rightly observes that these pioneering women would indeed feel at home in the feminist movement of the later half of the twentieth century. At a time when only women of the lower Strata of society and African-American women worked out of the house and that too out of sheer necessity, Charlotte Perking Gilman passionately advocated the economic independence of women. Her book, 'Women and Economics', carried a sub-title *A study of the Economic Relation Between Men and Women as a Factor in Social Evolution*, and quickly became the outstanding text for twentieth century feminism[3].

Similarly, it is significant to note that one of the earliest and most challenging voices against a wave of southern lynchings in the 1890s was that of Ida B. Wells. Wells was a figure closely identified with the efforts of coloured women to overcome the moral stigma attached to their reputations. She wrote articles against segregation and the inferiority of the schools Negro children had to attend as a result of that segregation. She launched a veritable one-woman anti-lynching crusade through the columns of many newspapers. Almost half a century before the formation of the NAACP, Ida Wells founded coloured women's clubs in Boston, New York, Chicago and the Middle-West[4].

This inspirational group of individuals, comprised of women who as early as the nineteenth century saw that they were at par with men and deserved to be treated as equals. They understood that at the heart of this inequality lay the inability of women to vote. As a result, in order to create a panacea for all the major problems faced by women, these activists fought for the vote, thus giving the women of the succeeding generations the precious gift of civil and legal equality. The work of Elizabeth Stanton, Susan B. Anthony, Carrie Chapman Catt, Charlotte Gilman and Ida Wells-Barnett in the field of raising awareness regarding women's and minorities' rights in a society ridden with conservatism makes them almost a century ahead of the society in which they lived. Eleanor Flexor has very correctly observed that, these women, "...would have felt at home in today's movement."[5]

The achievements of the pioneering women became more spectacular when one considers the time period of their activities. Had these women lived and worked in the later part of the twentieth century, they would not have had to suffer many of the hardships and difficulties which they had faced on the eve of the century simply because society was not ready to accept the concept of the legal equality of women. Elizabeth Stanton, born in the 1950s would already be possessing the right to vote and she could have worked against other kinds of sexual and racial inequalities. Similarly, in twentieth century, life for Ida Wells-Barnett as an African-American woman activist would have been much smoother and relatively safer and more secure from the life threatening opposition she faced in the nineteenth century.

The emergence and the development of the new women's movement in the 1960s and 1970s, was possible only because the generation of women before them had been aware of their rights and had struggled hard to secure them for themselves as well as for the generations of women to come. Since the women of the later half of the twentieth century already had the right to own property they now demanded equal opportunity in employment for earning that property. Since women by then already possessed the right to the custody of their children, they went a step ahead and demanded control over their own bodies and sought abortion as a legal option when their circumstances deemed it necessary. It was the effort of these pioneers at uniting and organizing the women which gave the later feminists the self-confidence and belief in their ability to be able to achieve the goals they had set for themselves. And most of all, it was the privilege of the right to vote which the earlier generation had won for their sisters and daughters which ensured that women's opinions made a difference. Political leaders were now willing to listen to the grievances of women. Presidents such as John F. Kennedy appointed the President's Commission on the Status of Women to delve into the needs and demands of women. And finally women were able to achieve the enactment of legislation like the Equal Employment Opportunities Act by the sheer weight of their votes. Hence it is evident that the recent feminists owed a lot to their predecessors[6].

However, these workers of the recent women's movement were not content with their inheritance of political and legal equality, they wanted more and were determined to work for it. Building upon their legacy, which gave them equality in the legal sphere, they took the women's movement into new directions of gaining equality in the economic sphere.

In 1964, the Congress passed the Civil Rights Act which aimed at ending racial inequality, but ignored gender-based discriminations. The federal government faced complaints from women charging sexual bias in employment. Such women's rights' advocates initiated the second wave of feminism when they founded the National Organization for Women in 1966. And through the NOW and other channels such as the National Abortion Coalition, Detroit Women's Liberation Coalition, this modern brand of feminism did make its mark upon the consciousness of America, affecting attitudes, customs and law, most notably in the case of equal opportunity in employment, as well as payment to the employees, rape, sexual harassment and abortion[7].

Just as the earlier movement for women's rights targeted mainly at political reform, the movement of the 1960s and 1970s also targeted at constitutional reforms and amendments. As imaginative public presentations, mass demonstrations and widespread publicity reinforced their lobbying, liberal politicians began to support the cause of the feminists. In 1972, after more than fifty years of sporadic debate, the most important of these reforms, the Equal Rights Amendment (ERA) was passed by both the House of Representatives and the Senate in 1972 and was then presented to the states for ratification. The Equal Employment Opportunities Commission (EEOC) stopped treating discrimination against women as a joke. Another major victory of the later feminists was the inclusion in Article VII of the Civil Rights Act, of the clause prohibiting discrimination on the basis of sex. Hence employers were no longer allowed to legally discriminate on the basis of sex. The feminists lobbied and ensured the passing of the Equal Pay Act, whereby no matter which profession or work was involved, the employer could not determine the remuneration on the basis of the sex of the worker. In a similar vein, Article IX guaranteed that no one will be denied access to higher education on the basis of sex[8].

Younger radical women pushed hardest for the issues that they felt struck closer to women's fundamental oppression—abortion and child care. When the movement began, the penal codes demanded corroborating evidence in rape cases and mostly followed the seventeenth century dictum that "rape is the easiest charge to make and the most difficult to prove." However, in course of the 1970s, most states rewrote their rape statutes and restructured the offence along feminist lines, largely because of the lobbying by the women's groups. John D'Emilio and Estelle B. Freedman emphasise the role of the women's movement in popularising the idea that rape was not an act of sexual passion, but rather a crime of violent assault perpetrated by strangers or even by acquaintances[9]. The women's movement also invented the phrase, 'sexual harassment' to describe the repeated and unwanted sexual advances that generations of female workers had experienced on the job. And before long, judges were recognizing the problem as an illegal condition of employment prohibited by the Civil Rights Act of 1964. According to John D'Emilio and Estelle Freedman, even though the feminist movement did not put an end to sexual harassment or violent assault, "it did identify sexual violence as the key element maintaining the subordination of women, provided women with new ways of understanding their situation, and expanded the sources that women had for fighting back."[10]

D'Emilio and Freedman believe that, Perhaps the most dramatic change provoked by the women's movement came in the area of reproductive rights[11]. Both the radicals in the women's liberation movement as well as the moderates in organizations such as the NOW recognized the fact that women's reproductive role occupied the central place in the structure of gender oppression. They believed that absolute control of fertility was essential in order to achieve full equality. Nineteenth century statutes still criminalized abortion, thus placing a barrier between women and full control of their bodies. In order to remedy this problem, the feminists recast the whole issue of abortion as one of "rights" over one's own body,and used militant tactics to achieve their goals. Radical feminists disrupted state legislative hearings on abortion law reform, and stormed the office of a county attorney who was prosecuting abortionists and staged guerilla theater performances at a convention of the American Medical Association. Responding to the pressure, a few states soon revised their statutes along lines closer to feminist models. And finally in 1973, in the case of *Roe* v. *Wade*, the Supreme Court acted and declared as unconstitutional any restrictions on abortion in the first trimester and made second trimester abortions easily available[12].

The feminist movement advocated choice not just in the sphere of reproduction but also in that of sexual orientation. Although initially divided on the issue of lesbianism the NOW eventually incorporated lesbian rights into its list of goals. Evidently, the radical ideas and cooperative forms of the women's movement were shaping the more conservative, tightly structured 'women's rights' branch of the movement. Sara Evans observes that by strengthening its position on issues like abortion and lesbianism, the NOW had considerably changed its style. According to Evans, "In several cities NOW became the chief instigator of new consciousness-raising groups." Such a process awakened women in different walks of life to their feminism. Theologian Mary Daly advocated women's rights in the church in her book, *The Church and the Second Sex* published in 1968[13].

While the nineteenth century movement saw legal and constitutional ways as the only ways to bring about change, the twentieth century movement is broader in scope. While the EEOC and the NOW ensured legal and constitutional changes, women in the second wave feminism also worked on a personal front by publishing literature raising the awareness of women regarding their rights in everyday life. A classic example of such literature is Pat Mainardi's liberation literature, especially her article on "The Politics of Housework." Like many militant feminists, she use the word politics to denote the basic power relationships in the culture of everyday lives and questions the age old custom if the assignation of housework to women[14]. Feminist ideas also penetrated mainstream institutions like business offices and publications. Textbooks were revised to eliminate blatant sexual and racial stereotypes. New words appeared in print such as "Ms.,", "chairperson" and "mankind" was transformed into "humankind".

To get a more comprehensive picture of the two movements, it is essential to briefly compare and contrast the two movements. According to Cott, while the nineteenth century movement enabled women to gain entry to political, economic, social and educational institutions, they were however not so successful in bringing about major transformations in the character and working of these institutions. This task was left to the twentieth century activists. Hence the twentieth century achievements such as the inclusion of Article ix and vii in the Civil Rights Act were in fact extensions of the nineteenth century breakthroughs.

The nineteenth century movement was not so concerned with sexuality, but during the twentieth century movement, demands for the reform of rape laws, reproductive rights and the question of sexual orientation appeared significantly on the feminist agenda. Another major difference in the latter part of the movement was that it became more mainstream than it was in the previous century, and aimed more at raising the awareness of women. Articles by Pat Mainardi and the introduction of terms such as "humankind" testify to this change.

The most significant change, as Cott writes that the feminist movement changed from a singular Woman's Movement to a pluralistic Women's Movement. Thus feminism became much broader in intent, presupposing a set of principles not necessarily beonging to every woman, thus attacking the earlier premise of unity. In the context of internal diversity, and the lack of consensus among women themselves, the feminist movement of the twentieth century made individuality and heterogeneity its underlying principles.

Considering the efforts made by the workers of the women's movement of both the previous generation as well as the generation of the 1960s and 1970s, and studying the underlying ideals and dreams of the activists of both the movements, it appears that the two movements should not be treated as isolated movements, but as phases of the same experience. It was an experience, which made women feel dissatisfied with the existing norms and conservatism which was prevalent in the society. It does not matter whether they were Susan B. Anthony, Charlotte Gilman or Ida Wells-Barnett asking for the vote, economic independence or an end to segregation in schools or whether they were Susan Casey Hayden, Dorothy Dawson or Ella Baker, fighting for civil rights and the end to segregation in public buses, the underlying principle was one—opposition to injustice along racist and sexist lines. The leaders of the 1960s movement did not start spinning a new yarn all by themselves—they simply picked up the thread from where the pioneers had left it and continued to weave another colourful patch in the rich fabric of the tradition of women's centuries of struggle against oppression.

REFERENCES

1. Eleanor Flexnor, Century of Struggle, *The Women's Rights Movement in the United States* (Cambridge, Mass. Belknap Press of Harvard University Press, 1975).
2. *Ibid.*
3. *Ibid.*
4. *Ibid.*
5. *Ibid.*
6. Sara Evans, Personal Politics: *The Roots of Women's Liberation in the Civil Rights Movement and the New Left* (New York: Vintage Books, 1979).
7. *Ibid.*
8. *Ibid.*
9. John D'Emilio and Estelle B. Freedman, eds., *Intimate Matters: A History of Sexuality in America* (Chicago: University of Chicago Press, 1997).
10. *Ibid.*
11. *Ibid.*
12. *Ibid.*
13. Evans, *Personal Politics.*
14. Pat Mainardi, "The Politics of Housework," *In The New Feminism in Twentieth Century America,* ed. June Sochen (Lexington: D.C. Heath, 1971).

13

...AND FINALLY THE VOTE WAS WON

Women's Suffrage Movement in the State of California

After the abolition of slavery, the issue which most divided the American nation into two distinct camps, was the question of women's suffrage. Partitioning the Americans into the suffragists and the anti-suffragists, the Suffrage Amendment reached the floor of the legislature of the nation as well as the states many times before it managed to become a law, giving women the right to vote. Surprisingly indeed, it happened so even in California, a state known for its immigrant culture and liberal traditions. California's community property law--inherited from Mexico—gave women control of the property they brought into a marriage and as early as 1870, women were voting in some school district elections.[1] Hence, in California women were given the right to own property, but were denied the right to vote. Women had to fight a long and hard battle of debating, appealing, canvassing and touring in order to win political rights at par with men.

The issue of the women's right to vote was initially brought up in 1896. The Californians however, were not willing to allow women to have a say in political decision-making. California suffragists had mounted a strong attack in the 1890s, and the legislature had approved an amendment for submission to the voters, who in turn rejected it by a wide margin in 1896. The Women's Christian Temperance Union supported the measure and many voters feared that women's suffrage would bring prohibition.

Women's suffrage next appeared on the ballot fifteen years

later in October 1911, as an amendment to the state constitution. During this Progressive era, upper-middle class club women from the cities, including San Francisco and its surrounding towns as well as Los Angeles were in the forefront of the campaign. Their state-wide organization was called the "California Equal Suffrage League". These leaders of the suffrage movement formed a coalition with the Republican Progressives. The debate between the suffragists and the anti-suffragists featured the standard arguments:

> The opponents arguing that a woman's place was in the home; advocates claiming that the women were already deeply involved in the public arena as workers and as advocates of social reform.[2]

The campaign reached virtually every constituency in California and utilized every conceivable tactic, including talking to people on the street, while touring in automobiles, as well as a precursor of today's direct mail effort. Another factor in favour of the women's suffrage cause in 1911, in contrast to 1896, was that temperance was now becoming more widely accepted as an important social reform. The amendment thus carried on the wave of the Progressive reform movement, but the vote was very close, the margin being slightly more than 3,000 votes.

This small margin of winning votes signifies that even in 1911, the state was almost equally divided into two divergent camps. Popular opinion still was not ready to accept the end of men's political monopoly and the beginning of equal political rights for men and women. One major source which reflects this cleavage in society and resounds the reluctance of many men and even many women to let go of the old system of political, legal and civil inequality, is the *San Francisco Chronicle*—the leading daily of California.

Catering mainly to a particular section of the society—the business class, the *Chronicle* which was a sort of a tabloid newspaper which represented the general anti-suffragist view prevalent amongst its readers. Even though in 1896 as well as in 1911, the Chronicle outwardly tried to appear neutral, by reporting news of the activities of both the camps, after reading in between the lines and studying various acts of omission and commission, the biased reporting of the Chronicle becomes clear.

This is an attempt to bring out the relationship between the society and the newspaper and see how the beliefs, desires and expectations of the former influence the content of the latter. This study will involve a critical review of these acts of omission and commission, which betray the true image of the Chronicle, in spite of its efforts to project itself otherwise. Even though the Chronicle tried to present itself merely as a neutral, detached, balanced reporter of events, certain news was ignored, while the other was highlighted and yet an other was blown out of proportion. Thus, even by not saying anything, the columns of the newspaper spoke volumes simply by reporting or ignoring certain news.

In 1896, the Chronicle, like the majority of the Californians was not at all ready to accept the question of women's suffrage. In fact, the issue was almost totally ignored. As it appears in the newspaper articles, the suffragists were not considered seriously at all and the question was not given much thought or coverage by the newspaper. There are solely two articles available on the subject in the Chronicle of June 1896, when the amendment was first put up for election. One of the articles states the events of the "State-Suffragists Meet" (Appendix 1) and the other article enumerates the activities of the "Anti-Suffrage League" (Appendix 2). Thus, ostensibly the Chronicle was trying to be neutral since it divided its paltry number of articles evenly between the two camps.

The first article began with the description of the venue:

> A flag sixty feet in length, formed a canopy under which sat the speakers of the day and many prominent guests. Huge palms, roses, sweet peas, nasturtiums and pinks were banked against the rostrum in small pyramids.
>
> (*San Francisco Chronicle*, June 13, 1896)

Thus, negating the seriousness of the reason behind the assembly of the people, making evident the seriousness or rather the lack of it, with which the Chronicle treated the subject of the Suffrage Amendment. The rest of the article went on to enumerate the number of people present and the names of the guests seated on the stage. The article, if it can at all be called so, concluded with excerpts from a speech given on the occasion and a list of the people who were to address the next convention.

The second article also followed in similar vein of detached reporting of a speech given by an anti-suffragist, the only bonus being that this time the reproduction of the speech was accompanied by sketch of, "Mrs. Carrie Murray, Principal Exponent of the Anti-Suffrage League" (Appendix 3).

Both these articles present a sense of dry enumeration of facts and events rather than 'reporting' in the true and sincere sense of the word. Morever, it was not what was present in the newspaper which was significant, but rather what was not. A critical analysis or an objective judgement of the events and the ongoing activities of these two groups was absent. The articles, instead of being thought-invoking, providing a direction or adding a new perspective to people's thinking, came across merely as space fillers or simply as token acknowledgements of the fact that the issue was then under much debate and voting. An editorial presenting a serious and focused look at the issue, discussing its various dimensions and implications was conspicuously missing from the *San Francisco Chronicle* of 1896, thus reflecting on how the society in general and the Chronicle's management, editorial staff and advertisers in particular thought about women's suffrage and how seriously or non-seriously they took the issue to be. This view is further highlighted by the fact that the entire suffrage issue was dismissed in a matter of two articles.

It took the Chronicle and the people of this state fifteen more years in coming around to giving this issue and its implications a serious thought. The Suffrage Amendment once again managed to elevate itself to the position of appearing on the ballot in 1911. The activities and the campaign organization of the suffragists had become more skilled and so had the editorial and journalistic tactics of the Chronicle. Even now, outwardly, the Chronicle played the game of being a neutral, passive onlooker of the activities of both sides. However, through subtle tactics it tried to let its faithful, conservative, mostly business class subscribers and advertisers know that it did indeed oppose women's suffrage. And thus, it betrayed its neutral image and exposed its espousal of the anti-suffragist cause.

Beginning on October 5, 1911, five days before the amendment was thrown open to vote, the Chronicle began to run parallel columns reporting the activities of both groups respectively, with joint captions such as "Both Sides of the Question Hotly Discussed". These were followed by parallel sets of sub-captions in the manner of, "Big Crowd Hears Anti-Suffragists" and "Women Make Plea for the Ballot" (*San Francisco Chronicle*, October 5, 1911) (Appendix 4).

This time, applying itself more seriously to the task of presenting to its readers, the latest developments on the issue, the Chronicle carried the news regarding women's suffrage everyday on page four, in the same columns and with a very similar appearance each day. The article, captioned sensationally, was usually supported by photographs of the suffragists and then followed the narrative. Often covering only one column as opposed to the two to three column wide caption, the narrative barely corresponded to the sensational quality of the caption.

These articles reproduced the speeches, arguments and counter-arguments of the advocates of both groups. The most famous of these debates, being the one between Colonel Irish and Dr. Aked. This debate between the former representing the anti-suffragists and the latter representing the suffragists, received considerable coverage in the *San Francisco Chronicle* and was presented under titles such as, "Forensic Battle to Take Place Tonight" (Appendix 5). The main issue brought up by the anti-suffragist speakers in their appeal to the people was the so called, "immigrant question" (*San Francisco Chronicle*, October 5, 1911). They used the tactic of fear appeal in their persuasive rhetoric stating:

> Before long California will face the immigrant question as New York now does. Hundreds of thousands of illiterate men arrive here and after a certain number of years are allowed the privilege of voting. Upon California's stand, to a certain extent depends the stand of the entire Nation in regard to women's suffrage and if the amendment is passed in this State, the wives of these immigrants will be allowed to vote because they become citizens automatically on their husband's receipt of his citizenship papers. These women are not fitted as well as their men to vote, because the men get practical experience during working

> hours that fits them to cope with the political situation with some degree of intelligence. With the women it would be different, and it is casting no disparagement upon my sex to declare that the immigrant vote would soon be a matter of money. It is our duty to oppose women's suffrage, a duty we owe to our country and to ourselves. (*San Francisco Chronicle*, October 5, 1911).

Colonel Irish based his opposition to the amendment on the grounds stating:

> The power to make laws and the power to enforce them, have always rested upon man, because (he said), that man alone has the two powers. A woman voter, (he said), would have the powers to make laws but not the physical power to endure the responsibility of enforcement and this one-sided condition (he declared) would destroy the principle of republican government. He dwelt at length upon the necessity of preserving the homes and said if suffrage is granted it would destroy domestic life, reduce men and women to a bestial state and eat away the vitals of good government with 'cancerous erosion'
> (*San Francisco Chronicle*, October 5, 1911).

The suffragists who were brought up in the same society and had their hands on the pulse of the conservatism and fears which the anti-suffragists were trying to invoke in the hearts of the people, were ready with well thoughtout, logical responses. They tried to allay the fears of their various audiences, be they people walking down the street, assembled in halls or members of women's clubs and associations. These suffragists had a massive task on their hands—that of dispensing political education among the men and women of California. This education involved the twin process: firstly, cleansing the minds of the naive audiences by ridding them of the images of the fearful consequences of women's suffrage, thus invoked in their mind by the anti-suffragist propaganda and the second task was, to impart to them the right information regarding women's suffrage by clearing their doubts and explaining to them the benefits of such a right being given to women. Responding to an enquiry of whether giving women the right to vote will lead to breaking up of the home, a suffragist speaker responded:

> "...the power of casting her ballot will not remove her from the home, as many of those opposed to equal suffrage are claiming. On the contrary, it will cement home ties for her. She is the partner of the man in the family life, in the family purse and should be his partner in making laws that influence these family ties."
>
> (*San Francisco Chronicle*, October 5, 1911).

The suffragists further explained that:

> "Politics will not take the woman out of the home, but on the contrary, will leave her just as motherly, just as housewifely, .if not more so, than before she was enfranchised. The right to vote in making laws and electing public servants will rouse women to feel, the things of outside influence on the home as well as the things inside.
>
> Many women are married, own property and support themselves. Should they not be allowed to vote say what shall be done with the money which is created for public funds by taxes on their earnings?; inquired a suffragist. Other women work with their husbands, helping to acquire homes and a little money in the bank. If the husband dies they are not recognized as owners of the property but must go to law to obtain it as an heir, is that right? Give women the right to vote, and change these things."
>
> (*San Francisco Chronicle*, October 5, 1911).

This debate apart from reflecting on the character of the reporting of the *San Francisco Chronicle*, also acts as a mirror of the society. It exposes the fears and the conservative and conventional views which were prevalent in the society. It also shows how the leaders of the conservative bloc, mainly men, played upon the fears of the masses, invoking images of destroyed homes and a total upside down picture of not only the society, social values, and socially acceptable norms, but also of the "republican government".

The press is usually considered a liberal and radical section of the society, often heralding the advent of civil rights movements and social revolutions. In case of the *San Francisco Chronicle*, however, this role of the press was either absent or was reversed. Women's suffrage which had the whole mass of California voters divided into two camps was an issue important enough to deserve front page coverage in a leading daily of the state such as the *San Francisco Chronicle*, however, before the elections, the only day when the suffrage amendment news appeared on the front page was on October 10, 1911 and that too was not because of the significance of the issue but because of the importance of the personality who had espoused the suffragist cause. (Appendix 6).

The issue got a lot of coverage on this day but every article centered around this musical celebrity, Lillian Nordica and her activities, more than it did around the issue. The second reason why the suffrage news was elevated to the position of being on the first page that day was that, just hours before the eve of the elections, the Chronicle decided, it was time to show some serious interest in the issue and this it did by deciding to issue bulletins on electoral returns on the Suffrage Amendment at the Scottish Rite Hall. (Appendix 6).

So far, (till the eve of the elections on October 10, 1911) the Chronicle had reported the latest developments on the suffrage in both camps, and this appeared to be a kind of a ritual reporting, dispassionate, detached and aloof from the issue. The article did not reveal on which side of the fence did the sentiments of the newspaper lie. They were written in the manner of what happened, when, where and who were the participants. The articles never tackled questions such as why things were developing the way they were, why women should be given the right to vote or why they should not, what will be the implications of their decision on the political, social, economic and moral life of the state.

As during 1896, in 1911 too the newspaper remained silent on how it stood on the issue, an editorial from a leading daily of the West Coast was much needed for by the readers but it was something they were never supplied with. There was merely one editorial which merely referred to all amendment proposals in general. In its editorial the newspaper very surprisingly claimed:

> The Chronicle has given its opinion in a detailed manner of the twenty three amendments which the voter will be called upon tomorrow to accept or reject. It insists, however, that it is far better that each elector decide fór himself how he shall vote... (the Chronicle) will refrain from further advice."
>
> (*San Francisco Chronicle,* October 9, 1911).

Thus, totally absolving itself of the duty which every responsible organ of the press has—one of channelling and adding new perspectives to public opinion. When an amendment as critical and controversial as women's suffrage was on the ballot, in an irresponsible manner, the editorial further went on to say: "The voters appear not to require much advice this year" (*San Francisco Chronicle*, October 9, 1911). The Chronicle was probably trying to justify its position of stubbornly refusing to take up any sides 'openly'.

The word 'openly' is of critical importance here, because it was only verbally that the Chronicle refused to choose sides. However, the other not so starkly legible tactics used by it show that the *San Francisco Chronicle* was indeed a conservative paper, supporting the anti-suffragists. The Chronicle catered to the convention ridden business class— its subscribers and more importantly its advertisers. Many of these businessmen were eager to avoid reforms such as temperance, laws regarding child labour and laws fixing the hours and working conditions for women workers. Therefore, they were opposed to an amendment which would give women,the right to vote since they thought that such a right would surely lead to the furthering of such reforms. Hence, the *San Francisco Chronicle* embraced their anti-suffrage cause as its very own. Fearful of the destruction of its neutral image, it did not openly advocate this view in its editorial section, however, there were many other ways which were less loud but which could successfully convey its endorsement of the anti-suffrage movement.

One of the ways, the Chronicle did so, was by placing a full page notice issued by "The Women of Northern California

Association Opposed to Woman Suffrage" (*San Francisco Chronicle*, October 9, 1911) (Appendix 7). The notice urged the voters:

> "...not to thrust the womanhood of this state into the political arena, at the request of the small minority of women who are asking for the ballot."

The notice went on to say:

> "The great majority of California women...do not want to vote; they depend upon the manhood of California to protect them from the responsibility of the ballot. They rely on manhood suffrage and Ya safe and sane government."
>
> (*San Francisco Chronicle*, October 9, 1911).

This notice not only exposes the fact that the men and women were blindfolded and brainwashed by such negative propaganda by other women, but also brings out the fact that by the very virtue of this notice being placed in the newspaper and that too across an entire page means that the *San Francisco Chronicle* did indeed belong to the anti-suffragist camp.

However, the most blatant of the Chronicle's act of its espousal of the anti-suffrage cause was the manner in which it reported the news of the returns of the elections.

On October 11, 1911 the Chronicle carried huge headlines: "WOMAN SUFFRAGE AMENDMENT DEFEATED BY 5000"

(San Francisco Chronicle, October 9, 1911) (Appendix 8) Notably, this was the case when the counting was not even over yet. Apparently, the lead of the anti-suffrage ballot in some constituencies was enough to reaffirm the Chronicle's belief in the imminent defeat of the Suffrage Amendment. However, this prediction seemed erroneous, as was evident the next day when the Chronicle, disheartened by the fast catching up of the pro-suffrage votes, was forced to report in a somewhat reluctant and, indeed small print, under the heading: "Suffrage May Prove Victorious When All Returns Are In" (*San Francisco Chronicle*, October 12, 1911) (Appendix 9). The said article gave a list of how different counties had voted on the amendment. And the final blow came on October 13, 1911, when the Suffrage

Amendment won. The significant nature of the news demanded its appearance on the front page, which it did indeed, however, the Chronicle made it obvious, how it felt about this victory. And this it did by sparing the news just one single left most column, under a non-sensationalized caption:

> "EQUAL SUFFRAGE WINS BY SAFE MAJORITY" (*San Francisco Chronicle*, October 13, 1911) (Appendix 10).

This news was sharply contrasted to the big headlines splashed all across the top of the front page just two days ago when the suffrage movement was just appearing to have been defeated in some counties. Moreover, the importance of this right for women in the eyes of the Chronicle is also evident by the fact that this news was allotted the same amount of space as another news connected with women which was considered important enough to be on the front page.

This article concerning matters such as:

"(The) lineless lady is going out of fashion...That's the latest news from the French capital." (*San Francisco Chronicle*, October 13, 1911) is being equated in the degree of its importance to women to a matter as grave and crucial as the right to vote.

In a similar vein, on October 13, 1911, a women's gossip columnist Helen Dare, tried to make light of the issue. In her article titled, "Now Come Those Obligations That Go With The Privilege" she treated the subject as frivolously as the editors of the *San Francisco Chronicle* nad treated it by placing an article concerning women's garments right next to it on the front page. This article began by giving the reason why women wanted the vote. She wrote:

> "It's no joke being a voter—least of all for the average woman who hasn't cared much about it, but only got keen about the ballot because she thought that the men didn't want her to have it."

Audaciously enough, she went on to predict how women would vote—on the basis of the candidates' looks. The article ended on a similar not with a question:

> "Will the suffragette registering in a dutch neck and elbow sleeves, and voting muffled to the chin

> and wrists, be insulted when called upon to establish her identity—and what will she do if a course of beauty treatment changes her?"

The flippancy with which this article addressed the issue of women's suffrage is indeed in consonance with the whole mood and atmosphere in which the *San Francisco Chronicle* had portrayed the issue.

The newspaper and its readers are like two interactive forces which are constantly acting and reacting upon one another. The newspapers print what their readers want to read, and vice-versa, the reader's views are shaped by the newspaper through its editorial. However, in case of the *San Francisco Chronicle*, this role is absent with regard to the crucial question of women's Suffrage Amendment. The *San Francisco Chronicle* true to its style, indulged in sensationalizing, reporting the colourful events of the campaigning of both the camps and sometimes completely ignoring the existence of the issue and thus in some way it represented the hopes, desires, aspirations and wishes of certain sections of the society. In spite of abandoning certain groups, just by its style of reporting, the presence of certain article or the absence of yet others and sometimes even the placement of these articles in the newspaper, the Chronicle, reflected on the needs, strengths, expectations and disappointments of the society and its various members.

Reading these newspapers, it becomes apparent that in spite of having had the experience of seeing five other states give their women the vote, without ushering in any social disaster or upheaval, California was still very reluctant to give this right to its women. Often referred to as the state of immigrants, it was in this very state that the earlier immigrants, who now considered themselves as citizens and residents of the state were trying to bar other immigrants from acquiring a status equal to theirs and they used this as an excuse to bar women both immigrant as well as native born from exercising the right to vote.

Moreover, seeing the heavy attack launched by these anti-suffragists, one comes to better appreciate the work of the suffragists, who had to struggle hard to achieve their goal. In a society where men were averse to the very idea of having to let their political monopoly go, a society where most of the women were brainwashed by a strong body of anti-suffragists, a society where women were against the prospects of being loaded with the responsibility accompanying the right to vote—this minority of suffragist men and women was indeed made up of people with vision and determination. They saw how critical the right to vote was for the improvement of the lot of the women in every sphere of their lives and were willing to fight an uphill battle in order to secure this basic political right.

APPENDICES

APPENDIX 1

The article on the activities of the Suffragists. (*San Francisco Chronicle,* June 13, 1896).

WANT THE BALLOT AND ITS BENEFITS.

STATE SUFFRAGISTS MEET.

ANIMATED SESSION AT MILLS TABERNACLE.

Mrs. Sargent Tells of the Work Already Accomplished by the Campaign Committee.

Oakland Branch Office of the "Chronicle," 950 Broadway, corner Ninth street.

OAKLAND, June 12.—The oppressive gloom of Mills' Tabernacle, with its great rough walls and network of unsightly scantlings, was transformed into a lively scene this afternoon when the State Woman's Suffrage Convention assembled. A flag, sixty feet in length, formed a canopy under which sat the speakers of the day and many prominent guests. Huge palms, roses, sweet peas, nasturtiums and pinks were banked against the rostrum in small pyramids.

About four hundred people gathered to hear the arguments of the suffragists. Upon the platform sat Mrs. A. A. Sargent, Mrs. John F. Swift, Mrs. L. A. Judd, Mrs. Knox Goodrich, Mrs. Holbrook Blinn, Mrs. Lloyd Baldwin, Mrs. F. C. Havens, Mrs. A. A. Moore, Mrs. Eliza Wilkes, Mrs. Henry Vrooman, Miss Hay, Mrs. Harper, Mrs. George Haight and Rev. J. K. McLean. State Organizer Miss Hay introduced the speakers.

Mrs. A. A. Sargent, president of the State Suffrage Association, made the opening speech, which was received with much enthusiasm and warmly ap-

APPENDIX 2

The article on the activities of the Anti-Suffragists. (*San Francisco Chronicle*, June 13, 1896).

THESE WOMEN DO NOT WANT TO VOTE.

THE ANTI-SUFFRAGE LEAGUE.

MRS. CARRIE MURRAY THEIR PRESIDENT.

Will Send a Committee to the Democratic Convention and Campaign the State.

Though Mrs. Carrie Murray, president of the Anti-Suffrage League, was disappointed in not having a meeting of her organization yesterday, she is still confident that a committee of at least ten will go to Sacramento Monday to labor for the defeat of the suffrage plank in the platform of the Democratic State Convention. She herself will go at the head of the committee.

The organization has had headquarters in the Mills building for several days, but no mass meetings in the campaign the organization has planned have yet been held. Mrs. Murray herself seems so far to have carried the burden of the movement on her shoulders alone. Although a meeting was called for yesterday afternoon, and another for the evening, Mrs. Murray was the only member of the organization who was on hand. Even the secretary, Miss M. A. Brown, did not appear. But Mrs. Murray is not discouraged. She heard from two women during the day who approved the objects of the Anti-Suffrage League. One of these expressed her belief that the suffrage movement was an effort on the part of women, who, by reason of being spinsters or of frivolous mind, did not know or did not appreciate how hard

APPENDIX 3

The sketch of Mrs. Carrie Murray, the principal exponent of the Anti-Suffrage League. (*San Francisco Chronicle*, June 13, 1896).

APPENDIX 4

Captions of the articles representing both camps. (*San Francisco Chronicle*, October 5, 1911).

Battle for Suffrage Rages

Both Sides of Question Hotly Discussed

Prominent advocates of woman suffrage who are taking prominent part in the meetings of the suffrage organizations.

BIG CROWD HEARS | WOMEN MAKE PLEA

PLEASE OPEN THIS FLAP TO READ THE TITLES AND SUBTITLES

APPENDIX 5

The article reporting a debate between the suffragists and the anti-suffragists. (*San Francisco Chronicle,* October 5, 1911).

Forensic Battle to Take Place Tonight

Colonel Irish Concedes Point to Dr. Aked in Debate on Equal Suffrage.

Those suffragettes and antis, who have been eagerly looking forward to the oft-debated debate between Colonel John P. Irish and Dr. Charles F. Aked, at which it is hinted fireworks

Can't Settle Terms of Suffrage Debate

Dr. Aked and Colonel Irish in a Muddle on Arrangements for Encounter.

Will the debate between Dr. Charles F. Aked and Colonel John P. Irish on equal suffrage occur? There seems to be a reasonable doubt that it will not, although yesterday morning it was

APPENDIX 6

Noted singer Lillian Nordica espouses the suffragist cause and the Chronicle decided to issue bulletins on the electoral returns. (*San Francisco Chronicle*, October 10, 1911).

Nordica Sings and Talks in Aid of Suffrage

Noted Artist to View 'Chronicle' Bulletins on Election Returns at Scottish Rite Hall

Madame Nordica, Miss Fannie McLean, Mrs. John Connell and Mrs A. B. Spencer, all of whom participated in the final street speaking of the suffrage campaign which took place last night about Union Square.

CHRONICLE INVITES WOMEN AND ESCORTS

Big Gathering Can Be Seated at Scottish Rite Hall to View Election Returns.

MUSIC AND PICTURES

Returns Will Also Be Displayed at "Chronicle" Office and Read in Theaters.

THAT the women readers of the "Chronicle," who have displayed such a keen interest in the campaign that has been waged for and against equal suffrage and the other amendments being voted on today, may learn the results of the election from every town, city and county in California, under the most comfortable conditions, the "Chronicle" has arranged to bulletin the returns this evening in the spacious Scottish Rite banquet hall, at Sutter street and Van Ness avenue.

This commodious auditorium, the entrance of which is on the Sutter-street side of the building, has a seating capacity of 1000, and only ladies and ladies accompanied by escorts will be accommodated.

NORDICA WILL BE THERE.

Mme. Lillian Nordica, whose keen interest in the success of the suffrage amendment was exemplified by her participation in the open-air exercises at Union square last evening, when she not only talked but sang to the big audience to show her earnest sympathy for the movement, will learn of the results of today's voting through the "Chronicle's" bulletins at Scottish Rite Hall tonight. Mme. Nordica will attend the Amato concert at the Scottish Rite auditorium this evening. The Scottish Rite banquet-room in the same building will be thronged with women and their escorts while the "Chronicle's" bulletins on the returns of the election are flashed on the screen, and her manager said last evening that while no definite programme of her movements could be made in advance, he was inclined to believe that Mme. Nordica would adjourn to the big banquet-room to

LILLIAN NORDICA SINGS FOR WOMEN

Marvelous Voice Heard in Union Square in Aid of Equal Suffrage.

Where the Returns Will Be Displayed

SCOTTISH RITE Banquet Hall, Sutter street and Van Ness avenue, entrance on Sutter street, where the "Chronicle" has provided specially for

APPENDIX 7

The notice issued by The Women of Northern California Association Opposed to Women suffrage. (*San Francisco Chronicle*, October 9, 1911).

TO THE VOTERS OF NORTHERN CALIFORNIA

We, the women of the Northern California Association Opposed to Woman Suffrage urge you not to thrust the womanhood of this State into the political arena, at the request of the small minority of women who are asking for the ballot.

Mrs. Harriet Stanton Blatch, one of the leaders of the world suffrage movement, in Pearson's Magazine, February, 1910, said:

"I've given up the American woman. She's hopeless. If it depends upon her, women will never have the ballot!"

The National Woman Suffrage Organization circulated an appeal in this State during this campaign in which, under the signature of Jessie Ashley, national treasurer, it is admitted that there are only 75,000 organized Suffragists in the United States, working among 93,000,000 people, and that the 75,000 organized Suffragettes are not sufficiently interested in the agitation to give a dollar each to the movement.

In 1895 the question of woman suffrage was put to a referendum vote of the women of Massachusetts. Out of nearly half a million women who might have voted on the question only 22,000 were sufficiently interested to cast a vote either way.

Since that time the Suffragists have fought every attempt to put the question to a vote of the women, even as they fought it here in California.

When in the polling booth, we ask you to remember that the vast majority of California women do not want to vote.

We ask you not to put upon our shoulders the responsibility of man's work.

The advance of woman—moral, intellectual and economic—has been made without the vote.

Woman now stands outside of politics and may appeal to any party on matters of education and reform.

and none of them dared help me. Women like Mrs. Mary C. Bradford and Mrs. Lafferty (who was a member of the last Legislature) took the platform against me and supported the System in its attempt to 'get' the Juvenile Court."

On page 306 of the same volume, Judge Lindsey says: "I talked to a number of school teachers . . . they told me they dared not make themselves conspicuous . . . the teachers were afraid of losing their positions."

On page 307 of "The Beast," Judge Lindsey says again: "If anyone believes that woman suffrage is a panacea for all the evils of political life, he does not know what those evils are . . . The women are as helpless as the rest of us . . . They are bound by the same bread-and-butter consideration as the rest of us. Their leaders in politics are politicians; when they get their nominations from the corporate machines, they do the work of the corporations, and there is almost no way . . . to get a party nomination except from a corporation machine. Women in politics are human beings; they are not 'ministering angels' of an ethereal ideality; and they are unable to free us, because they are not free themselves."

Suffrage Leaders Abuse Their Freedom.

Rev. Anna Shaw, President of the National Woman's Suffrage Association, says:

"I would make motherhood a Governmental institution. I would pension all mothers and have them provided for, first to last, by the State. I believe

Is This a Direct Blow at the American Home?

Mrs. Harriet Stanton Blatch, one of the leaders of the world suffrage movement, said in her discussion of the economic emancipation of woman that she rejoiced in every co-operative working woman's dwelling, because it aimed a blow at the isolated house, and she repeated her proposition regarding the institutional care of children.

Another leading Suffragist, in an article on woman's work in America, says: "Suffrage aims to benefit woman by recognizing her as a perfect equal of man, politically and socially, and by fixing woman's means of support by the State so as to render her independent of man."

Nothing Sacred to Suffragists.

The Suffragists have travestied the Bible, the Declaration of Independence and the American flag.

They have travestied the Bible with their "Woman's Bible," in which they take exception to the Creator as a Heavenly Father, instead of a Divine Pair.

They have travestied the Declaration of Independence—have mocked the most hallowed document of the Nation, and assert that man "has made her (woman), if married, in the eye of the law, civilly dead. He has endeavored, in every way that he could, to destroy her confidence in her own powers, to lessen her self-respect and to make her willing to lead a dependent and abject life."

APPENDIX 8

The huge headlines even before the votes were fully counted. (*San Francisco Chronicle*, October 11, 1911).

FFRAGE AMENDMENT DEFEATED BY 5000

M AND RECALL CARRIED BY BIG MAJORITIES

FROM ALL SECTIONS OF THE STATE SHOW THE FOLLOWING RESULTS

60,968 63,589 | No. 7 (The Referendum) Yes 85,746 No 27,747 | No. 8 (The Recall) Yes 90,367 No 28,728 | No. 16 (RR Commissioners) Yes 67,671 No 39,625

TOTAL VOTE CAST IN THE CITY AND STATE AT LARGE IS LESS THAN HALF NUMBER REGISTERED

Woman Suffrage Amendment Goes Down to Defeat—Railroad Passes and the Tax Exemption Measures Are Still in Doubt

ALL OTHER MEASURES CARRIED

Initiative and Referendum, the Recall and the Employers' Liability Are Given Big Majorities Throughout the Entire State

THE VOTE IN SAN FRANCISCO.

Complete returns from 290 Precincts in San Francisco out of 356 give:

No. 4 (Woman Suffrage)—	For	16,018
	Against	27,411
No. 7 (Initiative and Referendum)—	For	29,348
	Against	8,697
No. 8 (Recall)—	For	31,434
	Against	9,016
No. 16 (Appointment of Railroad Commissioners)—	For	24,138
	Against	11,355

The Vote on Amendments No's 4, 7, 8, 16 in the State

TURKEY SEEKING BASIS OF PEACE

Appeal to Powers May Bear Fruit When Italy Is Secure in Tripoli.

OLI BACK LOSSES

ar City he Guns Bat-

PLEASE TURN THE FLAP.

APPENDIX 9

A reluctant acknowledgement of the fact that the Suffrage Amendment may actually win. (*San Francisco Chronicle*, October 12, 1911).

Suffrage May Prove Victorious When All State Returns Are In

EARLY TOTALS FROM POPULOUS CENTERS MISLEAD

AMENDMENT LACKS 808 VOTES IN LATEST TOTAL

Many Scattering Precincts in Counties Favorable to Suffrage Unreported.

OTHER MEASURES CARRY.

Vote Was Remarkably Heavy One, Particularly in the Large Cities.

LATE returns received last night from the dilatory precincts throughout the State completely changed the situation in regard to the result of the fourth, or woman's suffrage amendment.

At an early hour this morning the balance against the amendment, from the returns then received, was but 808. It had been reduced from 3922 to that figure by the count of the last 421 precincts to be reported, and there were still 657 precincts yet to be counted. If this rate of gain should continue in the remaining precincts, the equal suffrage amendment will have carried by nearly 4000 votes.

Among the missing precincts at midnight were thirty-two in Los Angeles, where the vote was favorable to this amendment, and among the other missing precincts are few where any considerable majority against the amendment may be expected.

The latest count of 2462 out of 3121 precincts in the State gave 111,557 for the suffrage amendment and 112,365 against it, or an adverse majority of but 808.

From this showing it appears that the advocates of woman's suffrage may have been too hasty in admitting their defeat.

As the news went out by telephone

How the Counties Voted on Suffrage Amendment

RETURNS from 2462 precincts out of a total of 3121 in the State narrow the majority against suffrage down to 798. The totals, so far as returns have been received, are as follows:

For 111,557
Against 112,365

The vote by counties is as follows:

Counties.	For.	Against.
Alameda	10,385	12,686
Amador	478	823
Butte	1,436	909
Calaveras	694	441
Colusa	381	350
Contra Costa	1,560	1,548
Del Norte	305	198
El Dorado	815	350
Fresno	[illegible]	[illegible]
Glenn	562	345
Humboldt	1,894	1,106
Imperial	367	189
Inyo	334	173
Kern	1,594	1,463
Kings	206	227
Lake	409	268
Lassen	106	78
Los Angeles	35,542	30,793
Madera	269	203
Marin	949	1,449
Mariposa	122	120
Mendocino	489	851
Mono	78	103
Monterey	856	958
Napa	997	821
Nevada	1,774	1,797
Orange	1,659	1,585
Placer	623	407
Plumas	150	137
Riverside	1,003	773
Sacramento	3,111	2,907
San Benito	545	390
San Bernardino	2,324	2,228
San Diego	2,338	1,803
San Francisco	21,912	35,644
San Joaquin	2,326	1,981
San Luis Obispo	1,105	920
San Mateo	1,098	1,398
Santa Barbara	1,400	228
Santa Clara	4,856	3,083
Santa Cruz	1,388	856
Shasta	725	880
Sierra	35	45
Solano	580	582
Sonoma	2,384	2,323
Stanislaus	1,422	692
Sutter	301	358
Tehama	218	203
Trinity	200	130
Tulare	1,814	1,021
Tuolumne	487	346
Ventura	842	855
Yolo	859	891
Yuba	320	363
Totals	111,557	112,365

Latest State Totals on the Several Amendments

RETURNS compiled up to an early hour this morning from 2462 precincts out of a total of 3121 precincts in the State, including the complete vote from San Francisco and 369 out of the 401 precincts in Los Angeles, give the following vote on Suffrage, the Initiative and Referendum, the Recall, and the amendment making the Railroad Commission appointive by the Governor:

CONSTITUTIONAL AMENDMENTS.	FOR	AGAINST
No. 1 (Senate Constitutional Amendment No. 2)—Authorizing State inspection of weights and measures.	103,937	32,799
No. 2 (Committee Substitute to Senate Constitutional Amendment No. 5)—Permitting counties to frame and adopt charters.	83,243	45,668
No. 3 (Senate Constitutional Amendment No. 6)—Pro-	82,485	46,099

APPENDIX 10

The landmark event in the history of California and the Chronicle relegates it to one single column on the left most side of the front page. (*San Francisco Chronicle*, October 13, 1911).

EQUAL SUFFRAGE WINS BY SAFE MAJORITY

Amendment Is Two Thousand Votes Ahead, With Further Increase Assured.

MISSING PRECINCTS, 244.

The Counties Still to Be Heard From Confidently Claimed by the Women.

How the Vote Stands on Woman Suffrage

Counties—	For.	Against.
Alameda	10,6[illegible]	12,804
Amador	478	628
Butte	1,084	987
Calaveras	741	485
Colusa	347	389
Contra Costa	1,509	1,349
Del Norte	305	198
El Dorado	601	389
Fresno	3,017	2,427
Glenn	588	859
Humboldt	1,906	1,106
Imperial	307	189
Inyo	354	186
Kern	1,759	1,302
Kings	667	513
Lake	402	315
Lassen	243	150
Los Angeles	27,127	21,008
Madera	495	337
Marin	1,101	1,530
Mariposa	122	120
Mendocino	1,104	1,130
Merced	741	[illegible]
Mono	78	103
Monterey	1,146	1,151
Napa	907	821
Nevada	568	454
Orange	[illegible]	1,820
Placer	1,081	700
Plumas	895	221
Riverside	1,929	1,393
Sacramento	3,111	2,007
San Benito	545	390
San Bernardino	2,546	2,263
San Diego	2,786	2,120
San Francisco	21,912	35,844
San Joaquin	3,[illegible]	2,082
San Luis Obispo	1,[illegible]	1,038
San Mateo	1,1[illegible]	1,447
Santa Barbara	1,409	1,228
Santa Clara	4,913	3,113
Santa Cruz	1,3[illegible]	858
Shasta	1,100	815
Sierra	47	87
Siskiyou	375	
Solano	840	843
Sonoma	2,488	2,270
Stanislaus	1,472	682
Sutter	331	278

PLEASE OPEN THE FLAP

14

STATE FEMINISM IN CHINA

Has it Really Helped Women?

Initially, in the first half of the twentieth century, both the Chinese Communist Party (CCP) and the Nationalist Party (KMT) wanted women to join the ranks of the national movement. The KMT was more conservative, believed in capitalist ideology and adopted Confucian values, while the CCP on the other hand was definitely leftist in its approach and tended to appeal to the masses and was anti-capitalist in its stand. Consequently, the CCP was more enthusiastic about pursuing gender equality. For instance, on 30th, May, 1925, at a time when the nationalist government was complacent in its approach towards exploitative factory owners, the CCP instigated women workers to strike against foreign investors in Shanghai. As a result of this and numerous other such instances, women workers became sympathetic to the CCP, which promised them a genderless state.

However, in reality, politics is gendered and gender creates politics, hence when the Communists talked of bringing about gender equality, in reality what they instituted was a code of desexualization. The Communist control over the life of the Chinese people ranged all the way from literature to sex. The desexualization which affected women, robbed them of their femininity—they wore their hair short, were devoid of make-up, they could not wear dresses, rather they had to wear dull, dark-coloured, loose clothes to cover up their feminine form, and had to work very hard, like men. Even pregnant women till their eighth and ninth months had to keep working. This was ostensibly aimed at creating gender equality. Similarly, men were also desexualized because they could not speak out their minds against the government.

Ironically, gender equality within politics was a force; politics was not really gender blind, as, in fact, gender discrimination was embedded in politics. Women were not active participants in politics because their power was too weak before the overwhelming power of men in politics. Christina Gilmartin points out the fact that this discrepancy between the stated ideal of the Communist Party and the reality of the Chinese society existed not only in politics but even in the social sphere. She cites the example of Peng Pai, a high ranking Communist and the head of the bureau pushing for women's mobilization and gender equality, who brought home a young girl despite having a wife of many years. He had children with both and thus engaged in concubinage and polygamy.[1]

Despite such shortcomings, the CCP deserves some credit for enacting laws protecting women's rights. At the same time it is true that every policy had a downside. On 1st, May, 1950, the CCP passed the Marriage Law of China, whereby the feudal marriage system was abolished. In her book *Chinese Women in a Century of Revolution: 1850-1950* Ono Kazuko states that the new marriage law emancipated women who had been at the very bottom of the traditional family system.[2] She emphasizes that the marriage law clearly was a law for women. There was a freer choice since men and women now had a say in marriage and widows were free to remarry. Both men and women were equal partners in marriage and had equal right to get a divorce. Bigamy and concubinage were outlawed. As a result of enforcement of this law there were 1 million divorce cases in the subsequent three years and 75 per cent of them were initiated by women.

However, the down side to this was that an estimated 70,000 to 80,000 women were killed because of family disputes since women were now standing up against their husbands and in-laws. Two writers, Xiao Hong and Eileen Chang were outside the purview of Mao's guidelines and they wrote about women in the countryside, where Communist control was not so strong. They argued that these women were oppressed by husbands and mothers-in-law. Similarly, even urban women who married into polygamous households were a piteous lot. They competed with each other and spoke against each other to win the love of the unloving, disloyal and unworthy husbands. Hence in both cases, women were not aware of any sense of gender consciousness and neither were they aware of their oppression and subordination. So, even though the government could not really protect each woman individually, still, it did try to improve and strengthen women's position vis-á-vis the oppressive family and marriage system.[3]

Similarly, the government also gave female workers the recognition, which they deserved. Earlier female workers were seen as 'broken shoes.' This implied that their femininity and chastity was questionable in society and no respectable men wanted to marry such women. Now, however, the government exalted such women by calling them their 'heroes' and as 'good women', as opposed to the 'bad' ones who stayed at home. The government acknowledged the role of women workers by recognizing their contribution to the state. Their production was geared not just for the family but for the state as well. So, the judgment of female virtue was reversed. Hence the decade of 1950s have been aptly characterized as the 'age of innocent idealism.'

However, the government policy, which had the most far-reaching effect on women was the enactment of the birth control legislation. This policy is very controversial and poses a very painful issue for Chinese mothers. But China's population control policy has undergone many changes as a result of several factors—which are mentioned by Tyrene White.[4]

These factors include:

(a) economic training;

(b) the political movement involving the Cultural Revolution mindset as well as the post-Mao policy; and

(c) women's liberation under the Communist rule.

The biggest irony of the issue of birth control is that during the early part of the Communist Revolution, women in the cities wanted access to birth control, but later when they, had official access to birth control, they were not actually in control of the birth control.

Phases of the Birth Control Policy

Throughout the 1940s, up till the early 1950s, the general Birth Control Policy of the Communist Party was pro-natal. This was so because lots of lives were lost in the wars and consequently women were encouraged to have many babies. However, many women did not want to follow the Communist Party guidelines. They wanted less children because, either they were working or secondly, they did not want to be tied down by children because they wanted to participate wholeheartedly in the Communist Revolution. Despite, their desire for less children, women had no real access to birth control. Women needed the permission of the husband, the boss at the workplace and the doctor to be able to petition for birth control. Moreover, rural women still did not gain access to birth control.

The period from 1953 to 1956 was part of the 'First Five Year Plan' and all women were provided with access to birth control. However, in 1957, birth control suffered a blow from the persecution of people with progressive and supposedly western thoughts. From 1956 to the early 1970s, Chairman Mao asked Chinese women to have many children because of his fear of a US or Soviet atomic attack. Hence he wanted to double China's population. In 1965, the Chinese fertility rate constituted of six birth per couple. Hence, the mid-1970s onwards, the government was faced with the severe task of controlling the population growth. As a result, in 1980 the Chinese government formulated the 'One-Child Policy'.[5]

The population of China went from 673 million in 1962, to 1 billion in 1982. Thus, in spite of the loss of lives during the Cultural Revolution, there was still an increase of 300 million people.

Enforcement of the Birth Control Policy

The one-child policy was not enforced very strictly in the rural areas. The countryside experienced a relaxed control because it was very difficult to execute such policies in the villages, since the government found it hard to monitor each and every region. But it was enforced very rigidly in the urban areas. However, the high-ranking officials could get away with the policy, while the common masses had to bear the real brunt of the policy. Thus, it was the ordinary people who were oppressed, and especially so, the women.

In factories, both married and single women had to hand over their sanitary napkin to the birth control agent on a monthly basis. This was done to ensure that married women had only one child and that single women did not have any illegitimate children. Even when it was legal for a couple to have a baby, one had to go through a long process of petitioning and obtaining permits from the boss. Permits could be denied too. The head reviewed the petitions and decided which couple was in need of a child that particular year. Thus, newly married couples came in the low priority list.

The permit was valid only for a year because a quota had been fixed for the number of children who could be born in a particular year. As a result, women were under pressure to have the baby within a year since obtaining the permit. Consequently, women often went through induced labour and so there were many deaths during childbirth. If it was discovered that a woman secretly had more than one child, she was forcibly sterilized. This signalled an unjust sexual discrimination because men were not forced to sterilize. The man could remarry and have more children but the woman could not. Since after such secrets were uncovered through gossip, it is now evident that one of the major consequences of the Cultural Revolution was a destruction of human faith, leading to woman being pitted against woman.

Moreover, since every child had to be registered, a couple with a boy and a girl, registered only the boy and sent the girl to the countryside. Hence the girl being unregistered, lost out on education as well as food coupons. Moreover, such a practice creates an unbalanced sex ratio. At least on paper, boys far outnumbered women. Further on, since couples could have only one child, very often the female foetus was aborted and boys were much better cared for than the girls.

Other Implications of the One-Child Policy

A couple coming from one-child families is burdened with the task of caring for four older parents. Since there are more registered boys than girls, the lop-sided sex-ratio leads to problems in marriage. Moreover, the problem of domestic migration from rural to urban areas accentuates the problems resulting from the birth control policy.

The women who come to cities from villages are not given citizenship of the city and eventually have to return back. Very few of them want to return. Consequently, the government finds it difficult to keep track of them because they are in large numbers. Moreover, when the women cannot find respectable jobs, they resort to prostitution because they need to send money home. Even women who come to the city to get married to a person registered in the city cannot get citizenship of the city easily, since this citizenship also entails a number of other benefits which the citizen would be entitled to receive from the state. Nowadays, people are securing urban residency by bribing the officials.

Communist Ideology and Literature

During the Long March, Mao Tse Tung gave a lecture in the city of Yan'an which has become an important part of communist history in China. He said that writers should not write love stories or literature about one's intellectual pursuits because these constituted bourgeois literature. Rather, he urged the writers to serve the cause of the Communist Revolution, exalting a puritan sex-life in their writings, which was not only anti-prostitution, but also propagated a curtailment of sexual desires and pleasures within marital life itself. Communist literature aimed at advocating a puritanical work and love ethic. Such views were echoed in Communist policies which segregated men and women in separate communes and allowed couples to sleep together only once a week. During the 1930s and 1940s, Mao's guidelines regarding literature prevailed in the Communist controlled areas.[6]

Model operas were written in which young soldiers and peasants were in love with China and Mao, while private love being petty bourgeois, was missing. So women and men were desexualized and seen only as revolutionaries. As writer Ding Ling once wrote that she felt that her life was not her own, or her parents', rather it belonged to the CCP. During the Cultural Revolution, the literature did not reflect individuality because most of it focused on the common theme of showing how people were ready to self-sacrifice for China.

On 8, March, 1942 Ding Ling wrote an article on women's

need to think of themselves as independent, capable individuals. She complained about CCP's attitude of discouraging single women. The CCP ridiculed anyone who was over 25 years of age and still single. The official policy of the party ordered that such women to be spied upon. Ding Ling exposed the double standards of the CCP by writing that women who married and stayed at home were criticized for being, old-fashioned, while at the same time, those who left their children and husband at home and went to work at a high post were criticized for not being good wives and mothers. Ding Ling questioned the gender-based discriminatory policy of the CCP that men only had to be good revolutionaries but women had to perform a double duty as a good wife and mother as well as being a good revolutionary. She pointed out the poignant choice which many women made by deciding not to have children so that they did not come in the way of their being good revolutionaries. After Mao's death in 1976, China liberalized slightly and writers produced what is called the "literature of the wounded," wherein they used physical deformity to explain the mental torture the Chinese people underwent during the Cultural Revolution. Moreover, as Li Ziyun and Zhu Hong point out, women writers began writing on taboo subjects such as sexuality, marriage, divorce and love. Stories like *How Did Miss You* talk about how the CCP guidelines robbed women of their feminity and how they were no longer capable of being loved. Other stories such as *Silent Commemoration* and *The Tragedy of the Walnut Tree* talk about the continuance of old cultural remnants of feudal values such as stigma on widow remarriage and no real gender equality despite the political revolution.[7]

Any study of state feminism in China would not be complete without a discussion of the meaning of womanhood in Chinese Communist discourse. The term *funu* was coined by the *All Chinese Women's Federation* and denotes "a female subject in a socialist state." Tani Barlow explains the concept of *funu* and says that it entails that the woman has certain obligations towards the state and that she is not seen as an individual but rather as a part of society and state. This term was coined to remind the world that Chinese women were liberated by the Communist Revolution and was used in the early stage of the Revolution to make women think of themselves as equals to men and as members of the Chinese Communist society, capable of contributing as much as men. So this term had a heroic and noble connotation. The *Funu* were asked to go beyond family needs and to serve the state, and in return the government promised protection from imperialism, sexual discrimination and natural disaster.[8]

However, in reality, the Communist agenda did not give women many rights, neither did it spend resources in helping women build up their individuality because it did not fit the party's needs, which wanted women out of the house and into the labour force. As a result of all these reasons and the connotations attached to *funu,* women scholars were dissatisfied with the term as it reflected no individuality. So they coined the term *nuxing* or the 'female sex.' This term emphasized the characteristics which all women share, such as a commonality of history and shared universal experiences. Finally, however, the term *nuren* was coined to everyone's satisfaction. It means 'female person,' thus encompassing universality and individuality.[9] The *nuren* shares characteristics with all women by virtue of being a female, but as a person she has her own individual problems and likes and dislikes. Thus, this term localized as well as universalized Chinese women at the same time.

Communist Policy and its Repercussions: The Contemporary Scene

As stated at the beginning of the essay, the CCP recruited women workers into their ranks by promising to protect them. However, later this policy changed: whenever there was an excess of workers, women were the first to be laid off. They were asked to go home and be good socialist housewives. In her book *'Rewriting Gender,'* Ravni Thakur argues that the economic and political changes which occurred in post-Mao China had led to the emergence of a new set of guidelines and directives for women. Although the ideological underpinnings of women's roles remain grounded in the previous notions of female equality, today there is striking difference between the much publicized ideology of equality and the practice of female subordination.

Under Deng Xiaoping, China became capitalist in the economic sphere and this move was termed as "socialism of Chinese characteristics." This economic change depended on foreign investment, particularly from Taiwan. Especially so, as pointed out by Margaret Woo in the "special economic zones," which are exempt from implementation of the national requirements for the protection of women workers. So Taiwanese investors were given a free hand and laws safeguarding the health and safety of women workers were relaxed. Not surprisingly, women were the first to suffer in this pro-boss but anti-worker environment. Moreover, during phases of labour surplus, the first to be laid off are women in their forties and fifties.[10]

China's new premier Zhu Rongji devised the system of *Xia gang* which connotes, 'stepping down' voluntarily from one's official post. Not surprisingly, the first group which is forced to 'step down' is constituted of women, who are told that they are temporarily laid off and are to wait for a new assignment. In the course of this discussion one has to remember that theoretically speaking, China is still a socialist nation. Girls coming from the villages are given a year long work permit, and if they are found inefficient, they are fired at the end of the year. Thus, women, who are supposedly protected by the Communist state, are in fact controlled by the system which is only interested in maintaining a regular flow of dedicated, hardworking women.

In the recent years, however, as pointed out by Margaret Woo, the Chinese government has initiated protective legislation which focuses on the biological differences between men and women.[11] The government passed

1986—Women's Health Care Law;

1988—Women Workers' Protection Law;

1992—Women Workers' Rights Law;

to protect the interests of the women workers during critical periods of pregnancy, delivery and nursing the baby. However, these laws often backfired on women. Their removal from most hazardous employment also signalled their exclusion from the highest paying jobs. Moreover, during phases of labour shortage, these protectionist policies are not enforced.

The recent trend in women's lives has not been very encouraging. Earlier, the patriarch was at the helm of affairs, and was then replaced by the patriarch, but women in both cases were subordinate to an authority higher than themselves. Moreover, unfortunately, traces of misogynist, feudal gender bias are coming back. Bureaucratic views on women and chauvinistic attitudes still exist. Communist China today has pornography, Chinese women are very much present in the entertainment industry as prostitutes, escorts and sports models and women are being harassed sexually even in their workplace.

A very disturbing trend, whose roots can be traced back to the one-child policy, whereby many female babies went unregistered, has taken the shape of female trafficking. Since there are very few opportunities in the countryside, women want to live in the city. Moreover, the already lop-sided sex-ratio, which developed as a result of the one-child policy, creates a shortage of brides. Consequently, men kidnap girls in cities, who are then sold in open markets in the villages. China's huge size and diverse geographic areas make escape from a new and unknown area difficult for these poor women. Further on, if women who try to escape are caught, they are brutalized and neutered. Many Chinese girls are also sold as photo brides to other parts of South East Asia.

In the field of education also women lag behind men. Only 2 percent-3 percent of the Chinese population between the ages of 20 to 24 is enrolled in higher education and only 1/3 of this 2 percent-3 percent is constituted of women. 30 percent of the Chinese population is illiterate and 70 percent of this percentage is made up of women. This vast gulf between the number of educated men and women is the result of gender preference. If parents have both a son and a daughter, and they could afford to send only one to school, they would only send their son, because they believe that the daughter will ultimately marry out.

Employment Opportunities

Moreover, like Japan, in China, highly educated women find it hard to get a job because of a gender stereotypical concept of women doing low level jobs. Women with a college education find it extremely difficult to get good jobs because people believe men will refuse to work under her and so she cannot be a good manager. Thus, higher education puts women at a disadvantage. A survey of jobs open to women showed that they were usually hired for positions which require skills of public relations such as sales girls and title managers whose only job requirement involves offering tea to the clients or as PR ladies who are expected to take clients out to dinner. Hence in a way, even today the Chinese corporate world follows the traditional notion of *yin* attracting *yang*.

Chinese politics also reverberates with similar echoes, where the participation and contribution of women is concerned. During the Maoist period, the party's aim was to create gender equality, therefore some women did hold high political posts, but today there are few women in Central Committees and no women at all in the Politburo because today China's aim is to be a strong nation. Consequently, no more political handouts are being given to women. Today women are expected to prove their political mettle. However, this shift in priorities has proved disastrous for women because Chinese society is still in the traditional mould. As a result of this mindset, although in 1978, there were two women in the Politburo, there were no women in the Politburo in 1980. Similarly, in 1978, 11.1 per cent of the Central Committee members were women but in 1993, this figure fell to 7.5 per cent. Further on, out of the fortyone ministerial posts only three are with women.

Finally, the domestic household scene also proves that women are still suppressed in everyday life. Within the house, wife beating is still reported and men have extramarital affairs, despite the Communist Party's legislation against it. Chinese women are still taught to endure oppression and be chaste wives. Women's federations intervene and send petitions to the women's federation offices, yet it is to no avail. Hence even though there is equality in the legal documents, in reality communism did not bring about real equality for women. In fact, the traditional concept of 'separate spheres,' which says that men and women are supposed to do different kinds of chores still very much prevalent notion.

Even though women work outside for the same number of hours as men do and in much worse physical conditions, for instance till the eighth and sometimes the ninth month of their pregnancy, they are still expected to come home and perform the household chores such as cooking and cleaning. Moreover, the state expects them to be good workers and the society expects them to be good wives and mothers. The husband works only outside the home, and so his workday ends the minute he leaves work, but women have to come home and begin work there all over again. Thus, they carry a double work-day load. Hence, although in theory the Communists did try to bring about equality by enforcing uniform codes for men and women and by introducing the concept of state feminism, however, in reality, the Communist state only succeeded in desexualizing women, while not really helping them escape their fate as prescribed by the traditional male-dominated Chinese society.

Mayfair Mei-Hui Yang quotes Huang Shuqin, who says that both during the Cultural Revolution and today's commercialized China, the society is based on male power. Earlier men wanted women to become more masculine and now they want women to become feminine. Hence in terms of male power, both the periods are basically equivalent.[12] To conclude, it would suffice to say that although state feminism did much to release Chinese women from the hold of the traditional kinship and patriarchy, women were catapulted into the public sphere of labour and politics and the feminist agenda was forgotten with the decline of gender salience and women's transformation into state subjects in a new masculine state order.

REFERENCES

1. Christina Gilmartin, Ed., *Engendering China: Women, Culture and the State* (Cambridge: Harvard University Press, 1994).
2. Ono Kazuko, *Chinese Women in a Century of Revolution, 1850-1950* (Stanford: Stanford University Press, 1987), 13-186. Passim.
3. Gilmartin, *Engendering China*.
4. *Ibid.*
5. *Ibid.*
6. *Ibid.*
7. *Ibid.*
8. *Ibid.*
9. *Ibid.*
10. Gilmartin, *Engendering China*.
11. *Ibid.*
12. Mayfair Mei-Hui Yang, Ed., *Spaces of Their Own: Women's Public Sphere in Transnational China* (Minneapolis: University of Minnesota Press, 1999), 35-63. Passim.

SECTION 6

GENDER AT WORK

15

RYOSAI KENBO

THE CHANGING IDEAL OF JAPANESE WOMANHOOD IN THE WAKE OF POST-WAR CAPITALIST JAPAN

The Japanese society has witnessed various changes in the image of the ideal of womanhood through different periods of time. In post-Second World War Contemporary Japan, this ideal is symbolized by motherhood. Hence today an ideal Japanese woman is one who is a good and dedicated mother to her children. However, it is important to note that this has not always been the case in Japan. A brief survey of the views concerning ideal womanhood in the Tokugawa, Meiji and Taisho Japan reveals that the identification of the notion of ideal womanhood with the Concept of Motherhood is a recent development, significantly enough, it is a product of the Capitalist ambitions of Post-Second World War Japan.

The concept of ideal womanhood in traditional Japan constituted of *Ryosai Kenbo* or 'good wife, wise mother,' a Concept borrowed from Neo-Confucian philosophy regarding the role of women in the Tokugawa Period (1600-1868). During this period, the lifestyle of women differed depending on their social class and economic status. Thus, *Ryosai Kenbo* was the prescribed ideal only for the upper class and not so much for the lower class. While lower-class did not have many clear-cut gender distinctions, much more strict and rigid constraints were placed on the women of the upper classes. The ideal of *Ryosai Kenbo,* which was strictly imposed upon women of upper class, entailed women to be submissive and subservient. Further on, children became the primary responsibility of the mother, so mother was forced to stay at home and be subject to the three obediences, which ensured that they rendered abject obedience to their fathers, husbands and sons. At the time, even the merchant class tried to emulate the ideals of the upper class by transferring upper class ideals regarding the proper role and place of women to their own women. Ishida Baigan, a member of the merchant class, developed the notion of the "*Shingaku* woman," a pure and spiritual woman, who engaged in physical relations with her husband only to fulfil her duty of producing an heir, and then resigned herself to spiritual pursuits alone.[1] Thus, this ideal was also an offshoot of the concept of *Ryosai Kenbo.*

According to Jane Caplan, the Tokugawa order of society disassociated the roles of motherhood and childbearing on the one hand from femaleness and wifehood on the other.[2] Susan Orpett Long supports this argument and substantiates it by saying that historical and early ethnographic studies suggest that the association between women and nurturing was not so close in the past.[3] She emphasizes that from the Tokugawa through the Second World War, spanning across the Meiji and Taisho eras, other children, mothers in law, and even fathers frequently had major role in child care, while the major duty of the middle-aged women was to assist in the households' productive labour, whether in growing food, producing goods in Cottage industry or engaging in the family business. She further argues that even elder care was limited in scope, given the relatively short fifty year life expectancies in the era.[4] Hence Kathleen Uno, suggests that in pre-industrial Japanese household, the contribution of women to the productive activities of the peasant or craft household was at least as important as their reproductive and nurturing role.[5] Sharon H.Nolte and Sally Ann Hastings reiterate this view saying that motherhood was still a fairly vague concept in Japan in 1910. They point out the fact that in the two decades prior to 1910, Japanese state policy placed much more importance on a woman's responsibilities as a wife than on her function as a mother.[6]

From 1868 to 1912, Japan was ruled by the Meiji government, which aimed at modernizing Japan. As part of this modernizing drive, the Meiji government sought to promote the concept of

Ryosai Kenbo among all classes and even expected the lower classes to adapt their lifestyles to accommodate the ideal of *Ryosai Kenbo*. During this period, the government believed that if women were trained properly, they would make good wives and mothers. Thus, under the Compulsory education programme, girls were taught that womanhood meant *Ryosai Kenbo.* The central idea behind such teaching was to diffuse *Ryosai Kenbo* among all social classes, and not limit it just to the upper classes. Another method employed by the Japanese government was to extoll women's patriotic and feminine virtues for example, Shibata Hana taking care of retarded husband, sick parents and saving money for the Japanese National Army.

Susan Long says that recent researchers have shown that in the Meiji period (1868-1912) there was a purposeful government policy to create an image of Victorian genteel women while continuing to utilize female productive labour, a policy intended, according to Long, the improve Japan's image abroad and to maintain social control during rapid industrialization and social change at home.[7] The Taisho era symbolized the state's doubled expectations from women. They were expected to work and support the nascent industrialization and also be good wives and wise mothers. Yoshiko Miyake emphasizes the importance of the two solgans *Ryosai Kenbo* and *Fukoku Kyohei* (rich country, strong army) which aimed at the other role women were supposed to play as the reproducers of the next generation of the family system.[8]

However, during the Second World War, the government relaxed the state policy, of *Ryosai Kenbo* promotion. This led to modification and expansion of women's role as nurses, teachers, etc. But after the war was over, the government reverted back to its pre-war policy of encouraging 'Separate Spheres' and *Ryosai Kenbo.* In post-war Japan, the socio-economic and political atmosphere changed, thus, changing the concept of ideal womanhood from a multi-faceted role to one focusing mainly on motherhood. To begin with, the post-war government fired about three million women in 1945 in order to open their jobs to the returning soldiers. Thus, Japan's desire to emerge as an economic supergiant led to its changed stance regarding the best role for women.

The Japanese Capitalist society believes that without women's childbearing, childrearing and housework, the contemporary family would disintegrate and cease to meet the economy's demand for reproduction of an efficient labour force. Moreover, as Yoshiko Miyake points out, without women's care of the elderly and infirm, the state would have to increase social welfare expenditures.[9] Further on, since the Japanese work ethic requires regular overtime from men, a greater sharing of responsibilities at home between husbands and wives would interfere with the kind of total dedication of male workers to the workplace that characterizes the Japanese employment system. Miyake concludes her argument saying that the stability of the nuclear family is still crucial to the maintenance of social relations mandated by the post-war capitalist system. Hence, by expecting women to be temporary workers, and full-time mothers, the Japanese state is trying to balance women's reproductive role with their productive labour.[10]

Thus, even though the slogan *Ryosai Kenbo* was initially a part of the Meiji state's rhetoric, nevertheless it did not gain such a stronghold earlier, as it does in present day Japan. In the past the work ethic was not so harsh, and therefore, men and women could work side by side, however in the post-war era of the 'economic miracle' men are expected to work overtime and this necessitates that women stay at home to take care of the children and be good wives.

The work pattern of the majority of Japanese women shose that they submit to the social and state expectation from women by being *Ryosai Kenbo.* Both social expectation and pressure from colleagues and peers, are responsible for making women quit their job after marriage and definitely so after having children. Women and expected to take up the role of nurturers of children, be the care takers of the greying population, and also do all the housework. In her book *Urban Japanese Housewives,* Anne Imamura argues that in Japan's competitive world, it is increasingly expected that children will go on to higher education. This expectation coupled with the difficulties of the university examination system, concentrate a greater part of the mother's time and energy on the education of her children.[11] The term 'education mother' or *kyoiku mama* was coined to describe the woman who pushes her children ahead at all costs especially by involving herself deeply with the child's curricular activities and homework.[12]

June Allison describes her first-hand experience with a Buddhist Nursery School in Japan and describes the process of education in Japan, which is literally producing Mothers.[13] She refutes the earlier view of scholars that the role mothers comes of a later stage during the child's schooling, rather Allison emphasizes that, mothers were expected and even compelled to assist their children in adapting to school, such demands all in fact made by the school early on in the child's school life, right from nursery school itself. She shows how the institution of school expects mothers to carry on educational agenda into the very patterns and routines of daily life. Allison agrees with Imamura when she argues that the expectation that the mother must incorporate a continuous education into the vacations, play time and home, often burdens the mother with feelings of anxiety and doubt about the school system.[14] Seen in this light, the role of the *kyoiku mama* is neither simple, nor is it generated solely or even primarily by mothers themselves. Rather, as Allison points out, it is a realtionship between mothers, children and a school system that has been situated within the political and economic relations of Japan's post-industrial labour market. Norma Fields suggests that children are now being programmed at even earlier ages to assume a posture of productivity that will continue into later life. Allison adds to this view by suggesting that, Japanese mothers too all being programmed into and by the same model.[15] As S. Long states once children are born, most couples experience a greater separation of their daily activities, with the wife often retiring from paid employment at least until the children are in middle school.[16]

As discussed earlier, Japanese social convention and the attitude of colleagues forces women to quit their full-time jobs after having children. They often return to the work force as part-time workers and this trend puts most of the Japanese working women on what has come to be known as the M-Curve. The points A and B represent the two most active working periods of the Japanese women's lives. Point A represents women working full-time between the ages of 18 and 24 and point B symbolizes the return of the women to the work-force between the age of 30 and 50 after their children have at least finished their middle school. (see Appendix 1).

Such a pattern has been representative of women's participation in the workforce and it has been especially visible since the late 1960s onwards since Japan has experienced an increased need for part-time workers. The fall represents the period when women quit their work to have children. As discussed earlier, the high expectations, which society has from mothers and the pressure exerted by the school system make it impossible for mothers to manage both family and work. Since Japanese women are raised with the primary idea of producing good mothers, the prospect of having a career has never been very attractive to Japanese women. Moreover, even if it, does not seem attractive, very few women choose to forgo their family life to pursue a career. This pattern of choosing home over career is not only conducive to the Japanese economic system but is also at the same time a product of the same system. The working model of the M-Curve shows that when women return to the workforce, they are no longer young and attractive and can no longer be used as decorations in the office. As a result, now these women are used to fill up the numerous part-time jobs which men refuse to do. Not only do employers get part-time workers, they even succeed in reducing revenue loss by giving fewer perks and benefits. Moreover, while earlier the income ratio between men and women was $ 91.5 now it is only $ 51.2, so employers get cheap labour, because when women quit they give up their seniority and hence have to work for lower salary and perks. Further on, even when women work full-time, they have very limited options of employment. Out of all the administrative and managerial jobs only 8 per cent were open to women, consequently, women made up 70 per cent of the discouraged workers.[17]

To end discrimination against women, the Japanese women's movement and Committees representing workers' interest protested and rallied the support of international agencies. Under international pressure, the Japanese Government, in 1986 passed the Equal Employment Opportunities Law (EEOL).[18] This law aimed at guranteeing an end to discrimination against women if they pledged to work as hard as men and accepted transfer. However, women who accepted EEOL would automatically have to give up the protection offered by the Labour Standards Law of 1947.[19] Japanese women were also given the option of going on a maternity leave, which was part of the government's effort to ease motherhood along with full-time work. But this is not as ideal as it appears. Women who go on leave loose their seniority. Similarly, women who stay on the M-Curve loose salary and perks, however, the M-Curve at least gives them a chance to return to the labour market. Thus, in a way, it accommodates women's needs.[20]

Even though both the EEOL and the M-Curve are geared towards helping women remain connected to the labour market, however, the reality of Japanese society and its fixation with the ideal of motherhood does not allow women to reap the actual benefits of government legislation. As Miller R. Creighton says in her article "Marriage, Motherhood, and Career," a law such as the EEOL is based on foreign concepts, to appease international opinion and cannot be truly effective without a corresponding change in underlying Japanese social vales regarding gender roles and the relationship between work and domestic life.[21] She further argues that policies such as temporary retirement and reinstatement supported by the EEOL, did not correspond with Japanese values emphasizing the devout maintenance of on going personal relationships with all members of one's work group.

In a final analysis, Japan's cultural ideal of nurturance is not sufficient to explain the identification of ideal womanhood with motherhood. Women's focus on nurturing is not so much a cultural legacy, but rather as Long argues, it is reinforced by continued discrimination in the business world, that persists despite constitutional and legal guarantees of equal opportunity and non-discrimination. Companies may assert that discrimination against women workers is not technically based on gender but rather on seniority, because women retire more often than men to raise children or change jobs, and so they are likely to have less experience compared to men of their age.

Moreover when women return, they return to lower track positions with less pay, less work and less responsibility than men with similar educational background. Hence, Long argues that these considerations must enter a family's economic calculations when deciding if the wife should continue to work or retire. Thus, this reinforces the belief that marital roles are complementary. The wife may be more valuable and productive towards the family by supporting her husband's and children's careers and may render useful assistance through her provision of care for the chronically ill, elderly parents and in-laws. Hence the cultural ideal of women's nurturing, combines with the dictates of the capitalist economic system of Japan and together the two forces make motherhood the most rational choice for most Japanese women.

REFERENCES

1. Jennifer Robertson, "Shingaku Woman: Straight from the Heart," in *Recreating Japanese Women, 1600-1945,* ed. Gail Lee Bernstein (Berkeley: University of California Press, 1991).
2. *Ibid.*
3. Anne Imamura, ed., *Reimaging Japanese Women* (Berkeley: University of California Press, 1996).
4. *Ibid.*
5. Kathleen S. Uno, "Women and Changes in the Household Division of Labour," in *Recreating Japanese Women.*
6. Sharon H. Nolte and Sally Ann Hastings, "Meiji State's Policy Towards Women, 1890-1910," in *Recreating Japanese Women.*
7. Imamura, *Reimaging Japanese Women.*
8. Yoshiko Miyake, "Doubling Expectations: Motherhood and Women's Factory Work Under State Management in Japan in the 1930s and 1940s," in *Recreating Japanese Women.*
9. *Ibid.*
10. *Ibid.*
11. Anne Imamura, ed., *Urban Japanese Housewives: At Home and in the Community* (Honolulu: University of Hawaii Press, 1987).
12. *Ibid.*
13. Imamura, *Recreating Japanese Women.*
14. *Ibid.*
15. *Ibid.*

16. *Ibid.*
17. Yuko Ogasawara, *Office Ladies and Salaried Men: Power, Gender and Work in Japanese Companies* (Berkeley: University of California Press, 1998).
18. Lee Bernstein, *Recreating Japanese Women.*
19. *Ibid.*
20. *Ibid.*
21. Imamura, *Reimaging Japanese Women.*

16

BREAKING THE MOULD

The Changing Dynamics of Women Maquila Workers vis-a-vis the Triple Forces of Marianismo Patriarchy and Capitalism

The life experiences of female Maquila workers are marked by the contradiction of performing roles which are in contrast to society's traditional gender role expectations. This contradiction results from the interplay of three different forces: marianismo or the code of traditional female gender roles, patriarchy and capitalism. While marianismo and patriarchy are traditional forms of socio-cultural domination of men over women, capitalism is a new entrant in the field but is proving to be stronger than the other two vehicles of control. Not only has it taken away part of the power from patriarchy by instituting the concept of public patriarchy, but it has also forced both private patriarchy and marianismo to modify their definitions of the "proper" role of women. Economic forces have taken precedence over cultural ones and women have been let out into the public space constituted by the factory floor. Even though this release from confinement to the household walls, may not have necessarily spelt emancipation for all of them, since traditional forms of control have been replaced by new ones, however, in many cases, this move represents the crossing of the thresholds, stepping on the road to self-reliance, and gaining a better position within their respective domestic spheres.

This chapter focuses on the maquiladora industries located along the US-Mexico border and studies the impact of the triple forces of marianismo, patriarchy and capitalism, on the lives of maquila women workers. Here we shall briefly discuss these three concepts and show how these forces interact with each other and combine to influence the options available to the women and the decisions which they are sometimes forced to make and sometimes chose of their own accord. The central thesis of the essay argues that even though, in the initial phases of their establishment, in the 1970s and 80s, maquila industries exploited women by overworking and underpaying them, recent researches, especially those from 1990 onwards have revealed better scenarios. The conditions of maquila workers have improved a lot in certain sectors of the industry and hence it is erroneous to generalize the entire maquila experience as an exploitative one. Moreover, in many cases women have learnt to use their domestic and public situations to best suit their interets. Even though women have been exploited by virtue of their position as both the subordinate class as well as gender, nevertheless, they have now evolved their own sets of weapons to combat capitalist, male supremacy. Instead of being passive victims both at work and at home, they have begun to capitalize on their status as income generators, and have used it to bargain for more power in household decisions and in some cases women have even succeeded in modifying the lop-sided traditional concept of gender division of household chores, which were earlier seen solely as the women's responsibility.

The development of "Global Assembly Lines" or "off-shore production" units is a result of the capitalist trends prevalent in the post—World War II period. Since the 1970s onwards, a growing portion of the international capital has been invested in the transfer of manufacturing stages, particularly those involving labour intensive operations, from industrialized countries such as the US, Germany and Japan to developing areas such as China, Philippines and the Caribbean nations. In the US, writes, Fernandez-Kelly the south-bound flux of factory operations has spilled over the border into Mexico and has taken the form of maquiladora industries.[1] "Maquiladora" is the Mexican term for factories that assemble components, often of US origin, for export to world markets. Consequently, trademarks such as Sony, General

Motors, General Electric, Chrysler and Mattel-have set up off-shore production units which have linked workers, mostly women, halfway around the world by their inclusion in global assembly iines.[2]

Developing countries, such as Puerto Rico, Mauritius, (southern) Italy are undergoing momentous changes as a result of industrial relocation. The *zona libre* or the "Free Trade Zone" located along the Mexican-American border provides a classic example of the tremendous changes occurring as a result of the incorporation of a mainly female workforce.[3] Norma Inglesias Prieto points out that the firms stood to benefit financially by employing young women mostly between the ages of sixteen to twenty four.[4] This decision was based on the realization that Mexican women were reared with the idea of docility and were easily disciplined, thus promising increased productivity.[5] In 1982, between 80 per cent to 90 per cent of the EPZs or the "Export Processing Zones" workers were women. Thus, more than 150,000 Mexican women worked in electronics and garment industries. In 1982, the number of foreign-owned plants operating in the border town of Ciudad Juarez totalled 120 and employed a workforce of over 40,000 people, most of whom were women.[6] Even though in the recent years, the figures have fallen, by 1975, women formed 78 per cent of the maquila workforce, and in 1988, the numbers further fell to 64 per cent, nevertheless, women still form the majority of the maquila workforce.[7]

The high percentage of women workers in these off shore production units reflects not only the requirements of the maquiladora owners but also the attitude and cultural conditioning of the women who fill the ranks of maquiladora workforce. These women workers are representative of the patterns of gender roles which are perpetuated mainly through the process of socialization, especially within the family, since family is the primary locus of the socialization of the individual. In her article, "Women, the Family and Social Change in Latin America," Asuncion Lavrin stresses upon the social, economic and political ramifications of mothers socializing their daughters into *marianismo*.[8]

Marianismo is a socially defined organizing principle employed by historians and social scientists to study Latin American women. In the early 1970s, the concept of *machismo*, the undue stress of male values and male roles in Latin American studies was widely discussed and identified as a major cultural force behind behavioural patterns which upheld the preeminence of men in all aspects of decision making. To amplify and complement the notion of *machismo*, Evelyn Stevens posited the existence of *marianismo*, the idealization of female values, which confer on women a special form of authority within and outside the home, not only avoiding a confrontation with men, but carrying within itself, an understanding of the boundaries of the power of each sex.[9] Stevens describes *machismo* as the "cult of virility," whose chief characteristics are, exaggerated arrogance and sexual aggression in male to female relationships and emphasizes that, *marianismo*—"the other face of *machismo*, is just as prevalent in Latin America and is characterized as the "cult of feminine spiritual superiority," which teaches that women are semi-divine, morally superior to and spiritually stronger than men. Among the characteristics of the ideal of the "real women" are infinite capacity for humility and sacrifice, self-denial, and patience with men. And submissiveness before the demands of men—husband, son, father, brother, and today this list has been modified by the inclusion of the male maquila floor managers. Beneath the submissiveness, lies the strength of conviction which helps women in forgiving the incompetence, obstinacy and foolishness of men. Consequently, women under marianismo are depicted as long suffering and sad.[10]

A brief history of the evolution of the concept shows that although *marianismo* is not a religious practice, the term derives from ecclesiastical imagery, which has as its object, the special veneration of the figure of the Virgin Mary. Stevens argues that *marianism* or *Mariology*, as most theologians prefer to call the religious movement, has provided a central figure and a convenient set of assumptions around which the practitioners of *marianismo* have erected a secular edifice of beliefs and practices related to the position of women in the society.[11]

Researchers such as E. Stevens and Ann Pescatello trace back the antecedents of *marianismo* to the figure of the *Mater Dolorosa* or the grieving and searching mother.[12-13] Gradually, "Mother of God"–Mary was integrated into Christian dogma, and this cult of *Marian* migrated to the New World and in mid-seventeenth century Virgin Mary was given the name of *Our Lady of Guadalupe* and proclaimed as the patroness of entire Latin America. Such religious beliefs were translated into legal codes and thus reinforced the passive, submissive role which women were expected to play in society.[14] Tracy Ehlers writes that in the colonial period, women were taught to emulate the virtues of the Virgin Mary.[15] The Spanish fostered a non-temporal, spiritual and secondary role for women by creating laws and codes limiting women's rights and defining women as subservient. Ehlers argues that the tradition was quickly established, thus relegating the unquestioning, obedient women to the home, the church and the family.[16]

Stevens asserts that all classes of Latin American Mestizo cultures exhibit a well defined pattern of beliefs and behaviour centered on popular acceptance of a stereotype of the ideal woman. This stereotype, like its *macho* counterpart is ubiquitous to every social class, thus distinguishing the Latin American version of "separate spheres" from those present in the rest of the world, where the concept is confined to the upper-middle class alone and does not cut across class boundaries.[17]

Probably, inspired by the North American debate over the validity of the concept of "separate spheres," most significantly contested by historian Nancy Hewitt, Tracy Ehlers also dismisses the concept of "*marianismo*" as a construct of the privileged middle class.[18] In her article, Hewitt describes two exceptions to "separate spheres": slave women who united in defense of same class women and in defiance of other class women; working class women who felt one with their male co-workers rather than with their sisters from the upper class. Hence, Hewitt concludes that there is no single women's culture or sphere unifying women of all classes, instead, she emphasized that, there was only a culturally dominant definition of separate spheres, promulgated by an economically, politically and socially dominant elite. Ehlers transfers this theory to the context of her study of Guatemalan wives, and argues that *marianismo* is a concept derived from normative middle class Latin America, where women are socially segregated and discouraged from working and are exclusively identified with the home. She further elaborates on the subject and says that non-working wives are exhibited as symbols of material prosperity. Ehlers argues that the *marianismo* model ceases to work in the context of the millions of poor women for whom work is a necessity.[19]

This theory negates the significance of the fact that, even many working class women aspire to the *marianismo* ideal. As Sarah Levine's study among lower class, urban Mexican women shows that the popular cultural belief holds that the husband should earn enough, so that the wife does not have to take on *doble jornada* or double work-load of working outside and within the home.[20] Thus, acceptance of Ehlers' theory that *marianismo* is limited to a middle class minority would amount to the denial of the most distinguishing feature the ubiquitousness regardless of class barriers, of Latin American version and extension of "separate spheres" or *marianismo*. Hence, while this argument holds true for the North American culture, it is not so readily applicable to Mexico of colonial as well as contemporary times. Even in late twentieth century Mexican women of all classes, especially those from the lower classes try to model their lives according to *marianismo's* ideals.

In Mexican maquila towns, *marianismo* is prevalent among members of almost all social classes, and those who cannot afford to follow it due to economic constraints, indeed, at least aspire to it. Unlike other regions of the world, where women of the upper classes alone were confined to the domestic sphere, in Mexico, this tendency is rampant and very much alive among the lower class even today. Maria Patricia Fernandez-Kelly, Susan Tiano, Norma Inglesias Prieto and Altha J. Cravey have studied the *maquiladora* or the "off shore production" units on the US-Mexican border and conclude that both women's productive as well as reproductive activities in this region are controlled to a significant extent by traditional ideals regarding female roles, in other words, *marianismo*.[21] Lavrin writes that the reproductive role of these workers includes not just creating the next generation of labour force, but also instilling in them the same traditional social roles and structures.[22]

Levine asserts that the women themselves are to blame for the perpetuation of such attitudes, since as mothers, women teach their sons *exigir* or "to demand" and their daughters *cumplir* or "to give in."[23] In the same vein, Lavrin adds that female roles are shaped within the family as part of the education of children of both sexes and are later translated into practical forms of subordination in social life.[24] Lavrin further explains that the cultural roots of gender role models lie in a tradition of authoritarian fathers and submissive mothers, which contributes to the continuity of female dependent roles within the family. She argues that the significance of this situation goes beyond the confines of the home and its bearing on social behaviour outside becomes obvious. Thus, according to Lavrin, *marianismo* dictates gender behaviour models which affect politics, legislations, education and occupational patterns. Women will accept less challenging careers and defer to men in politics or receive less education if they are socialized to accept specific forms of behaviour believed to be appropriate to their sex.[25]

Fernandez-Kelly argues that as these women enter the realm of paid labour, they bring forth particular kinds of behaviour and attitudes which are linked to their socialization.[26] She further adds that these female workers move in a world pervaded by ideological notions about women's work, femininity and women's proper role in the social environment. Fernandez-Kelly makes a valid observation when she says that, although they may share working and migratory backgrounds, women and men behave in and are expected to respond to their environment according to gender-specific criteria[27]. In a similar vein, Cravey also emphasizes the strategic importance of gender in the lives of the women workers. She defines gender as "a set of culturally defined traits labelled masculinity or femininity," thus, gender is a socially constructed concept and not an inherently psychological one. She asserts that gender contracts within a locality or a region reflect deeply embedded ideas about masculinity and femininity.[28]

This argument finds support in Tiano's statement that despite a meager family wage, many men want their wives to stay at home because they are brought up thinking that the women's place is in the home, and that keeping women at home is a sign of upward mobility.[29] Women also see their income as only supplementing the main income of the male head of household. While in real life, in the twentieth century, women do not really follow the rigid rules such as those regarding mourning and sexual relations, laid down by *marianismo*, such codes have now been translated into practical forms of behaviour such as: upholding marriage and motherhood as being the primary duties of women, a general submissive and compliant attitude expected from and rendered by women to men, and conversely, the exercise of over arching patriarchal rights and powers by male heads of household, with growing industrialization, this power is extended to the male supervisors of women on factory floors. Hence today, patriarchy does not have to dominate women physically, but can use indirect market control to limit female independence, and marginalize their role as economic actors.[30]

Since these women were reared with a view of making them submissive and obedient, so that they make ideal wives in the tradition of *marianismo*, they also prove to be excellent labour material for the multinational corporations. Fernandez-Kelly points out that, the fact women form the majority of maquila workforce is not the result of inherent feminine or masculine psychological determinants, but rather this fact is explained by the economic and political position of men and women vis-a-vis international capitalism.[31] She adds that the incorporation of women with acute economic needs, into maquila industries represents, in objective terms the use of the most vulnerable sector of the population to achieve greater productivity and larger profits.[32] In contrast, argues Fernandez-Kelly, if men were employed, then the industries would have to pay higher wages, provide better working conditions and accommodate more flexible work schedules, and all these would amount to lesser capitalist gains.[33] Hence it is obvious that these corporations represent the growing contemporary tendency of international capital to invest in areas where labour is cheap, docile, unskilled or semiskilled and abundant in supply. This exploitative combination of requirements is both the cause as well as the result of the rapid incorporation of large contingents of young, formerly "unemployable" women into the workforce of the manufacturing industrial sector. Maquila industries work on the principle of minimization of labour conflict, minimization of cost and maximization of profits.[34]

Cravey argues that even though, in its efforts to maintain the flow of foreign capital, the Mexican government plays a pivotal role in mediating gender contracts, however, in the process of eliminating old forms of gender subordination, the state constructs new gender inequities within social and industrial policies which are reworked to promote growth.[35] The freedom from existing labour laws and employees health protection codes, which the multinational corporations experience in these "Free Trade Zones" leads to situations where, according to Cravey, "private" forms of patriarchy have come to be more "public."[36]

In order to understand this transfer of power, it is first imperative to broadly define patriarchy as male control over female labour and sexuality, that is, over women's productive and reproductive role.[37] While earlier the primary locus of patriarchy was the home, Helen I. Safa, argues that with the development of industrial capitalism, it has shifted to the workplace, or from the private to the public sphere.[38] She adds that patriarchy works at various levels of gender subordination and is manifest in the male control over female labour in the home where women are charged with domestic responsibilities and at the workplace, where women are segregated into poorly paid, unstable jobs.[39]

Thus, women workers hold a disadvantaged position both as the subordinate class and subordinate gender.[40] Tiano says that, the social relations of production structuring the capitalist mode organize people on the basis of class relations which reflects their access to, or exclusion from productive resources. She further says that the relations structuring the domestic mode organize people on the basis of gender relations which reflect social meanings attributed on the basis of biological sex. Thus, while capitalism as an overarching political economy, defines class relations, on the other hand, patriarchy, as a system subordinating women to men, defines gender relations.[41]

The study of the maquiladoras deems it necessary to understand the crucial relationship between patriarchy and capitalism. Tiano, establishes this relationship by discussing that the primary locus of patriarchy is the household, where production and reproduction relations are maintained by the ideology emphasizing male authority. Yet, argues Tiano, patriarchy's influence ramifies beyond the domestic mode to organize relations in the capitalist mode. Similarly, even though the primary locus of capitalism is the market economy, however, its influence permeates the household to structure relations in the domestic mode. Hence, the two are intertwined systems. Tiano believes that the decision to go into wage labour mirrors the relations of production and reproduction in both capitalist and domestic modes, at the root of which is the gender-based division of labour and its supporting ideology of defining "appropriate" roles for men and women.[42]

In the light of the above discussion, it is important to note that when women participate in capitalist production, the ideology and relations of reproduction colour the terms of their labour.[43] Women tend to be viewed by society, their employers and often even by themselves as actual or potential wives and mothers, with men to support them economically. Regardless of their domestic status, their primary obligation is assumed to be to their families, and not to their employers. Tiano further adds that their wage work is seen as temporary pastime to occupy them until they marry and have children, when they will be expected to leave work and take up solely domestic tasks. Safa argues that a woman's dependence on a male breadwinner is not only reflected, but is even reinforced by certain policies at the workforce.[44] Thus, gender-based division of domestic labour is thus, restructured within the capitalist mode when capitalism uses patriarchy and its ideology of reproduction to satisfy the labour force.[45]

Although with increasing number of women working outside the home, the image of women simply as "housewives," is inconsistent with the circumstances of most women in core and peripheral societies, who either head their own households or are unable to subsist on single wages. Yet the image effectively maintains women as a surplus labour reserve that responds to the cyclic fluctuations of the capitalist economy.[46] Brought up to view themselves primarily as mothers and wives, women's ambivalence about their roles as "wage workers" makes them willing to work under unstable and temporary conditions and to enter or leave the labour force according to the system's labour needs. Tiano further points out that such flux is possible because households are flexible enough to release women when the expanding economy requires their labour and to absorb them when economic contradictions make their labour superfluous.[47] Thus, the "cult of the home" or *marianismo*, facilitates women's movement into and out of the labour force without leading to political instability or jeopardizing the efficient functioning of the economy.[48]

The relationship between patriarchy and capitalism also becomes very significant when one looks at the techniques of labour discipline adopted by the maquila owners. Cravey highlights three main methods which the managers employ to ensure obedience and discipline among the ranks of women workers.[49] These techniques are founded on the premise of the cultivation and reinforcement of rigid gender roles. One of the techniques makes use of existing gender hierarchies. This technique is very much visible in the use of male floor managers alongside female line workers. The other method involves the super-imposition of foreign gender hierarchies over existing ones. This takes the form of invitations by the owners to cosmetic vendors, to come within the factories premises to promote western ideals of beauty and femininity. The third, and age old method is constituted by the sexual harassment of female workers by male managers. This technique of labour discipline, according to Cravey often extends beyond working hours.[50] She reports that in Mexican maquiladoras, women who socialize with the supervisors, are referred to as, "waged concubines."[51] These women are rewarded, while those who refuse the advances of the male supervisors are ostracized or even threatened with termination.[52] Prieto's study of Tijuana's maquiladora plants also shows that gender plays a very crucial role in the lives of these women workers. The manager becomes a benevolent dictator or the public patriarch, and in many cases his privileges include sexual exploitation of female workers. Thus, Prieto argues that the male manager or the owner of the factory, perceives the working women not just as docile, able, attentive and patient, but also as sexual objects.[53]

The industry takes over the power of the household patriarchs in other ways also and exercises public patriarchal control over the personal lives of the women workers. Firstly, the building of the factory itself separates them from the rest of the community. Secondly, family relations are temporarily broken, when the women reside in dormitories. This places these women under the direct control of their managers. Thirdly, since job is a prerequisite for the housing, the arrangement is insecure, sickness, pregnancy and even personality conflict can result in both job and housing loss. Nogales is unique in this regard, for Cravey informs that this maquila town has dormitories for the workers. Women here are crowded into unhealthy living conditions, moreover, workers are still under control, even beyond the shop floor and after working hours.[54] Thus, the factory regime penetrates into the daily life of the workers.

Thus, these are new ways of introducing gender inequities, combined in addition to increased power and control of the employers over their employees, as reflected in the company run dormitories of Nogales.[55] These dormitories represent a novel form of household in Mexico. For workers who must accept this control, both productive and reproductive activities are strictly regulated by their trans-national employers, resulting in a loss of autonomy and privacy. Thus, the employers extend the discipline of the shop floor into off-duty hours in the dorms.[56] This phenomenon is explained by Tiano, who is in conjunction with Safa and Cravey, when she writes that under the maquila industries, private patriarchy is giving way to public patriarchy and the employers are becoming the new patriarchs, who dominate women by virtue of not only their gender, but also class. Thus, a gender subordination and patriarchal control continues to exist in the lives of the women workers.

This public patriarchal supervision is motivated by a desire for profit maximization, rather than from a concern for the well-being of women workers. Cravey provides supporting evidence by showing that in early 1998, the results of a six month long study of NAFTA's (North American Free Trade Agreement). National administrative office demonstrated that export assembly Trans-national Corporations were regularly violating Mexico's labour laws by firing harassing and intimidating workers who become pregnant. This, of course, saves the employers a considerable amount of money that might be spent on maternity benefits. The research also documents discrimination against pregnant women which takes place during initial employment interviews. Young women, says Cravey, are clearly considered productive and profitable employers as long as they *are not* and *do not* become pregnant.[57]

Drawing from the above study, Cravey argues that the experiences of Mexican women working in the maquila industries provide a theoretical understanding of the relationship between gender and capital. This study demonstrates how tightly the two systems are bound together, such that one cannot understand many of the complexities of capitalism without scrutinizing the systems of gender-subordination.

When women enter the labour force, their involvement subordinates them to the interacting forces of capitalist exploitation and patriarchai oppression. Capitalism takes advantage of pre-existing patriarchal relations to create a gender-stratified labour force in which women are forced to occupy a subordinate position. The notion that women's waged work is an unnecessary and temporary adjunct to their "proper" roles as wives and mothers is used to legitimate this arrangement.[58] The maquila managers and owners use this ideology to justify the confinement of women in low-status, poorly paid jobs that afford them minimal security and little or no opportunity for advancement. Moreover, as Tiano points out, the typically intense competition for the jobs available to women keeps wages low and contributes to their docility.[59]

Fernandez-Kelly quotes maquila managers as saying that women are hired because of their willingness to comply with monotonous, repetitive and highly exhausting work assignments. These views reflect on the way the maquila industrial units shape their hiring practices to exploit to the fullest possible extent, the socially prescribed docility of women.[60] In 1994, eleven years after Fernandez-Kelly's work Tiano observed similar attitudes among the Trans-national employers, who they still claimed preference for female labourers because of the qualities which women are assumed to acquire through their traditional gender-role socialization. These included: a tolerance for tedious work, a manual dexterity which suits them for minute tasks, and most important of all, a docile nature that enables them to withstand the pressure of rapidly paced, closely supervised production.[61] In 1997, the preference of recruiters still remains similar to the one prevailing during Fernandez-Kelly and Tiano's research.[62]

Moreover, the managers explicitly confess that women's docility discourages organizing efforts by union leaders. They emphasize that the use of female labour in maquila conditions reduces the bargaining capacity of the working class as a whole. Tiano also highlights the fact that since women assume these paid jobs in addition to childcare and household duties, they have no time to unionize or organize and press for better working conditions.[63]

Prieto's study, published in 1997, reflects on the impact of a predominantly young, female labour force on the labour movement in the border region and argues that this group of population was previously excluded from industrial production and since the social lives of these women were circumscribed mostly by domestic responsibilities, the entry of these women in large numbers into the industrial labour force has conditioned the form and content of labour organizing along the border.[64] She points out that even in 1997, the labour movement was not so extensive in this region, since women workers are bound by the constraints of family and household responsibilities. She observes that even when women strike, they still have to prepare food, take care of the household chores and often have to bring children to the strike site, a problem, which male strikers never have to face.[65]

The socialization of men and women into believing that child rearing and housework is primarily a woman's work, leads to the problem of "double burden." This is the foremost problem faced by many women workers with families and children to manage. Like most female workers, women in maquila sectors are also subject to a double work day. Hence, the analysis of the contribution of female workers is much more complex than that of the contribution of their male counterparts.[66] Prieto echoes Tiano's views by linking the issue of women's unionization with their gender and says that as a result of their status as the subordinate, submissive gender, women face limitations in terms of achieving a broader degree of organizing and mobilization. These limitations are closely linked to the convergence of contradictions which reside and unfold in the life of each and very female maquila worker: on the one hand they feel grateful and indebted to the firm which gave them a job, on the other, they feel exploited and insecure in their job.[67]

While women are influenced by those tenets of *marianismo*, which preach docility and obedience, they are even more influenced by the Marian ideology of the veneration of motherhood as the ideal of womanhood. Consequently, in the Mexican culture, women aspire, and are encouraged to become mothers and housewives and dedicate their lives to the well being of their families. Hence, many female maquila workers tend to leave their job after an average of three years at a time.[68] In most cases, premarital as well as post-childbirth, the decision of the woman to work, stems from the economic need of her family. The family of the average maquila worker comprises 7 members, which surpasses even the local standards of 5.3. Hence, young girls are forced to enter the workforce.[69] Fernandez-Kelly argues that the function of the household structure is a necessary precondition that determines labour supply vis-a-vis the requirements of international capital. In most cases, young unmarried girls migrate to and seek employment at maquila sites as members of kin networks for whose survival their earnings are vital. Statistics show that one-third of the female maquila workers are sole earners of their families. Most of these young women fall between the ages of seventeen and twenty five and they form 70 per cent of the total female workforce in the maquila industries.[70] They hand over more than half of their income to their families. These women usually work for short periods, an average of about three to five years.[71] They get off the labour market for a few years, usually in their mid-twenties to get married.

After marriage, women start families of their own and Fernandez-Kelly argues that in almost all cases, women opt to leave the workforce in order to respond to the pressures of their male-counterparts who urge them to leave their jobs and give full attention to the home and children and thus fulfil what is considered to be their "normal" or "proper" role.[72] However, children also represent growing financial needs, and so these women have to re-enter the labour market. Thus, they follow the M-curve, which is representative of the pattern followed by female workers in countries, such as Japan where the social norm prescribes wifehood and motherhood as the ideal roles for women. (See Appendix 1) The two peaks A and B represent the two periods when women's first enter and then re-enter the labcur force, point C represents the period when women leave the workforce, in order to have children and to see them through middle school.[73] The women workers in the maquila industries follow a similar pattern. The diversity of maquila industries offers women a chance to re-enter the labour force. Fernandez-Kelly's case study of the Mexican maquila town of Ciudad Juarez shows that despite being members of the same gender, women have different experiences working within different sectors of the maquiladora.

The industry and labour force in Ciudad Juarez is divided into two sectors: electronics and apparel, in the ratio of 70: 30.[74] The former employs mostly young women who are better educated, and have been living in an urban area for most of their lives. These women gave more than half their salary to their parents or their siblings with whom they lived. When women re-enter the labour force, their age and the existence of offspring act as handicaps in a highly discriminate labour market in which single, childless women are preferred for maquila work. Tiano also testifies that re-entering the labour force often proves to be difficult because there are fewer opportunities for older women.[75] Thus, these women fill the ranks of the apparel industry and are characterized by their older age and married status. They are less educated, and usually hail from a rural background, and have lived in the urban area of Ciudad Juarez only for the last five years or so. They used their salary to bear the expenses of their children. Around a third of them are the only breadwinners of their families and had been forced to work due to death or desertion by a spouse.[76]

Hence, Fernandez-Kelly rightly concludes that women's strategies of economic sustenance depend on their age, marital status and health. She observes that the portrayal of mothers and daughters as breadwinners is "marked by diversity rather than uniformity."[77] However, the study of women workers in these two different sectors shows that the goal of women in both cases are almost the same. They are both earning mainly because of economic necessity, although in some cases individual motivation may be a crucial determinant. Based on her study of maquila plants in the Caribbean countries, Safa concludes that working class women's paid employment is commonly justified in terms of their family's need rather than in terms of personal fulfilment.[78] In the case of both the younger and older women, the beneficiaries of their income are their families, either of birth or of procreation. Thus, for most women, work represents financial needs rather than symbolizing economic emancipation. Lavrin writes that, "whether single or married, women regard their work as contributing to the family survival, but do not attempt to establish their economic independence through it."[79] She adds that cultural values of male predominance within the family have for too long been reinforced by education, by national development policies, by the realities of unequal employment, and by salary practices. Since only highly qualified and exceptional women earn as much as men in the same position, women with lesser earning power, such as those within the maquila industry, are forced to accept their ancillary position as wage-earners within the family.[80]

The issue of the impact of patriarchy and capitalism on the position of women workers within the maquila industries has been the focus of considerable academic debate in which two streams of thought, represented by the Exploitation thesis and the Integration thesis, have emerged.[81] The former emphasizes the hardship of maquila employment and the latter stresses the industry's benefits for women workers. The Exploitation thesis is consistent with socialist-feminist analyses of women's role in the capitalist society. Most literature describing the nature and consequences of women's participation in assembly processing industry is consistent with the assumptions of the Exploitation thesis. Fernandez-Kelly represents scholars of this school of analysis. She believes that Trans-national corporations invest in the Third World because there they can easily exploit the inexpensive female labour which performs tedious monotonous tasks in return for minimum wages, with little job security or opportunity for advancement.[82] Fernandez-Kelly argues that, contrary to common belief, involvement of women in paid industrial labour does not necessarily imply the improvement of their alternatives as individuals and as members of families. Rather, she contends that their employment in maquiladora may be a symptom of their economic vulnerability. In the absence of jobs for them and for the men in their families, women opt for the only employment available.[83] Fernandez-Kelly admits that this affords the survival, but says that it is hardly adequate for expanding choices for the working class, whom she sees as the backbone of the advancement of the nation. She maintains that the argument is not against participation of women in paid work, but rather against perpetuation of sexual segregation in the labour market which fosters under-development and economic atrophy.[84] Related to this kind of gender segregation in the labour market is the concept of occupational sex-typing. Even though, today the total percentage of women in the maquila industry is falling, while that of men is rising, in the earlier years, especially the mid-1980s, as a result of the process of socialization in traditional values, certain occupations were believed to be specifically feminine. Lavrin argues that this led to the creation of "feminine labour enclaves."[85] A feminized occupation, such as the apparel industry, loses its appeal to men and becomes wage-depressed. Feminization becomes evident in the numerical imbalance of women in managerial or supervisory positions on the maquila factory floors. These jobs are usually the domain of men while women are employed as workers under the control of a male supervisor. Although cultural in nature, Feminization reinforces stereotypes and adversely influences the economic situation of many women.[86] Low wages could also weigh in the family's decision to keep women at home, rather than sending them out to work, thus reinforcing the tradition of keeping women at home, though more from economic, rather than cultural motivations.

The proponents of the Exploitation thesis point out that the maquila managers encourage high turnover in order to avoid paying the seniority-related wage hikes. The maquila sector does not encourage permanence, the women workers are either fired or asked to quit voluntarily. Managers can afford to indulge in such practices, or rather, they are able to avoid spending money on giving benefits to long-term employees by firing women periodically and replacing them with new ones from an abundant pool of workers. Prieto writes that the maquila managers generally dismiss women older than twenty five to thirty years of age and replace them with younger workers from whom greater productivity is anticipated.[87] Like Fernandez-Kelly, Prieto also maintains that this rotation of female workers is made possible by the vast reserve army of labour that could be used or discarded in accord with the industry's interests and needs.[88] This thesis highlights the fact that although the work exposes women to dangerous chemicals, and other hazards, which might result in sight impairment and other ailments, they are frequently denied insurance and disability benefits.[89] Likewise Prieto also brings out the frequent dangers facing maquila workers in a workplace which is characterized by inattention to accident and occupational ailment prevention.[90] she traces this dehumanization to the policy which results from giving priority to production values rather than to workers' health.

Advocates of this school believe that women enter work in Export Processing Zones not as individuals but as members of patriarchal families. This view rests on the belief that the survival of the family depends on the daughters' wage, and so the daughters are not encouraged to marry or live alone. They are expected to hand over their wages to the fathers, who decide how to dispose of it. Usually these daughters support the education of younger siblings, especially that of their brothers. So women work not out of choice but rather because of family pressure. Hence, they stay in alienating conditions within the factories, for the sake of their families. The Exploitation thesis holds that patriarchal relations also structure relations of production on the factory floor. Referring to the beauty pageants, make-up demonstrations and cooking classes conducted on factory premises, this school of thought concludes that such activities reinforce the traditional notions of femininity. Advocates of the Exploitation thesis, highlight the fact that the supervisors act as parent "surrogates" for their "girls," closely monitoring not only their productive output but also their personal lives. This, the proponents of this thesis conclude that instead of encouraging notions of self-reliance and autonomy, work in the assembly plants is assumed to deepen obeisance to patriarchal authority and acquiescence to traditional female gender roles.[91]

In contrast, the central tenet of the integration thesis holds that development liberates women by involving them in their society's political economy.[92] Scholars of the schools believe that modernization enriches women's opportunities and that labour force participation is a liberating experience for women. Waged work offers them an alternative to financial dependence on a male partner and increases their bargaining power within the household. Moreover, considering the economic crisis in Mexico, assembly line work is seen as an improvement over other forms of employment options available to women. Even though, in the 1970s and 1980s, women's employment was characterized by minimum wage and hardly any benefits, towards the late 1980s and the beginning of 1990 onwards, employees in many sectors of the industries began receiving various health and medical benefits. Susan Tiano's study of the electronics industry in Ciudad Juarez in 1994 shows that, the health and safety standards parallel those prevalent in the US' factories. Workers get the full complement of benefits mandated by the state for formal sector workers, added incentives include factory subsidized transportation and factory cafeterias. Hence, certain sectors of the industry provide different experiences for the women, and so it is incorrect to generalize the experiences of women workers in all sectors of the industry as being highly exploitative.[93] Linda Lim's study in 1990 compares the Mexican maquiladoras to those in Asia and says that both regions reveal similar trends, where many assembly line workers claim to enjoy the prestige attached to working in Trans-national firms and point to the widespread job-satisfaction and the perception of women that the jobs are materially and personally rewarding.[94]

Maquila employment enables women to challenge patriarchal relations in the household and society at large, moreover, formal employment in the maquiladora gives women material resources and self-respect to negotiate effectively with male members of the household. Safa reiterates that the increasing importance of women as wage earners challenges the status of men as principal breadwinners.[95] Both Exploitation thesis as well as the Integration thesis concur that women must earn an income to themselves and their families. Advocates of the Exploitation thesis also admit that jobs in the Export Processing Zones are superior to women alternative options. Even Fernandez-Kelly, who represents one of the leading voices of the Exploitation thesis accepts that majority of the jobs in the service sector offer no stability, rather, some of the prestigious, professional jobs offer very meager salary. Her study in Ciudad Juarez in 1983 showed that many maquila operators had acquired at least six years of schooling, many had attended commercial academies where they had acquired typing and accounting skills. Of the women who had worked before joining the assembly lines, 40 per cent were former nurses, beauticians, seamstresses and computer technicians, thus proving that maquila work offered the best employment alternatives in Ciudad Juarez.[96] One of the most significant factors to be taken into consideration is that compared to salaries in other types of employment in Mexico, assembly line workers earn more, thus, Ellwyn Stoddard argues that, "only distortions induced by dubious comparisons of American working women with Mexican maquila female workers minimize these as work opportunities for women who must find work."[97]

The Exploitation thesis errs by viewing these women workers as passive, helpless victims of Trans-national companies embodying the so-called, "tripartite oppressions" of patriarchy, capitalism and imperialism. However, in the context of her research in the Caribbean maquiladoras, Safa refutes this contention by arguing that, women were not passive victims of patriarchal control, rather they actively resisted it in the home as well as the workplace.[98] Tiano's study in Mexicali also shows that although women are victimizes by a couple of host conditions, they are "not necessarily passive."[99] Tiano's analysis conceptualizes women workers as active agents taking responsibility for their lives within the limiting parameters of their structural and cultural conditions.[100] Her approach represents the middle ground between the two theses and assumes that the interacting systems of capitalism, patriarchy and social relations that emanate from them, create the structural conditions in which women must operate when they formulate their lines of action. Although these structures constrain women's options, they however, do not entirely determine them. She argues that women have some leeway in: making choices from alternatives and in reshaping these parameters through their actions, thoughts and perceptions.

Tiano argues that although alienated, women lack the autonomy to believe in their ability to change their condition, their awareness of oppression and their rejection of the relations that engender it create a basis for future collective resistance if they acquire a framework to interpret or challenge their discontent. Tiano highlights the value of feminist organizations such as Juarez based COMO, for providing educational and organizational support to catalyze their collective action.[101]

Susan Tiano further highlights the gradual ebbing away of the conventional belief that women's employment leads to destruction of the family by interfering with their reproductive role. Researches by Tiano, Prieto and Cravey show that this view is giving way to a reinterpretation of women's work. Female wage labour is now being seen as the woman's means to support their households, most women in the studies, expressed a contradiction between their views of women's ideal roles as full-time housewives, and their own desire to remain in paid employment. This ambivalence is understandable given the sweeping changes in

Mexican women's roles and role expectations occurring during the course of their lifetimes.[102]

However, despite the contradictory feelings women might have regarding their waged work, the reality is that traditional social views regarding women's work are changing. This is a major factor behind women's increased participation in paid employment. Economic needs have forced even the patriarchs to modify their ideology which focused on women's role in reproduction and defined waged work as inappropriate for Mexican women. When women began leaving the house to enter the ranks of workers in increasing numbers, the fact of their employment impacted upon the old ideology, and modified it to justify their employment. The patriarchs claimed that as long as it occurs within certain limits, as a way to strengthen the family by ensuring its economic support, female employment was legitimate. However, ironically, women's employment has been justified in terms that reinforce, rather than transform their symbolic assignment to the reproductive sphere in the role of the wife and the mother—the caretaker of the family.[103] Even though, work participation of women is only one of the necessary conditions to erode patriarchy, and has to be accompanied by legal, cultural and socio-economic changes that undercut patriarchal relations regulating women's employment, still, the personal consequences which paid employment work has had for some individual women is noteworthy.[104] In her article, Ehlers delineates an economic basis for female subordination and shows how *marianismo* idealizes the harsh reality of women's lives.[105] She argues that, due to their economic dependence on men, women passively accept male responsibility, or suffer a threat to their very survival. She believes that economic reasons are crucial to women's tolerance of abusive husbands. Thus, women continue in bad marriages because they have no alternative.[106] Levine admits that while the economic factors are crucial to the perpetuation of *marianismo*, since many women confided in her that they would tolerate marital infidelity as long as their husbands continued to support them economically because they could not affords to turn back on economic security. Levine admits that while the economic factors are crucial to the perpetuation of *marianismo*, since many women confided in her that they would tolerate marital infidelity as long as their husbands continued to support them economically because they could not affords to turn back on economic security.[107] Hence, Ehlers theorizes the *marianismo* is a product of economic necessity more than a mere social construct. Ehlers substantiates her argument by pointing out that *marianismo* is no more than a strategy for psychological survival, necessitated by women's exclusion from income-generating activities.[108]

In the light of such arguments, women's work becomes all the more crucial in determining their status in their domestic lives. In capitalist economies, access to material resources depends on cash income generation by paid employment, Tiano rightly points out that, this is often the only way women can get financial resources necessary to confront private patriarchy, and to be able to bargain better in a male-dominated relationship. Extra domestic work has expanded women's options for confronting patriarchy, they can now muster the resources necessary for leaving an abusive husband or a bad relationship. Evidently, women's gender consciousness and bargaining power in the household have increased as a result of their massive incorporation into the labour force in the recent decades.[109]

However, Tiano points out that there is an underlying paradox in the whole situation of women's increased freedom from patriarchal relations, because this freedom is achieved through their immersion in capitalist relations of production in which they hold a subordinate position. Hence, the price paid for gaining access to resources, to gain leverage over private patriarchy is the acceptance of a labour contract that limits their autonomy in a different way by subjecting them to capitalist and patriarchal relations at the workplace. So women trade one kind of autonomy for another.[110]

When questioned about their feelings regarding the trade-off between household and workplace autonomy, women related their experiences, which can be divided into two distinct scenarios. Some women claimed that they would gladly retire from the labour force if their wages were not essential for their family's subsistence. For them the alternative to working was not lack of independence, but rather economic destitution. Moreover, for female heads of household, working solely from economic necessity, autonomy over private patriarchy was a moot issue. For these women, the only benefit of waged work was that it provided food and clothing for their children and avoided them the humiliation of relying on other family members.[111]

On the other hand, there were many women who had developed a commitment to their wage-earning roles that went beyond mere economic need. These women believed that the gains from their employment were well worth the toll of their labour contributions. Many among this group desired to remain economically active because it increased their self-esteem which arose from: their economic self-reliance, creative fulfilment of operating in a realm beyond the isolating confines of the domestic spheres and by their increased independence from their male partners or parents.[112]

Neither one of these two perspective is in itself, adequate in explaining women's diverse motivations for employment, yet each is useful for explaining the forces that lead women to and make them remain in paid employment. Fernandez-Kelly's analysis if Ciudad Juarez, Tiano's study in Mexicali in 1994, Prieto's study in Tijuana, Cravey's research in Nogales and Ciudad Madero all show that the economic reason was the main motivation for joining waged work in the initially. However, once involved, many women developed a commitment to their wage earning roles that transcends the economic imperative. Their continued participation reflects the positive incentive stressed by the Integration thesis as well as the negative constraints emphasized by the Exploitation thesis. Women who occupy a privileged position in the labour market are more apt than their less fortunate counterparts to respond to the non material incentives envisioned by the Integration thesis. The case is not simple enough to be generalized, as discussed earlier, women in the electronics industry are privileged and enjoy greater perks and benefits as compared to women working in the apparel industry, where many of them earn only the minimum wage.[113]

Moreover, there exists a key contradiction between capitalism and patriarchy, as pointed out by Tiano. Capitalism takes advantage of patriarchal relations to create a vulnerable, low-waged labour force whose labour increases the rate of capital accumulation. Yet, at the same time, the large-scale, longtime mobilization of women into the labour force may create a female proletariat whose interests are more or less the same as those of male workers and thereby they may undermine patriarchy by threatening the dichotomous gender-division of labour, and the ideology on which it depends. This point weighs down in favour of the Integration thesis which sees hope for women, and believes that gradually they will come around to manipulating the capitalist system in their own interests.[114]

Prieto admits to the exploitation of women workers in maquila industrial zones, but she tends to share the optimism characterized by the Integration thesis. The period of her study is a crucial determinant in shaping her belief that the socialization involved in the work experience favours a widening of famale horizons previously focused on the routine problems of the family.[115] Her study was conducted in 1997, almost two decades after the maquila industries first started operating in the region. By this time, women were better acquainted with the factory ways, they had heard about the experiences of their mothers or sisters, aunts who had previously worked in maquila labour, thus they were better equipped than the previous batches of women workers, to handle the pressures of the job and tried to derive meaningful relationships and at least some amount of satisfaction from their work. Thus, the social experience of work facilitates the possibility that the women workers are no longer in absolute subordination to their feminine condition which, Prieto argues is a construct of the patriarchal structure of the household and the economy.[116]

Cravey believes that the Mexican industrial and capitalist transition has been facilitated by a restructuring of gender relations, both in the household, as well as the private lives of the workers. Her study further shows that the predominantly nuclear household form supported by a male breadwinner, which was the norm in the state-led factory regime, has given way to a multiplicity of forms in which workers devise new strategies for survival.[117] Cravey observes a positive change in women's life as a result of their incorporation within the maquila industries. She asserts that, in conjunction with the reconstitution and reorganization of the household unit, the increased participation of women in waged-work has had an impact on the division of domestic labour. She argues that even though the traditional division of domestic labor still perpetuates in many regions such as Ciudad Madero, an optimistic trend is noticeable in Nogales. Nogales represents the more recent factory regime, while, Ciudad Madero is an older maquila town. Cravey emphasizes that "child care" has been the arena for the most dramatic change, with some Nogales men contributing to household labour on a regular basis through a sequential scheduling strategy. Cravey's study reveals that men in Nogales also may help with cooking, laundry and grocery shopping in a more systematic fashion than in Ciudad Madero, where such male contribution is less regular and less sustained.[118]

Time is a very crucial determinant in this regard, since changing times symbolize changing trends. While Fernandez-Kelly's study constitutes one of the earliest works in the field, Prieto and Cravey's studies show some of the latest trends in the area. Hence the differences in their conclusions and outlook towards the exploitative or beneficial role of maquiladora reflect the different stages through which ranks of women workers has passed and the various strategies they have adopted in order, firstly to survive through the ordeal of harsh working conditions and secondly, to use the situation as women and workers in their best possible interest. One such strategy is visible in Nogales, where many women workers have successfully enlisted the support of their husbands. Thus, Cravey's study departs from earlier studies, in that it shows the restructuring of households and the flexibility of the very notion of maleness and femaleness.

Patriarchy is slowly loosening its hold, at least within the realm of the household. Correspondingly, concepts of gender division of labour and the "traditional female tasks" are eroding slowly in the face of the reality of women working outside, and hence, the rise of the practical need for the other parent to take care of children and help with household tasks. Hence, the present trend reflects in a practical way the optimism of the Integration thesis which was not so easily acceptable around a decade ago in writings of Fernandez-Kelly. Increasing employment has forced women to redefine their role within the home and to challenge the myth of the male breadwinner. The inability of men to earn an adequate family wage and be the sole supporters of the family on the one hand, has been countered by the emergence of women as wage earners on the other, and has thus resulted in weakening men's position of absolute authority within the home and breaking the image of women as obedient subordinates of men. Today there are visible signs to prove the contention that slowly but surely, the hold of patriarchy is loosening and there is a gradual movement towards gender role-sharing by the two earning heads of the household.

REFERENCES

1. Maria Patricia Fernandez-Kelly, *For We Are Sold, I and My Poeple: Women and Industry in Mexico's Frontier* (Albany: State University of New York Press, 1983), p. 191.
2. *Ibid.*, p. 191.
3. Norma Inglesias Prieto, *The Beautiful Flowers of the Maquiladora: Life Histories of Women Workers in Tijuana* (Austin: University of Texas Press, 1997), p. xxiv.
4. *Ibid.*, p. xix.
5. *Ibid.*, p. 33.
6. Fernandez-Kelly, *For We Are Sold,* p. 191.
7. Susan Tiano, *Patriarchy on the Line: Labour, Gender and Ideology in the Mexican Maquila Industry* (Philadelphia: Temple University Press, 1994), p. 24.
8. Asuncion Lavrin, "Women, the Family and Social Change in Latin America," *World Affairs* 150, No. 2 (Fall 1987): 109-121.
9. Evelyn P. Stevens, "Marianismo: The Other Face of Machismo," in female and *Male in Latin America: Essays*, ed. Ann Pescatello (Pittsburgh: University of Pittsburgh Press, 1973), p. 90.
10. *Ibid.*, pp. 90-91.
11. *Ibid.*, pp. 92-95.
12. Ann Pescatello, ed., *Power and Pawan: The Female in Iberian Families, Societies, and Cultures* (London: Greenwood Press, 1976), pp. 4-7.
13. Stevens, "Marianismo," pp. 92-95.
14. *Ibid.*, p. 95.
15. Tracy Ehlers, "Debunking Marianismo: Economic Vulnerability and Survival Strategies Among Guatemalan Wives," *Ethnology* (1990): p. 3.
16. *Ibid.*
17. Stevens, "Marianismo," p. 96.
18. Hewitt, Nancy, "Beyond the Search for Sisterhood: American

Women's History in 1980s," *Social History* 10, No. 1, (1985): pp. 299-321.

19. Ehlers, "Debunking Marianismo," p. 4.
20. Sarah Levine, *Dolor y Alegria: Women and Social Change in Urban Mexico* (Madison: University of Wisconsin Press, 1993), p. 83.
21. Fernandez-Kelly, "Mexican Border Industrialization, Female Labour Force Participation and Migration," in *Women, Men and the International Division of Labour,* eds. June Nash and Maria Patricia Fernandez-Kelly (Albany: State University of New York Press, 1983), Altha J. Cravey, *Women and Work in Mexico's Maquiladoras* (Lanham, Md: Rowman and Littlefield, 1998).
22. Lavrin, "Women, the Family and Social Change," p. 114.
23. Levine, *Dolor y Alegria*, p. 93.
24. Lavrin, "Women, the Family and Social Change," p. 112.
25. *Ibid.*
26. Fernandez-Kelly, "Mexican Border Industrialization," p. 207.
27. Ibid., p. 208.
28. Cravey, *Women and Work*, p. 8.
29. Tiano, *Patriarchy on the Line*, p. 39.
30. Ehlers, "Debunking Marianismo," p. 5.
31. Fernandez-Kelly, "Mexican Border Industrialization," p. 219.
32. *Ibid.*
33. *Ibid.*
34. Fernandez-Kelly, *For We Are Sold*, p. 191.
35. Cravey, *Women and Work*, 133.
36. *Ibid.*, p. 8.
37. Helen I. Safa, *The Myth of the Male Breadwinner: Women and Industrialization in the Caribbean* (San Francisco: West View Press, 1995), p. 38.
38. *Ibid.*, p. 39.
39. *Ibid.*
40. Tiano, *Patriarchy on the Line*, p. 34.
41. *Ibid.*
42. *Ibid.*, p. 36.
43. *Ibid.*

44. Safa, *The Myth*, p. 39.
45. Tiano, *Patriarchy on the Line*, p. 37.
46. *Ibid.*, p. 39.
47. *Ibid.*
48. *Ibid.*, pp. 39-40.
49. Cravey, *Women and Work*, pp. 7-8.
50. *Ibid.*
51. *Ibid.*
52. *Ibid.*
53. Inglesias Prieto, *Beautiful Flowers*, pp. 76, 99.
54. Cravey, *Women and Work*, pp. 16-17.
55. *Ibid.*
56. *Ibid.*
57. Cravey, *Women and Work*, p. 135.
58. Tiano, *Patriarchy on the Line*, p. 40.
59. *Ibid.*
60. Fernandez-Kelly, "Mexican Border Industrialization," p. 219.
61. Tiano, *Patriarchy on the Line*, p. 44.
62. Prieto, *Beautiful Flowers*, pp. xix, 3-5.
63. Tiano, *Patriarchy on the Line*, p. 40.
64. Prieto, *Beautiful Flowers*, p. 100.
65. *Ibid.*, pp. 88-93.
66. *Ibid.*, pp. xxv, 32-34.
67. *Ibid.*, pp. 28, 59-60, 99-100.
68. Cravey, *Women and Work*, p. 6.
69. Fernandez-Kelly, "Mexican Border Industrialization," p. 216.
70. *Ibid.*, p. 214.
71. Inglesias Prieto, *Beautiful Flowers*, p. 99.
72. Fernandez-Kelly, "Mexican Border Industrialization," p. 220.
73. Anne Imamura, ed., *Re-Imaging Japanese Women* (Berkeley: University of California Press, 1996).
74. Fernandez-Kelly, "Mexican Border Industrialization," p. 214.
75. Tiano, *Patriarchy on the Line*, pp. 26-28.
76. Fernandez-Kelly, *For We Are Sold*, p. 193.

77. *Ibid.*, p. 7.
78. Safa, *The Myth*, p. 57.
79. Lavrin, "Women, the Family and Social Change," p. 111.
80. *Ibid.*
81. Tiano, *Patriarchy on the Line*, p. 37.
82. *Ibid.*, pp. 219-20.
83. Fernandez-Kelly, *For We Are Sold*, p. 192.
84. *Ibid.*
85. Larvin, "Women, the Family and Social Change," pp. 115-16.
86. *Ibid.*
87. Prieto, *Beatiful Flowers*, pp. xxi-xxii, 7, 36-38, 98-99.
88. *Ibid.*, p. 99.
89. Fernandez-Kelly, *For We Are Sold*, p. 193.
90. *Ibid.*, pp. 19-23, 25.
91. Tiano, *Patriarchy on the Line*, p. 46.
92. *Ibid.*, p. 38.
93. *Ibid.*, pp. 26-28.
94. *Ibid.*, p. 46.
95. Safa, *The Myth*, p. 39.
96. Fernandez-Kelly, "Mexican Border Industrialization," p. 217.
97. Tiano, *Patriarchy on the Line*, pp. 46-47.
98. Safa, *The Myth*, p. 40.
99. Tiano, *Patriarchy on the Line*, p. 221.
100. *Ibid.*
101. *Ibid.*, p. 222.
102. *Ibid.*
103. *Ibid.*, p. 224.
104. *Ibid.*
105. Ehlers, "Debunking Marianismo," pp. 5, 13.
106. *Ibid.*, p. 13.
107. Levine, *Dolor y Alegria*, p. 90.
108. Ehlers, "Debunking Marianismo," pp. 5, 10-11.
109. Safa, *The Myth*, p. 58.

110. Tiano, *Patriarchy on the Line*, p. 225.

111. *Ibid.*

112. *Ibid.*

113. *Ibid.*, pp. 26-28.

114. *Ibid.*, p. 43.

115. Prieto, *Beautiful Flowers*, pp. 34-35, 70-72.

116. *Ibid.*, p. 100.

117. Cravey, *Women and Work*, pp. 135-36.

118. *Ibid.*, pp. 137-38.

WORKS CITED

BOOKS

Agarwal, P. *Passage From India; Post-1965 Indian Immigrants and Their Children.* Palo Verdes: Yuvati Publication, 1991.

Alexander, Mina. *The Shock of Arrival: Reflections on Postcolonial Experience.* Boston: South End Press, 1996.

Alexander, M. *The Shock of Arrival: Reflections on Postcolonial Experience.* Boston: South End Press, 1996.

Austen, Jane, *Pride and Prejudice*. London: Octopus Books, 1987, *Sense and Sensibility.* London: The Zodiac Press, 1956.

Austen, Jane, *Mansfield Park,* Ed. James Kinsley. Oxford: Oxford University Press, 1998.

Carroll Smith-Rosenberg, *Disorderly Conduct: Visions of Gender in Victorian America* (New York: A.A. Knopf, 1985).

Chang, Pang-Mei. 1996. *Bound Feet and Western Dress*. New York: Doubleday.

Chaffee, John W. and Wm. Theodore de Bary. *Neo-Confucian Education: The Formative Stage*. Berkeley: University of California Press, 1989.

Childs, Margaret Helen, Trans., *Rethinking Sorrow.* Ann Arbor: Center for Japanese Studies, 1991.

Cole, Richard C., Ed., *The General Correspondence of James Boswell, 1766-1769.* Edinburgh: Edinburgh University Press, 1993.

Cott, Nancy F. *The Bonds of Womanhood: "Woman's Sphere"* in *New England*, 1780-1835. New Haven: Yale University Press.

Daniels, Roger. *Coming to America: A History of Immigration and Ethnicity in American Life.* Princeton: Harper Collins, 1990.

Daniels, R. *The History of Indian Immigration to The United States.* New York: The Asia Society, 1989.

Dasgupta, S.S. *On The Trail of An Uncertain Dream: Indian Immigrant Experience In America.* New York: AMC Press, 1989.

D'Emilio, John and Freedoman, Estelle B. Ed., *Intimate Matters; A History of Sexuality in America.* Chicago: University of Chicago Press, 1997.

Diner, Hasia R. *Erin's Daughters in America: Irish Immigrant Women in the Nineteenth Century.* London: The Johns Hopkins University Press, 1983.

Divakaruni, C.B. *Arranged Marriage.* New York: Doubleday, 1995.

——— *Black Candle: Poems About Women From India, Pakistan and Bangladesh.* Corvallis: CALYX Books, 1991.

——— *Leaving Yuba City: New and Selected Poems.* New York: Doubleday, 1997.

Du Bois, Ellen Carol and Ruiz Vicki L. eds., *Unequal Sisters: A Multicultural Reader in U.S. Women's History.* New York: Routledge, 1990.

Eaves, T.C. Duncan and Kimpel, Ben D., Eds., *Pamela; or, Virtue Rewarded.* Boston: Houghton Mifflin, 1971.

Edward, Louise P. *Men and Women in Qing China: Gender in the Red Chamber Dream.* New York: E.J. Brill, 1994.

Erikson, Erik. *Childhood and Society.* New York: Norton, 1964.

Fernandez-Kelly, Maria Patricia. 1983. *For We Are Sold, I and My People: Women and Industry in Mexico's Frontier.* Albany: State University of New York Press.

——— "Mexican Border Industrialization, Female Labour Force Participation, and Migration," In *Women and Men and the International Division of Labour*, ed. June Nash and Maria Patricia Fernandez-Kelly, pp. 205-23. Albany: State University of New York Press, 1983.

Furth, Charlotte. *A Flourishing Yin: Gender in China's Medical History.* Berkeley: University of California Press, 1999.

Gilfoyle, Timothy. *City of Eros: New York City Prostitution and the Commercialization of Sex, 1790-1820.* New York: W.W. Norton, 1992.

Gilmartin, Christina, Ed., *Engendering China: Women, Culture and the State.* Cambridge: Harvard University Press, 1994.

Glenn, Susan A. *Daughters of the Shtetl.* Ithaca: Cornell University Press, 1990.

Halsband, Robert, Ed., *The Complete Letters of Lady Mary Wortley Montagu.* Oxford: Clarendon Press, 1965-1967.

Handlin, Oscar. *Boston's Immigrants.* Cambridge: The Belknop Press of Harvard University Press, 1959.

Harris, Alice Kessler. *Out To Work.* New York: Oxford University Press, 1982.

Hawkes, David. The *Dream of the Red Chamber,* Vols. 1-5. London: Penguin Books, 1973.

Hawkins, Joyce M. and Allen, Robert Ed., *The Oxford Encyclopedic Dictionary* (Oxford: Clarendon Press, 1991), p. 1174.

Hill, Bridget, Ed., *The First English Feminist: Reflections upon Marriage and Other Writings by Mary Astell.* Aldershot: Gower/Maurice Temple Smith, 1986.

Huang, Martin W. *Literati and Self-Representation: Autobiographical Sensibility in the Eighteenth Century Chinese Novel.* Stanford: Stanford University Press, 1995.

Imamura, Anne Ed., *Urban Japanese Housewives: At Home and in the Community.* Honolulu: University of Hawaii Press, 1987.

Imamura, Anne, Ed., *Reimaging Japanese Women.* Berkeley: University of California Press, 1996.

Kazuko, Ono. *Chinese Women in a Century of Revolution,* 1850-1950. Stanford: Stanford University Press, 1987.

Khare, B.B., ed. *Asian Indian Immigrants: Motifs on Ethnicity and Gender.* Dubuque: Kendall/Hunt Publishing Company, 1997.

Kelly, Joan. *Women, History and Theory: The Essays of Joan Kelly.* Chicago: University of Chicago Press, 1984.

Kerber, Linda. *Toward an Intellectual History of Women: Essays.* Chapel Hill: University of North Carolina Press, 1997.

Ko, Dorothy. *Teachers of the Inner Chambers: Women and Culture in Seventeenth Century China*. Stanford: Stanford University Press, 1994.

Lebsock, Suzanne. *The Freewomen of Petersburg: Status and Culture in a Southern Town, 1784-1860.* New York: Norton, 1985.

Levine, Sarah. *Dolor y Alegria: Women and Social Change in Urban Mexico.* Madison: University of Wisconsin Press, 1993.

Louise P. Edwards, *Men and Women in Qing China: Gender in The Red Chamber Dream* New York: E. J. Brill, 1994.

Mann, S. *Precious Records: Women in China's Long Eighteenth Century*. Stanford: Stanford University Press, 1997.

May, Elaine. *Great Expectations: Marriage and Divorce in Post Victorian America* (Chicago: University of Chicago Press, 1980).

McCullough, Helen Craig Trans., *Genji and Heike: Selections from The Tale of Genji and The Tale of the Heike.* Stanford: Stanford University Press, 1994.

McLaren, Anne E., Trans. *The Chinese Femme Fatale: Stories from the Ming Period.* Sydney: Wild Peony, 1994.

McMahon, Keith. *Misers, Shrews and Polygamists: Sexuality and Male-Female Relations in Eighteenth Century Chinese Fiction*. London: Duke University Press, 1995.

Ogasawara, Yuko. *Office Ladies and Salaried Men: Power, Gender and Work in Japanese Companies*. Berkeley: University of California Press, 1998.

Pescatello, Ann. Ed., *Power and Pawan: The Female in Iberian Families, Societies, and Cultures.* London: Greenwood Press, 1976.

Prieto, Norma Inglesias. *Beautiful Flowers of the Maquiladora: Life Histories of Women Workers in Tijuana.* Translated by Michael Stone with Gabrielle Winkler. Austin: University of Texas Press, 1997.

Rischin, Moses, Ed., *Grandma Never Lived in America: The New Journalism of Abraham Cahan.* Bloomington: Indiana University Press, 1985.

Ropp, Paul S. *Dissent in Early Modern China: Ju-lin wai-shih and Ch'ing Social Criticism.* Ann Arbor: The University of Michigan Press, 1981.

Safa, Helen I. *The Myth of the Male Breadwinner: Women and Industrialization in the Caribbean.* San Francisco: West View Press, 1995.

Saran, P. *The Asian Indian Experience in the United States.* Cambridge: Schenkman Publishing Company, 1985.

Seidensticker, Edward, Trans., *The Gossamer Years: A Diary by a Noble woman in Heian Japan.* Tokyo: Charles E. Tuttle Company, 1973.

Shah, N. *The Ethnic Strife: The Study of Asian Indian Women in the United States.* New York: Pinkerton and Thomas Publications, 1993.

Shesgreen, Sean, Ed., *Engravings by Hogarth.* New York: Dover, 1973.

Snitow, Anne. Christine Stansell, Sharon Thompson, eds., *The Powers of Desire.* New York: Monthly Review Press, 1983.

Smith-Rosenberg, Carroll. *Disorderly Conduct: Visions of Gender in Victorian America.* New York: A.A. Knopf, 1985.

Sprigge, Timothy L. S., Ed., *The Correspondence of Jeremy Bentham.* London: Athlone Press, 1968.

Stansell, Christine. *City of Women: Sex and Class in New York, 1789-1860.* Chicago: University of Illinois Press, 1987.

Tiano, Susan. *Patriarchy on the Line: Labour, Gender and Ideology in the Mexican Maquila Industry.* Phialdelphia: Temple University Press, 1994.

Tomaselli, Sylvana, Ed., *A Vindication of the Rights of Man: With, A Vindication of the Rights of Woman, and Hints by Mary Wollstonecraft.* Cambridge: Cambridge University Press, 1995.

Ulrich, Laurel Thatcher. *A Midwife's Tale: The Life of Martha Ballard Based on her Diary, 1785-1812.* New York: Vintage Books, 1990.

Vaisey, David, Ed., *The Diary of Thomas Turner, 1754-1765.* Oxford: Oxford University Press, 1984.

Watson, R.S. 1991. *Marriage and Inequality in Chinese Society.* Berkeley: California University Press.

Women of the South Asian Descent Collective, *Our Feet Walk the Sky: Women of the South Asian Diaspora.* San Francisco: Aunt Lute Books, 1993.

Yang, Mayfair Mei-Hui. Ed., *Spaces of Their Own: Women's Public Sphere in Transnational China.* Minneapolis: University of Minnesota Press, 1999.

POEMS AND SHORT STORIES

Divakaruni, Chitra Bannerjee. "Yuba City School," in *Leaving Yuba City: New and Selected Poems.* New York Doubleday, 1997.

———. "Doors," in *Arranged Marriage.* New York: Doubleday, 1995.

———. "My Mother at Maui," in *Black Candle: Poems About Women from India, Pakistan and Bangladesh.* Corvallis: CALYX Books, 1991.

———. "The Garba," in *Black Candle: Poems About Women from India, Pakistan and Bangladesh.* Corvallis: CALYX Books, 1991.

ARTICLES IN BOOKS

Ali, Zainab. "Becoming Agents of Our Identity," in *Our Feet Walk the Sky: Women of South Asian Diaspora,* Ed. The Women of South Asian Descent Collective. San Francisco: Aunt Lute Books, 1993.

Feuerwerker, Yi tse Mei. "The Chinese Novel," in *Approaches to the Oriental Classics*, Ed. Wm. Theodore de Bary. New York, 1959.

Gandbhir, Lalita. "To My Beloved Teenager," in *Our Feet Walk the Sky: Women of the South Asian Diaspora,* Ed. The

Women of the South Asian Descent Collective. San Francisco: Aunt Lute Books, 1993.

Ganesan, I., "Food and the Immigrant." In *Half and Half: Writers on Growing Up Biracial and Bicultural,* ed. O'Hearn, C.C., New York: Pantheon Books, 1998.

Garcia, Alma M. "The Development of Chicana Feminist Discourse," in *Unequal Sisters: A Multicultural Reader in U.S. Women's History.* New York: Routledge, 1990.

Glenn, Evelyn Nakano. "The Dialectics of Wage Work: Japanese American Women and Domestic Service, 1905-1940," in *Unequal Sisters.*

Kohli, Aarti. "Thrka," in *Our Feet Walk the Sky: Women of the South Asian Diaspora,* Ed. The Women of South Asian Descent Collective. San Francisco: Aunt Lute Books, 1993.

Mani, Lata. "Gender Class and Cultural Conflict: Indu Krishnan's *Knowing Her Place,"* in *Our Feet Walk the Sky: Women of the South Asian Diaspora,* Ed. The Women of South Asian Descent Collective. San Francisco: Aunt Lute Books, 1993.

Mann, Susan. "learned Women in the Eighteenth Century," in *Engendering China: Women, Culture and the State,* Ed., Christina Gilmartin. Cambridge: Harvard University Press, 1994.

Matsumoto, Valerie. "Japanese American Women during World War II," in *Unequal Sisters: A Multicultural Reader in U.S. Women's History.* New York: Routledge, 1990.

Miyake, Yoshiko "Doubling Expectations: Motherhood and Women's Factory Work Under State Management in Japan in the 1930s and 1940s," in *Recreating Japanese Women.*

Mukherjee, B. "A Father." In *Charlie Chan is Dead: An Anthropology of Contemporary Asian American Fiction,* ed. J. Hagedorn, New York: Penguin, 1993.

Nolte, Sharon H. and Hastings, Sally Ann "Meiji State's Policy Towards Women, 1890-1910," in *Recreating Japanese Women.*

O'Brien, Denise "Women's Writing in Heian Japan: Expressions of Power," in *Configurations of Power: Holistic Anthropology in Theory and Practice*, ed. John S. Henderson and Patricia J. Netherly. London: Cornell University Press, 1993.

Patel, Sajani. "Viewpoint From a Female," in *Our Feet Walk The Sky: Women of the South Asian Diaspora,* Ed. The Wornen of South Asian Descent Collective. San Francisco: Aunt Lute Books, 1993.

Pessar, Patricia. "The Role of Gender in Dominican Settlements in the United States," in *Women and Change in Latin America*, Eds. June Nash and Helen Safa. Massachusetts: Bergin and Garvey Publishers, Inc., 1985.

Pinto, Lorna Gonsalves. "Breaking Through the Borderlands on the U.S. Ethnoscape," in *Asian Indian Immigrants: Motifs on Ethnicity and Gender,* Ed. B.B. Khare. Dubuque: Kendall/Hunt Publishing Company, 1997.

Preety, "Home," in *Our Feet Walk the Sky: Women of the South Asian Diaspora,* ed. The Women of the South Asian Descent Collective. San Francisco: Aunt Lute Books, 1993.

Robertson, Jennifer. "Shingaku Woman: Straight from the Heart," in *Recreating Japanese Women, 1600-1945,* Ed. Gail Lee Bernstein. Berkeley: University of California Press, 1991.

Ruiz, Vicki L. "A Promise Fulfilled: Mexican Cannery Workers in Southern California," in *Unequal Sisters: A Multicultural Reader in U.S. Women's History.* New York: Routledge, 1990.

Sanchez, George J. "'Go after the Women:' Americanization and the Mexican Immigrant Woman, 1915-1929," in *Unequal Sisters: A Multicultural Reader in U.S. Women's History.* New York: Routledge, 1990.

Stevens, Evelyn. "Marianismo: The Other face of Machismo." In *Female and Male in Latin America:* Essays, ed. Ann Pescatello, 90-101. Pittsburgh: University of Pittsburgh Press, 1973.

Susan Mann, "Grooming a Daughter for Marriage: Brides and Wives in the Mid-Ch'ing Period," in *Marriage and Inequality in Chinese Society*, Ed. Rubie S. Watson. Berkeley: University of California Press, 1991.

Tonomura, Hitomi "Re-envisioning Women in the Post-Kamakura Age," in *The Origins of Japan's Medieval World,* Ed. Jeffrey P. Mass. Stanford: Stanford University Press, 1997.

Uno, Kathleen S. "Women and Changes in the Household Division of Labour," in *Recreating Japanese Women.*

Vasudev, Amita. "Journal Entry," in *Our Feet Walk the Sky: Women of the South Asian Diaspora* Ed. The Women of South Asian Descent Collective. San Francisco: Aunt Lute Books, 1993.

Yung, Judy. "The Social Awakening of Chinese American Women as reported in Chung Sai Yat Po, 1900-1911," in *Unequal Sisters: A Multicultural Reader in U.S. Women's History.* New York: Routledge, 1990.

JOURNALS

Bargen, Doris A. "Spirit Possession in the Context of Dramatic Expression of Gender Conflict: The Aoi Episode of the Genji Monogatari," *Harvard Journal of Asiatic Studies* 48, June 1988.

Ehlers, Tracy. "Debunking Marianismo: Economic Vulnerability and Survival Strategies among Guatemalan Wives." *Ethnology,* 1990.

Furth, C. 1987. "Concepts of Pregnancy, Childbirth, and Infancy in Ch'ing Dynasty China." *Journal of Asian Studies* 46: 7-37.

Ho, Clara Wing-Chung. "The Cultivation of Female Talent: Views on Women's Education in China During the Early and High Qing Periods." *Journal of the Economic and Social History of the Orient* 38, No. 2 (May 1995): 191-223.

Hewitt, Nancy, "Beyond the Search for Sisterhood: American Women's History in 1980s". *Social History* 10(1), 1985.

Lavrin, Asuncion. "Women, the Family and Social Change in Latin America." *World Affairs* 150(2), Fall 1987.

McMahon, Keith. "A Case for Confucian Sexuality: The Eighteenth Century Novel 'Yesou puyan'," *Late Imperial China*, 9 (2) December 1988: 47,

DISSERTATIONS

Shankar, R. "The East Indians of the Greater San Francisco Bay Area of California: A Study of An Ethnic-Status Community." Ph.D. diss., Boston College, 1976.

Index